Internet and E-mail for Seniors
with Windows XP

Addo Stuur

Internet and E-mail
for Seniors
with Windows XP

For everyone who wants to learn to use the Internet at a later age

This book has been written using the Visual Steps™ method.
Translated by Grayson Morris, Lorri Granger, Marleen Vermeij
Copyright 2005 by Visual Steps B.V.
Cover design by Studio Willemien Haagsma bNO

Second printing: August 2005
ISBN 90 5905 054 1

Would you like more information?
www.visualsteps.com

Do you have questions or suggestions?
E-mail: info@visualsteps.com

Website for this book:
www.visualsteps.com/internet
Here you can register your book.

Register your book
We will keep you aware of any important changes that are necessary to you as a user of the book. You can also take advantage of our periodic newsletter informing you of our product releases, company news, tips & tricks, special offers, etc.
www.visualsteps.com/internet

Table of Contents

Foreword

The Internet has ushered in a whole new era. Until a few years ago, most computers were isolated from one another. Since the emergence of the Internet, the computer has become a device that allows you to communicate worldwide with other computers. The Internet has gradually become so vast that you can browse in even the most obscure libraries and communicate with people and organizations no matter where in the world they are. More and more applications are being created that have advantages for computer non-experts as well. For example, e-mail is increasingly replacing the telephone, regular mail and the fax. This book has been written specifically to first acquaint you with the Internet, then teach you all the skills you'll need to take full advantage of all the Internet has to offer at this moment.

We've created a special website to accompany this book, where you can safely practice what you've learned before you set out on your own on the Internet.

I hope you enjoy this book and wish you a pleasant journey on the Internet.

Addo Stuur

P.S. Your comments and suggestions are most welcome. My e-mail address is: addo@visualsteps.com

Introduction to Visual Steps™

The Visual Steps™ manuals and handbooks offer the best instructions on the computer expressway. Nowhere else in the world will you find better support while getting to know the computer, the Internet, *Windows* and other computer programs.

Visual Steps™ manuals are special because of their:
- **Content**
  Your way of learning, your needs, your desires and your know-how and skills have been taken into account.
- **Structure**
  You can get straight to work. No lengthy explanations. What is more, the chapters are organized in such a way that you can skip a chapter or redo a chapter without worry. The small steps taken in Visual Steps also make it easy to follow the instructions.
- **Illustrations**
  There are many, many illustrations of computer screens. These will help you to find the right buttons or menus, and will quickly show you whether you are still on the right track.
- **Format**
  A sizable format and pleasantly large letters enhance readability.

In short, these are manuals that I believe will be excellent guides.

Dr. H. van der Meij

Faculty of Applied Education, Department of Instruction Technology, University of Twente, the Netherlands

What You'll Need

In order to work through this book, you'll need to have a few things on your computer.

The most important requirement for using this book is that your computer has the US version of **Windows XP**. You can check this yourself by turning on your computer and looking at the welcome screen.

You need a number of things in order to use the Internet.

You need a working **Internet connection**.
For help adjusting the settings for your connection, you can consult *Chapter 9, Appendix A* and the information your Internet Service Provider gave you.

The following programs for working with the Internet should be installed on your computer:
- *Internet Explorer* version 6.0
- *Outlook Express* version 6.0

These programs come standard with *Windows XP*. They might still need to be installed, however.

In *Windows*, the group *Accessories* should be installed and should contain the following programs:
- *WordPad*
- *Paint*

If these programs haven't been installed on your computer yet, you can read how to do that in *Appendix A.*

Prior Computer Experience

This book assumes a minimum of prior computer experience. Nonetheless, there are a few basic techniques you should know in order to use this book. You don't need to have any prior experience with the Internet. But you do need to be able to:

- click with the mouse
- start and stop programs
- type and edit text
- start up and shut down *Windows*

If you don't know how to do these things yet, you can read the book **Windows XP for Seniors** first:

How This Book Is Organized

This book has been written so that you don't have to work through it from beginning to end. It is a good idea, however, to work through the chapters containing basic techniques first.

The Basics

connecting to the Internet	Chapter 1
surfing the Internet	Chapters 1 and 2
sending e-mail	Chapter 5

After you've mastered these basic techniques, you can choose among the following chapters. Each one can be worked through seperately. These cover the following subjects:

Optional Subjects

searching the Internet	Chapter 3
saving text and pictures	Chapter 4
your address book and e-mail attachments	Chapter 6
formatting e-mail	Chapter 7
downloading files	Chapter 8
relaxing on the Internet	Chapter 10

Last but not least, there's a chapter specifically devoted to adjusting your computer's settings so that you can comfortably use the Internet.

adjusting your computer's settings	Chapter 9

How to Use This Book

This book has been written using the Visual Steps™ method. It's important that you work through each chapter **step by step**. If you follow all the steps, you won't encounter any surprises. In this way, you'll quickly learn how to use the Internet without any problems.

In this Visual Steps™ book, you'll see various icons. This is what they mean:

Techniques
These icons indicate which technique you should use:

⌨️ The mouse icon means you should do something with the mouse.

⌨️ The keyboard icon means you should type something on the keyboard.

☞ The hand icon means you should do something else, for example turn on the computer.

Sometimes we give you a little extra help in order to work through the book successfully.

Help
You can get extra help from these icons:

⇨ The arrow icon warns you about something.

✖ The bandage icon can help you if something's gone wrong.

✓ The check mark icon appears in the exercises. These exercises help you independently practice the techniques you've learned.

👣1 Have you forgotten how to do something? The number next to the footsteps icon tells you where you can find it in the appendix *How Do I Do That Again?*

This book also contains a great deal of general information and tips about the Internet, computers and *Windows*. This information is in seperate boxes.

Extra Information
Information boxes are denoted by these icons:

 The book icon gives you extra background information that you can read at your convenience. This extra information is not necessary for working through the book.

 The light bulb icon indicates an extra tip for using *Windows* and the Internet.

The Screen Shots

The screen shots in this book were made on a computer running *Windows XP* with *Service Pack 2. Service Pack 2* is an extension to *Windows XP* provided by Microsoft. If you don't (yet) have *Service Pack 2* on your computer, some of the images may differ from what you see on your screen.

Test Your Knowledge

Have you finished reading this book? Test your knowledge then with the test *Internet and E-mail*. Visit the website: **www.ccforseniors.com**

This multiple-choice test will show you how good your knowledge of Internet and e-mail is. If you pass the test, you'll receive your free computer certificate by e-mail.

For Teachers

This book is designed as a self-study guide. It is also well suited for use in a group or a classroom setting. For this purpose, we offer a free teacher's manual containing information about how to prepare for the course (including didactic teaching methods) and testing materials. You can download this teacher's manual (PDF file) from the website which accompanies this book: **www.visualsteps.com/internet**

1. Starting Out on the World Wide Web

The Internet consists of thousands of computers that are connected to one another by cables, the telephone network and satellite links. The *World Wide Web* is one of the most enjoyable and widely-used parts of the Internet. The *World Wide Web* is just that: a "spiderweb" of computers containing information on many diverse subjects.

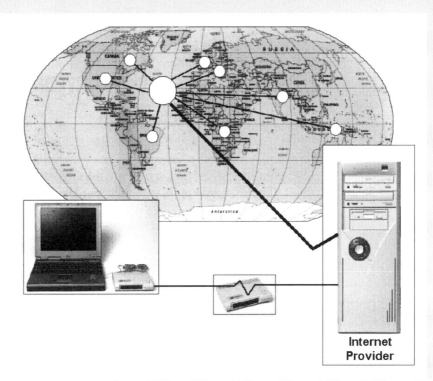

A computer connected to an Internet Service Provider

You can use your computer to open and read these sources of information no matter where you are in the world. These information sources on the Internet are called *websites*. You can move from one page to another with a click of the mouse. You can move from one website to another just as easily. This is called *surfing the Web*.
In order to access the Internet, you must make contact with a computer that is already connected to the Internet. You do this through an *Internet Service Provider*, also called an *ISP*.

If you want to use the Internet, you'll need a subscription with an Internet Service Provider. You'll be given a username and a password, and the ISP will provide software to set up your computer. This gives you access to the Internet.
Once you're connected to the Internet, you're *online*. In this chapter, you'll go *online* in order to *surf*.

In this chapter, you'll learn how to:

- start *Internet Explorer*
- connect to your Internet Service Provider
- use a web address
- browse forward and back
- use the scrollbar
- move from one window to another
- increase or decrease the text size
- disconnect from the Internet

 Please note:

You must have a working Internet connection in order to use this book.
Contact your Internet Service Provider or your computer store if you need help.
- If this applies to you, you can read the tips on *Connecting over a Telephone Line* at the end of this chapter.

Starting Windows

Windows starts automatically when you turn on your computer.

  Turn on your computer

After a short while *Windows* starts and you see the *Desktop* containing several icons:

⇨ **Please note:**

The screen illustrations used in this book were made with the *Windows XP* default settings. However, these may be very different from what you see on your screen. The settings for *Windows XP* can be adjusted in many ways.
The Internet changes on a daily basis. For this reason, the images in this book taken from the Internet may appear different on your computer.

Is Your Modem Ready?

Many people use a **modem** and a telephone line to connect to the Internet. A modem is a device that connects your computer to your telephone line. Sometimes it's in a separate box, called an *external modem*. In many modern computers, however, the modem is already built in – an *internal modem*. Before you connect to the Internet, it's important to check that your modem is ready to begin.

☞ **Make sure your modem is connected to the telephone line**
You can read the tips on *Connecting over a Telephone Line* at the end of this chapter if you need to.

Do you have an external modem?
☞ **Turn the modem on**

Do you have an internal modem?
☞ **You don't have to do anything**

Starting Internet Explorer

The program you'll use to contact the World Wide Web is called *Internet Explorer*. Here's how you start this program:

☞ Click on ⊞ start

☞ Click on
   Internet
   Internet Explorer

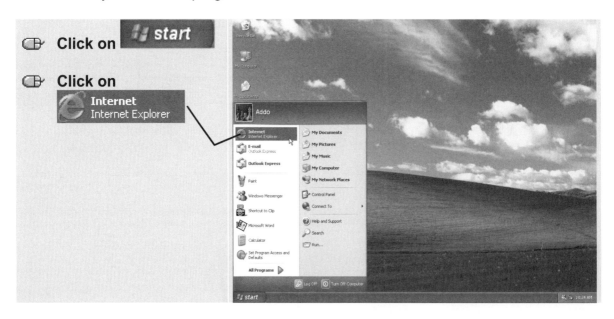

The program starts. Now you can connect to the Internet.

First you see the *Dial-up Connection* window:

Take note:
If you are connected to the internet by cable or DSL, then this Dial-Up Connection screen will not appear. Your computer is already connected to the internet. In this case, you can continue on page 28.

If you have an Internet service subscription, your Internet Service Provider has given you a **username** and **password**. If everything's been set up properly, both items are already displayed in the window.

Are your username and password already filled in?

☞ **Click on** [Connect]

Are these items not yet filled in?

⌨ **Type your username and password in the white fields**

☞ **Then click on** [Connect]

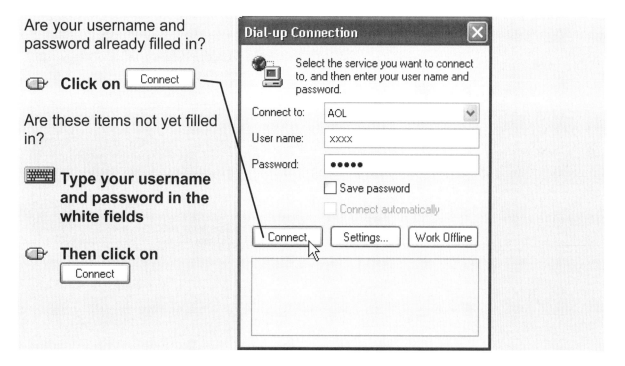

Connecting to Your Internet Service Provider

Your computer will now connect to your Internet Service Provider through your modem. If your modem is connected to your telephone line, these are the steps it will take:

- The modem dials your ISP's telephone number.
- The modem connects to your ISP's computer.
- Your computer sends your username and password.
- Your ISP checks the username and password.
- You're given access to the Internet.

If your modem is connected to your telephone line, you can usually hear beeping and static during this process. If you have a cable or ISDN connection, this process is quick and noiseless.

You can follow the progress of your connection in the window:—

> Dialing...1-456-456-4556

Are you connected to the Internet?

You will now see a webpage in the *Internet Explorer* window. If you haven't changed any settings, this is probably the home page for *Microsoft Network (MSN).*

On the right-hand side of the taskbar, two little computers let you know you're connected: —

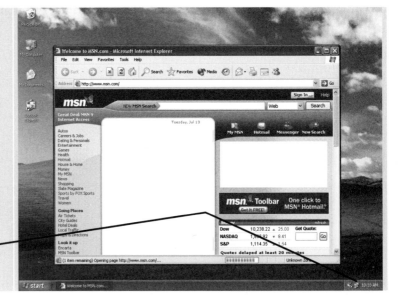

The modem is busy when the little screens on the computers blink:

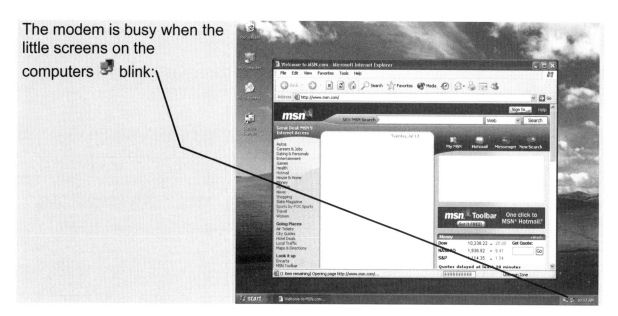

 Please note:

The home page above might be different on your computer. You might see your Internet Service Provider's home page, for example.

 HELP! There's no connection.

Are you not connected to the Internet?
This can happen if your Internet Service Provider's number is busy:

```
Dialing...
Dialing...
Dialing...
Unable to establish a connection.
```

 HELP! I'm still not connected.

Are you still not being connected to the Internet after several tries?
Then your computer is probably not set up correctly. Contact your Internet Service Provider for help.

Typing an Address

Every website has its own address on the *World Wide Web*. These are the famous **www** addresses you see organizations and companies advertising.
A website can be found on one of the thousands of computers connected to the Internet by using this www address. The address for my website is:

www.visualsteps.com

Click in the white field

next to `Address`

You can type the address into this box:

Type:
`www.visualsteps.com`

Press `Enter ⏎`

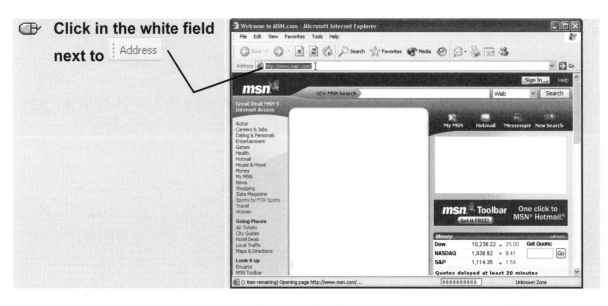

HELP! Where's the Enter key?

The Enter key is on the right-hand side of your keyboard:

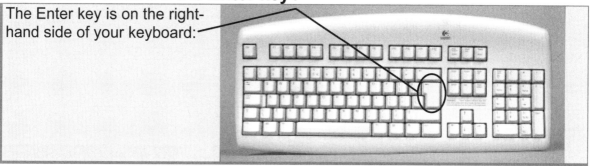

After a short while, you see the home page for my website:

Maximizing the Window

You can maximize the *Internet Explorer* window at any time, so that it fills the entire screen. This makes it easier to view a website. Here's how you do it:

Click on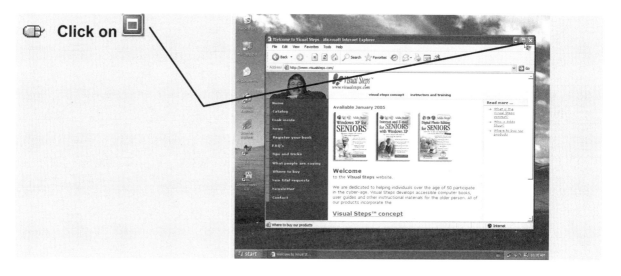

The window now fills the whole screen:

This makes it easier to view a website.

💡 Tip

Unfortunately, *Internet Explorer* doesn't automatically start with a maximized window. Go ahead and click on right after it opens.

A Wrong Address

Sometimes you may type in an address incorrectly, or the address may no longer exist. This latter isn't all that unusual, because the Internet changes every day. Web addresses in particular go through a lot of changes.
When you type in a web address, pay attention to the following:

- Sometimes you'll see **http://** in front of an address. That's extra information telling your computer you're looking for a website.
  In *Internet Explorer,* you don't have to type in **http://** yourself. The program automatically assumes you're looking for a website.
- Make sure the periods and slashes are in the right place. Otherwise you'll get an error message.
- Never type spaces in a web address.

Even a missing period can cause an error message. Give it a try:

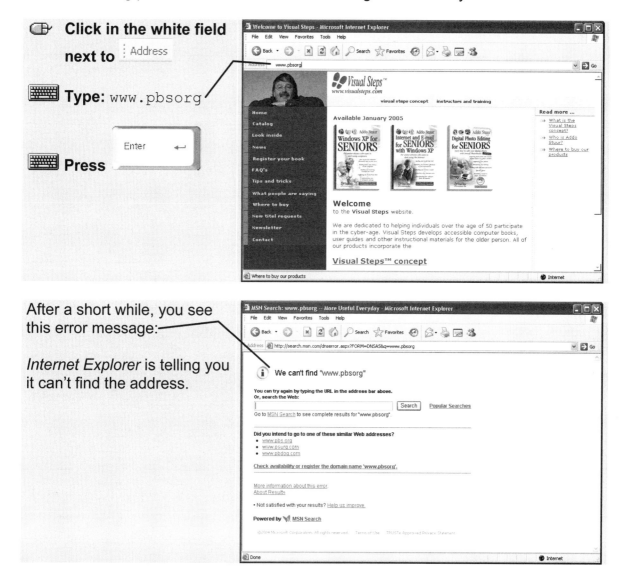

Click in the white field next to Address

Type: `www.pbsorg`

Press Enter

After a short while, you see this error message:

Internet Explorer is telling you it can't find the address.

And indeed it can't, because the address is incorrect. The right address for the Public Broadcasting Service is:

www.pbs.org

Now give the right address a try:

 Type: www.pbs.org

Press [Enter ←]

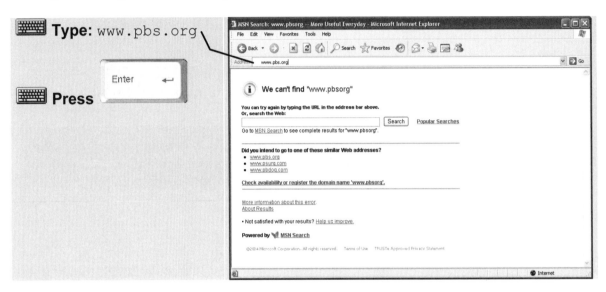

After a short while, you see the home page for the Public Broadcasting Service:

Now you've seen that forgetting even a period can keep a website from being found.

⇨ **Please note:**

The website above may look different now. The Internet changes daily.

Refreshing a Page

Sometimes a page isn't shown properly on the screen. In that case, you can tell *Internet Explorer* to fetch the page again. Take a look at what happens:

☞ **Click on** 🔄

You see that the window is cleared:

At the bottom you see the little computer screens blinking to signal that information is being retrieved:

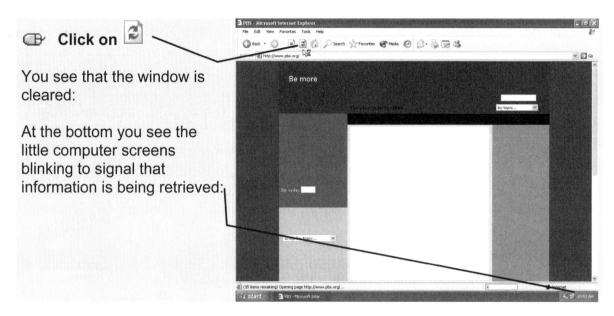

Everything you see on your screen must be sent to you through the phone line or the cable. This takes time. It may appear as if nothing's happening. But *Internet Explorer* is very busy. You can see this in various ways:

The program is busy when the little flag in the top right corner is waving:

A green bar at the bottom of the window indicates that information is being retrieved:

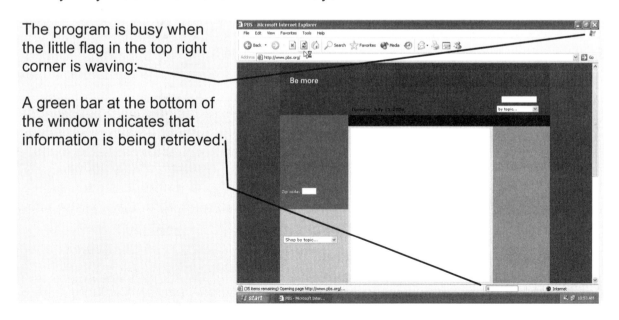

The information does not appear at once on the screen; the page is built up slowly.

Forward and Back

You don't have to type in the web address again if you want to revisit a website. *Internet Explorer* has buttons that let you navigate on the Internet.

☞ **Click twice on**

You'll leave the PBS website and go back to a website visited earlier.

First you'll see the window with the error message, and then you'll see the home page for my website.

Now you see my website, which you visited earlier:

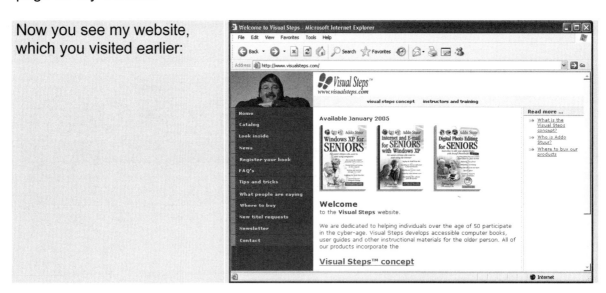

Maybe you noticed how quickly this happens. This is because *Internet Explorer* stores recently-visited web pages in its memory, so you can view them again quickly without all the information having to be sent over the telephone line or the cable again.

☞ **Click on** **again**

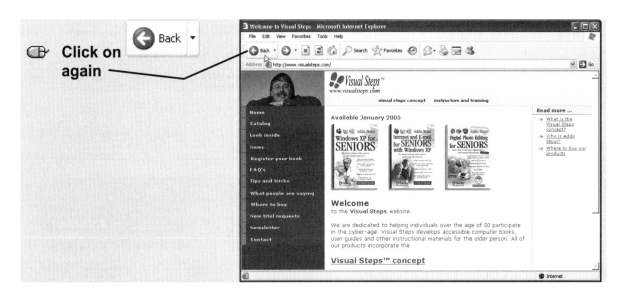

Now you'll see the website you looked at before this one.

Now you see the initial web page with which you began:

You can't browse backwards anymore. After all, this was the first website you opened.

The [Back] button is now gray and no longer active:

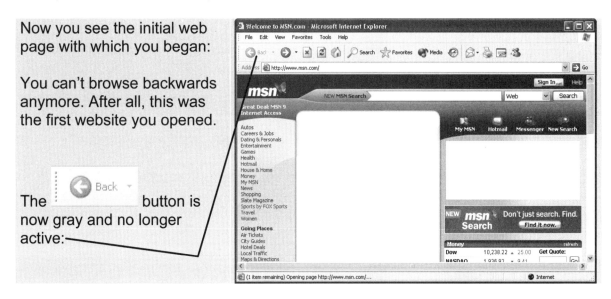

You can browse in the other direction, however. There's a button for that, too.

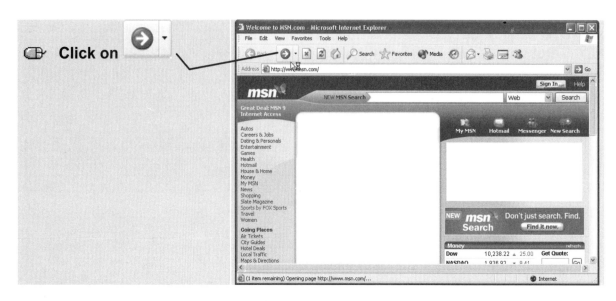

Now you see my website on the screen again:

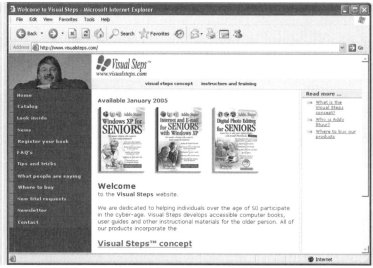

You can use the ⊕ ▾ and ⊙ Back ▾ buttons to easily move from one previously-visited website to another. You can "surf" the Internet this way.
These websites aren't permanently stored in the memory, however.

If you close *Internet Explorer,* the ⊕ ▾ and ⊙ Back ▾ buttons will lose their memory of the pages you've visited this time.

Subdirectories

Some websites have an additional website added onto the main web address. This extra website is in a subdirectory. The subdirectory is separated from the main address by a / (*slash*). Take, for example, the practice website for this book:

⊞ Click in the white field next to Address

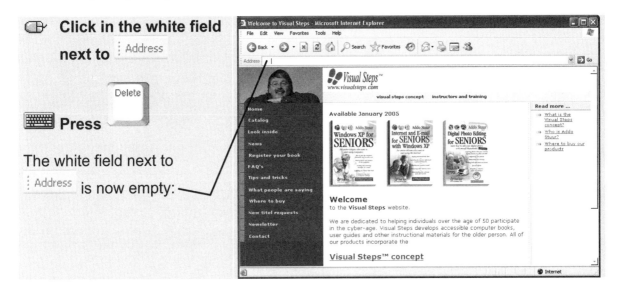

⌨ Press Delete

The white field next to  is now empty:

HELP! Where's the Delete key?

The Delete key is in the group above the cursor keys:

You can now type in the entire address including subdirectory. Later on in this book, you'll see that this *Address* field is full of useful tricks that can save you a lot of typing.

 Type:
www.internetforsen
iors.com/practice

 Press

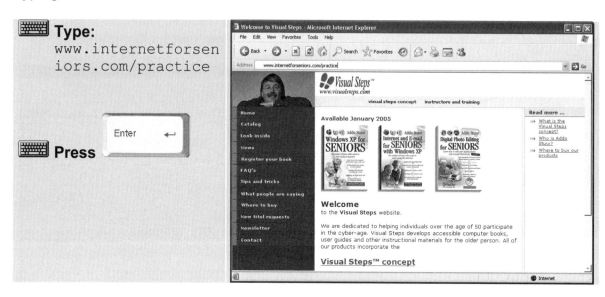

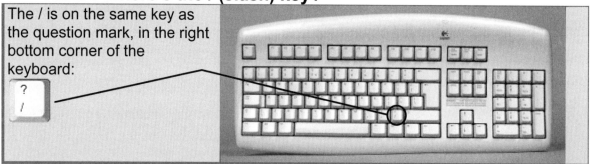 HELP! Where's the / (slash) key?

The / is on the same key as the question mark, in the right bottom corner of the keyboard:

After a short while, you see the practice website for this book:

Browsing by Clicking

Every website has a page with a table of contents summarizing the subjects you can find on the site. This website has one too. You can see the subjects in a column on the left-hand side. By clicking on one of the subjects, you can go to another page:

☞ **Place the mouse pointer on**

Practice website

You see the mouse pointer change into a little hand 🖑 :

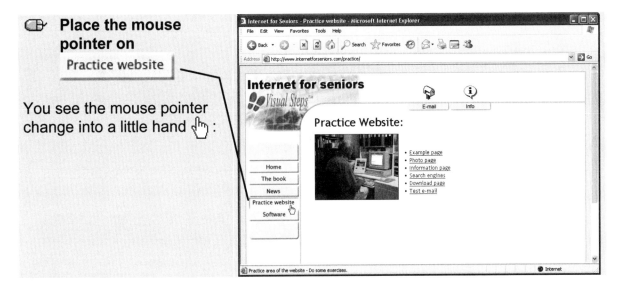

You can click anywhere on a web page where you see the little hand appear. You can click on not only a button, but also a bit of text or an image. A word, a button or an image on which you can click is called a **link**. Sometimes the word **hyperlink** is used.

On the page you see various links to other pages:

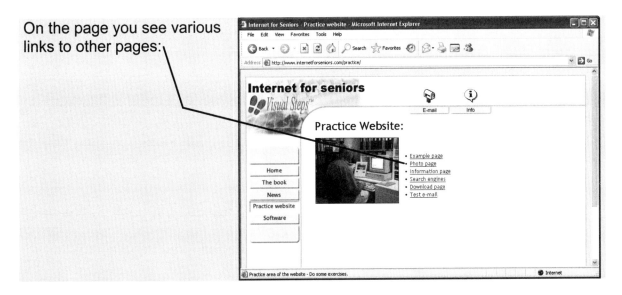

You can also click on these words:

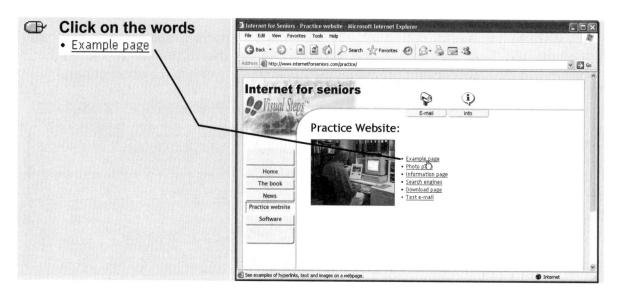

⟨⎘ **Click on the words**
- Example page

On the example page shown here, you see that the bottom part of the page is off the screen:

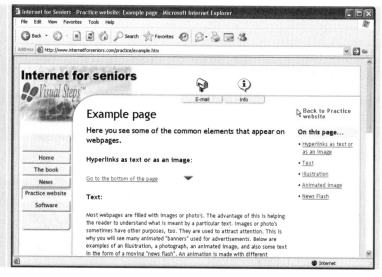

You'll have to use the scrollbar to read that part.

Using the Scrollbars

You'll have to use the scrollbars a lot when you're on the Internet. Not all information fits into one window. In order to see the rest of the page, use the vertical scrollbar:

Click on ⌄ **at the bottom of the scrollbar**

You see the page slide upwards:

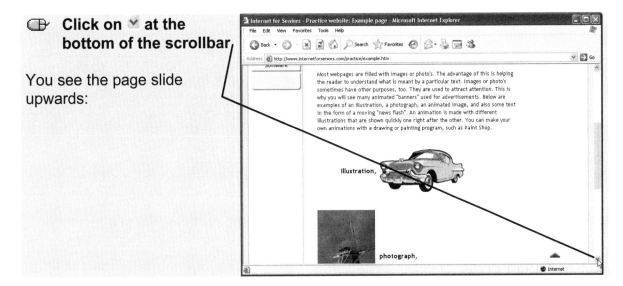

You can move the page back down so you can see the top again.

Click on ⌃ **at the top of the scrollbar**

You see the page slide back down:

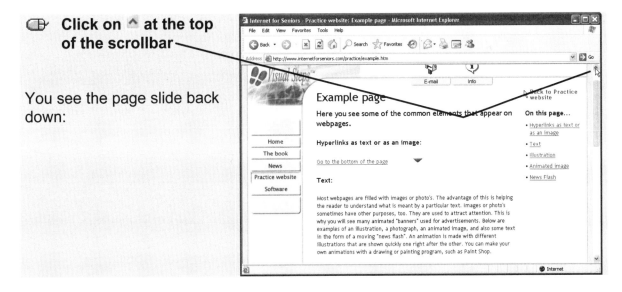

You can move the page very precisely by **dragging** with the mouse. Here's how you drag:

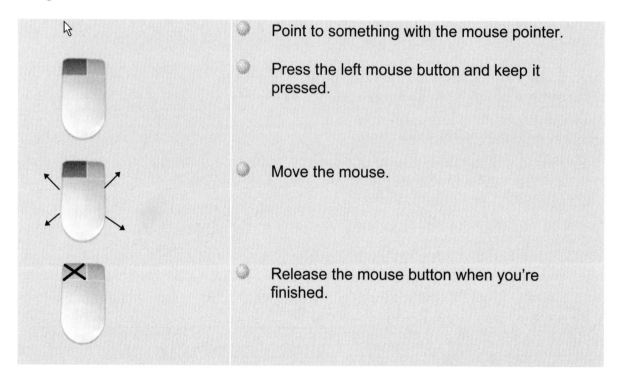

Point to something with the mouse pointer.

Press the left mouse button and keep it pressed.

Move the mouse.

Release the mouse button when you're finished.

By dragging with the mouse, you can move the slidable part of the scrollbar, called the slider. Give it a try:

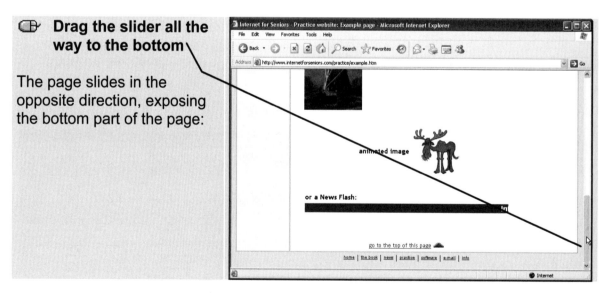

Drag the slider all the way to the bottom

The page slides in the opposite direction, exposing the bottom part of the page:

This window sliding is called *scrolling* in computer language.

Tip

The Wheeled Mouse

The increase in Internet usage has led to an additional feature of the mouse: the scroll wheel. By turning this wheel with your index finger, you can scroll the contents of the window. This is exactly the same effect you get by using the scrollbar, but much easier and faster.

In addition to the classic mouse shape, there are also *ergonomically*-shaped mice with extra buttons for your thumb, for example. You can give these different buttons specific functions.

A *trackball* is a kind of "reverse" mouse. The device remains stationary on the table while you turn the ball with your fingers to move the mouse pointer. The trackball also has a scroll wheel for the Internet and multiple buttons.

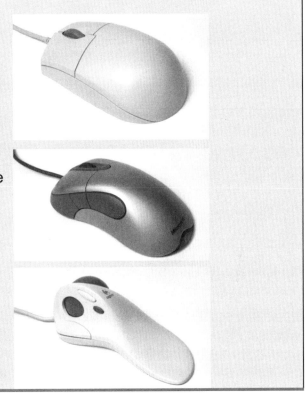

Back to the Home Page

A good website is designed so that you can move easily from one page to another without losing your way. Usually there's a *Home* button you can use to return to the opening, or *home* page for the website.

Click on home

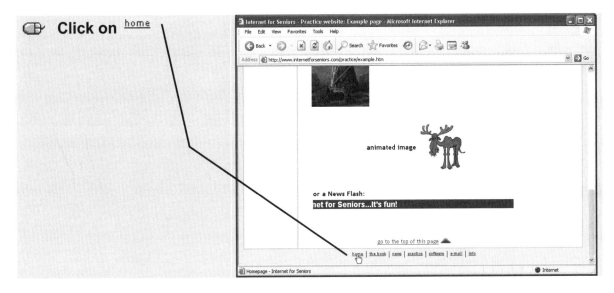

You see the home page again:

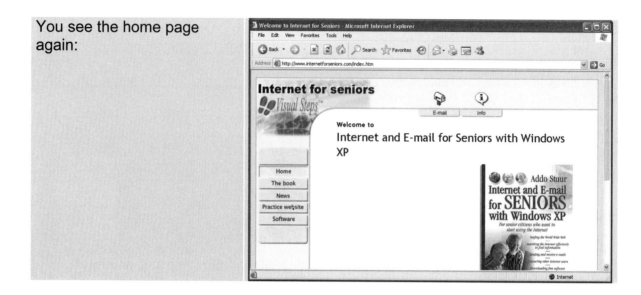

A Second Window

Up to this point, you've viewed all the web pages in a single *Internet Explorer* window. However, a website can be designed so that a new window is opened when you click on a hyperlink. You don't have any control over this, because it's been programmed into the website and happens automatically. There's a hyperlink like this on the practice site. Give it a try:

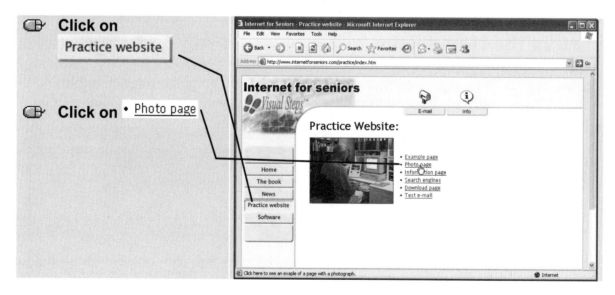

You see a new window
containing a photo:

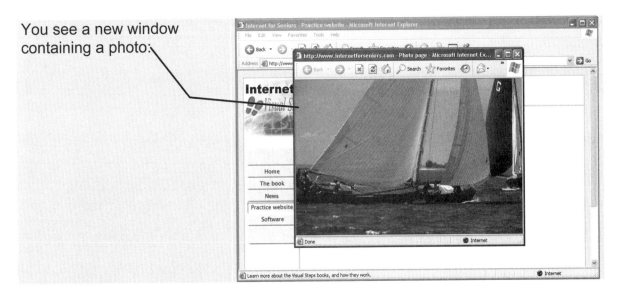

If you want to keep this window available and not close it completely, you can
minimize it.

Minimizing a Window

Making a window small is called *minimizing*. This allows you to better see the
underlying window.

Click on

The window containing the
photo is minimized.

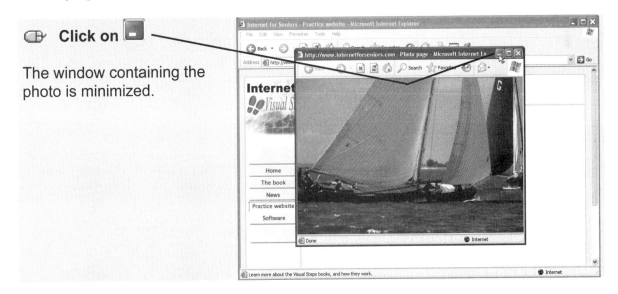

Now you see the practice website window again:

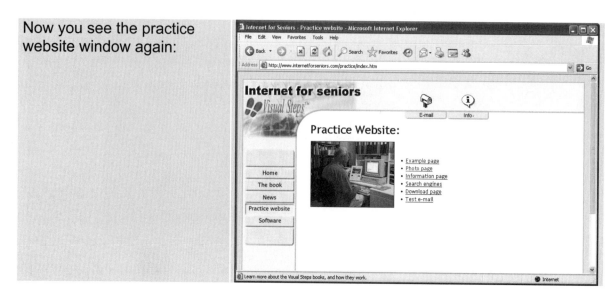

You can also minimize the window for the practice site:

👆 **Click on** 🔲

The practice site window is minimized.

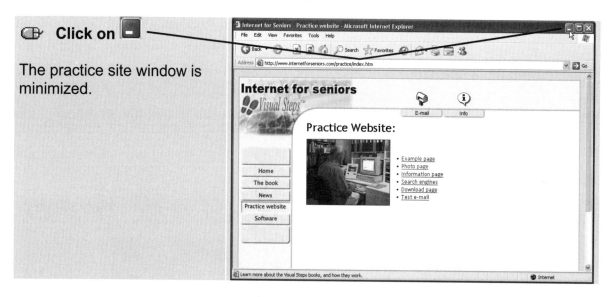

Now you've minimized two windows: the practice site and the window with the photo.

Both windows have been
minimized and have a button
at the bottom of the screen:

The blue bar next to 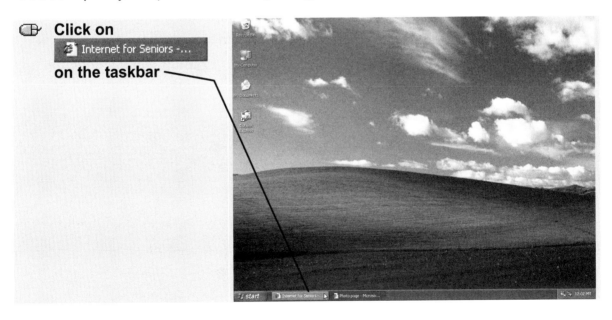 is called the **taskbar**. The taskbar always contains
the buttons for the windows you're currently using.

Opening a Window

You can quickly re-open a window by using the taskbar buttons:

☞ **Click on**

       📄 Internet for Seniors -...

on the taskbar

You see the window for the practice site again:

You can open the window with the photo the same way:

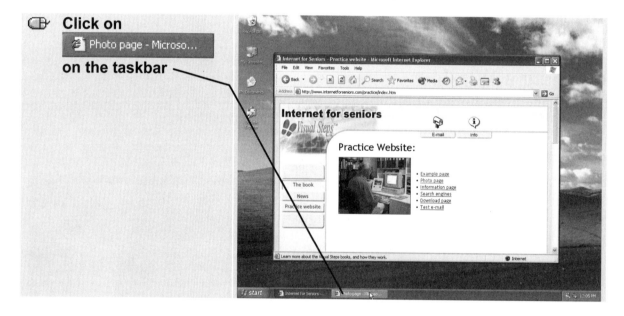

☞ **Click on**

📄 Photo page - Microso...

on the taskbar

The window with the photo opens:

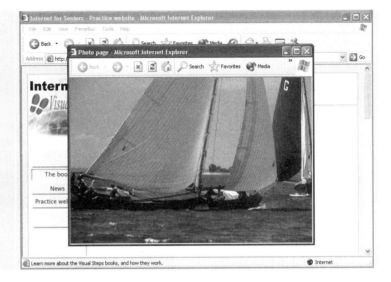

The window with the photo is now in front of the window for the practice site. That's easy to change, however.

Going from One Window to Another

You can use the taskbar to quickly move from one window to another:

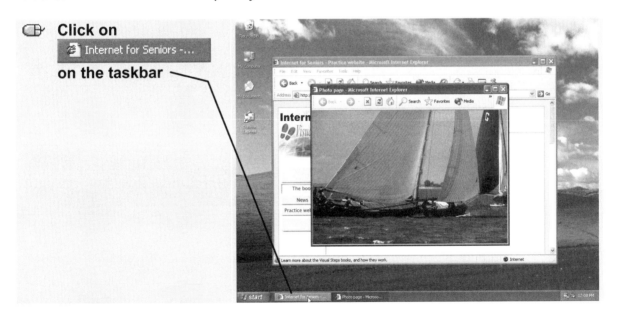

☞ **Click on**

Internet for Seniors -...

on the taskbar

The window with the photo now disappears behind the window for the practice site.

Click on

> Photo page - Microso...

on the taskbar

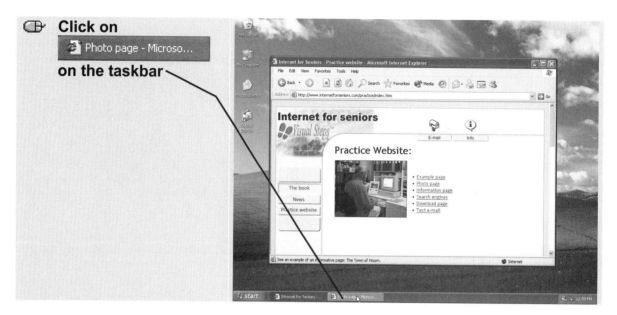

The window with the photo pops in front again:

The window for the practice site is once again behind it.

You can easily switch between different windows this way.

Closing Windows

After you've opened several windows, you can always close the ones you no longer need.

 Please note:

Always keep at least one *Internet Explorer* window open, or the connection to the Internet may be broken.

In this case, you can close the window with the photo.

Click on ⊠ in the window with the photo

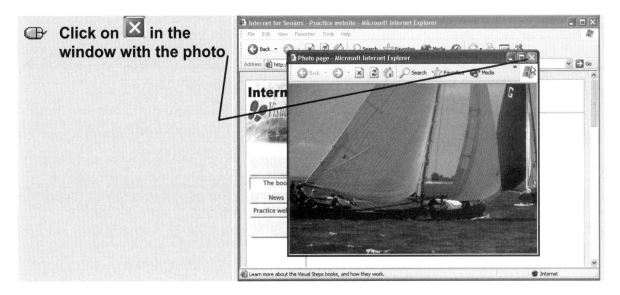

The window closes and its button on the taskbar disappears.

Larger or Smaller Text

You can make the letters of the text on web pages larger or smaller. Sometimes this helps make them more readable. You should realize, however, that some text, such as text on buttons, has a fixed size and can't be changed. You can see the effect on the example page:

You see the *Internet for Seniors* practice website:

☞ **Click on** • Example page

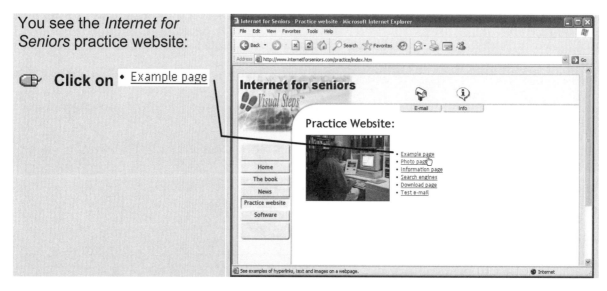

You see this page:

Take a good look at the size of the text in the right-hand frame:

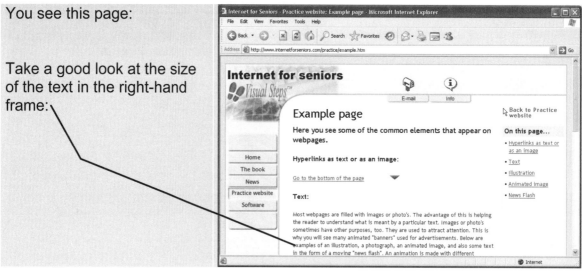

You can start out by choosing the largest size:

Click on `View`

Click on `Text Size`

Click on `Largest`

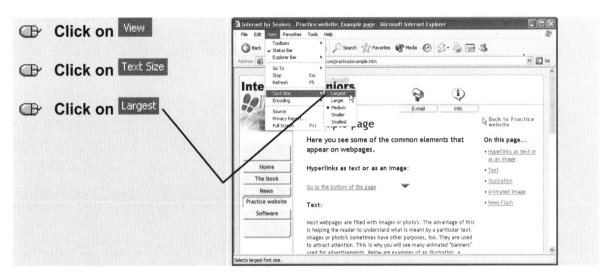

The letters of the text in the right-hand frame are now quite a bit larger:

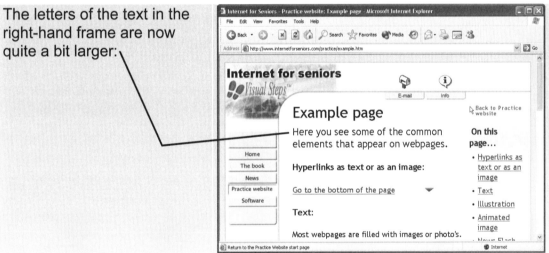

You can also decrease the text size:

Click on `View`

Click on `Text Size`

Click on `Smallest`

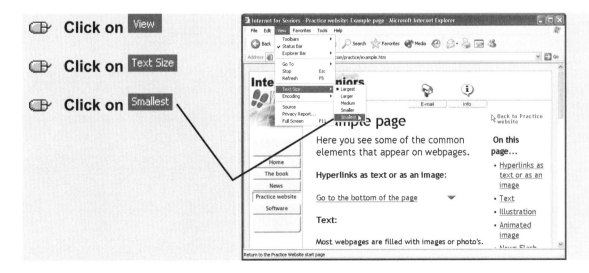

The letters of the text in the right-hand frame are now quite a bit smaller:

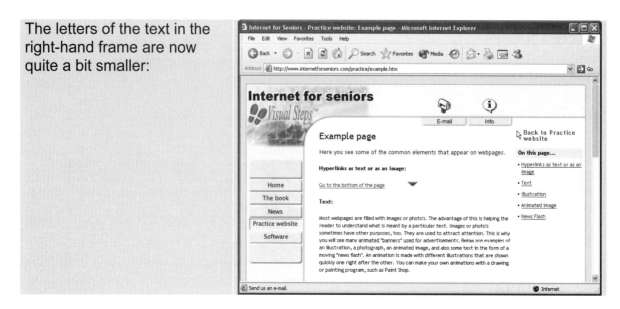

Internet Explorer saves this setting. If you chose smaller letters last time, then the next time the program is started, this setting with smaller text will be used.

If the letters are too small for you to read them, you should change this setting. You can restore the font to the standard size:

Click on View

Click on Text Size

Click on Medium

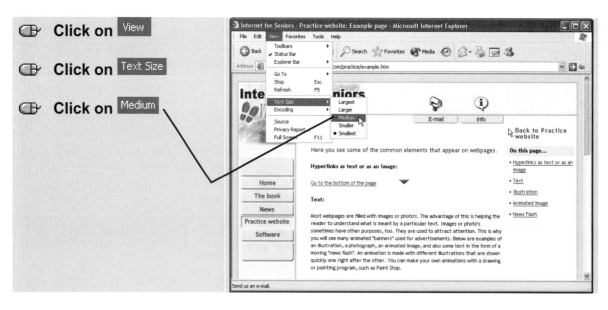

Now *Internet Explorer* will start up with regular letters next time.

Disconnecting from the Internet

Do you have a telephone line connection? Then it's important that you break your connection to the Internet when you're finished looking at web pages. No other calls can come through to you as long as you're connected to the Internet.
You can close the *Internet Explorer* window this way:

👉 **Click on** File

👉 **Click on** Close

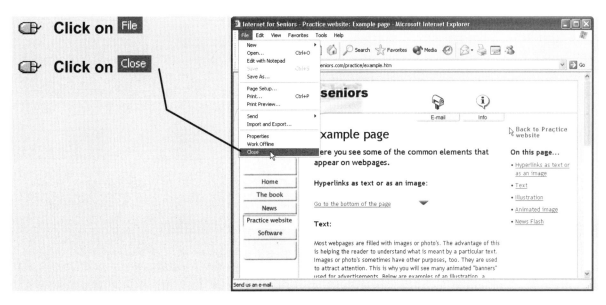

Windows asks you if the connection should be broken:

👉 **Click on** Disconnect Now

The little computers 💻 will then disappear from the taskbar:

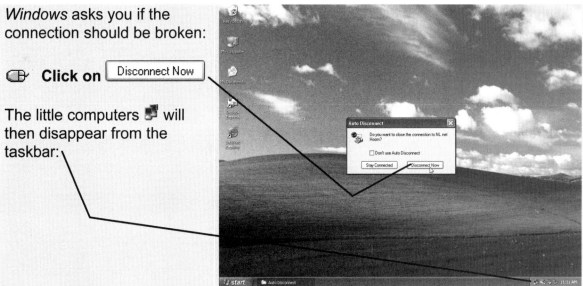

The connection has been broken. You can practice these techniques in the following exercises.

HELP! My connection isn't broken.

Have you not been asked if you want to break the connection?
Are the little computers 🖳 still on the taskbar?
Then the connection hasn't been broken yet. You can do that like this:

🖱 **Double-click on the taskbar on** 🖳

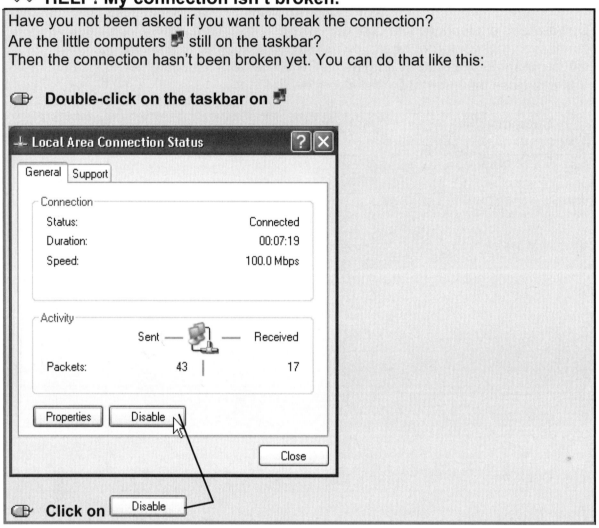

🖱 **Click on** | Disable |

Exercises

The following exercises will help you master what you've just learned. Have you forgotten how to perform a particular action? Use the number beside the footsteps to look it up in the appendix *How Do I Do That Again?*

Exercise: Surfing

Going from one website to another is called surfing. In this exercise, you'll surf among previously-visited websites.

✓ Start *Internet Explorer*. [1]

✓ Connect to the Internet. [3]

✓ Type in the address of the Public Broadcasting Service: www.pbs.org [4]

✓ Type in the address: www.internetforseniors.com [4]

✓ Go back to www.pbs.org [6]

✓ Refresh the page. [8]

✓ Go forward to www.internetforseniors.com [7]

✓ Click on Practice website .

✓ Click on • Example page .

✓ Look at the bottom of the example page. [9]

✓ Go back to the top of the example page. [10]

✓ Go back to the Public Broadcasting Service website. [6]

✓ Close *Internet Explorer*. [2]

✓ Break the connection to the Internet if necessary. [5]

Exercise: Windows

In this exercise, you'll practice opening and minimizing windows.

✔ Start *Internet Explorer.* $\ell\ell^1$

✔ Connect to the Internet. $\ell\ell^3$

✔ Type in the address: www.internetforseniors.com $\ell\ell^4$

✔ Click on ___Practice website___ .

✔ Click on • <u>Photo page</u> .

✔ Minimize the photo page window. $\ell\ell^{11}$

✔ Minimize the *Internet Explorer* window. $\ell\ell^{11}$

✔ Open the window with the photo by using the taskbar. $\ell\ell^{12}$

✔ Close the window with the photo. $\ell\ell^{13}$

✔ Open the *Internet Explorer* window by using the taskbar. $\ell\ell^{12}$

✔ Close *Internet Explorer.* $\ell\ell^2$

✔ Break the connection to the Internet if necessary. $\ell\ell^5$

Background Information

The Modem

It's easy to understand why the telephone network is used to connect computers that may be thousands of miles apart. After all, nearly everyone has a telephone line. Cable TV providers have also entered the Internet market, using the cable network for Internet connections. You need a special device to connect to the Internet via a telephone line or a cable connection: the **modem**. A modem makes it possible for your computer to communicate with your ISP's computer.

There are two kinds of modems.

The first is a separate box that is connected to your computer with a cable. This is called an **external modem**. Another cable connects the modem to the outlet for the telephone line or the cable TV connection.

External modem

Almost all new computers have a built-in modem. This is called an **internal modem**.

The only part of this you see is a plug for a telephone cable or for a cable connection on the back of your computer.

Internal modem

The modem for the telephone network is connected to the telephone jack in your home by a regular telephone cable. You can also use a splitter if you want to keep your telephone connected to this same jack.

Telephone splitter

Domain Names
A web address associated with a particular name is called a domain name. Every web address has a suffix such as *.com*.

For example: *www.visualsteps.com*

There are several variations on this suffix. In Europe, a country code is often used:

For example: *www.visualsteps.nl*

Other country codes include **.be** for Belgium and **.de** for Germany.
Outside Europe and in the United States, a different system is used. The suffix indicates the type of organization:
.com   commercial company
.edu   educational institution
.org   non-profit organization

The History of the Internet
Soon after the introduction of the first computers, people in offices began connecting them using cables so that every employee could exchange information with others. Computers that are connected to one another are called a *network*.
The first of these networks began in America at the end of the 1960s. The Department of Defense had a network called ARPANET. ARPANET was an experiment. The DoD wanted to develop a technology that would allow all the defense computers to communicate with one another, even if part of the connection fell away because of a nuclear attack, for example. The problem was solved by a method that works just like the highway network. If a road is blocked, you can usually still get to your destination by taking a different route. This technique worked. Similar networks appeared in other countries. At the end of the 1980s, all these networks were connected to one another. The Internet was born. At first, mainly universities and research institutions were connected to the Internet, but in 1990 individuals and commercial companies also gained access to it. From that moment on, the number of users has grown phenomenally, a growth that continues up to this day.

Internet Service Providers

Connecting to the Internet is often made over a telephone line. Computers can communicate with one another over the telephone network. Connecting your computer to others usually happens with the help of an *Internet Service Provider* (ISP). This ISP gives access to the Internet by means of a large number of computers, all of which are connected to the Internet. When you make contact with one of the ISP's computers, you enter the Internet.

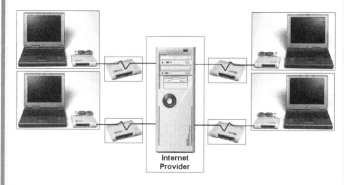

The Internet Service Provider offers access to many users

Most large ISPs have so many *access numbers* (the telephone number for the ISP that your own computer will call) that you can always call locally. If there is no local number in your area, the ISP usually offers a toll-free number you can call. That means accessing the Internet won't cost you a lot of money on your telephone bill. There are two kinds of subscriptions: free and premium. In practice they offer the same options, though some providers distinguish between them. With a premium subscription, the paying customer will get faster access and more disk space for his own website. You don't have to feel sorry for the free providers, though – they make their money on advertisements placed directly on your screen.

What services do ISPs provide?

- access to the *World Wide Web* (viewing information on the Internet)
- e-mail (electronic mail);
- FTP (download files from other computers)
- newsgroups (discuss topics with a group of other users)
- chatboxes (chat in real time with other users)

During the time you're connected to the Internet, you, the *client*, are in contact with your ISP's computers. These computers are called *servers*. The computers work together according to the *client-server* model.

How the Computer makes a Connection

If you have an internal modem, a cable runs from the modem in your computer to the telephone jack. If you use a splitter, you can plug both your telephone and the modem into the same jack.

Computer with internal modem and splitter

If you have an external modem, the modem box is located somewhere between your computer and the telephone jack:

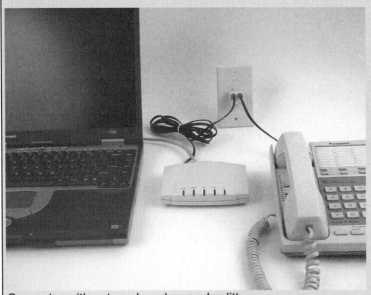

Computer with external modem and splitter

The modem is connected to the computer with a separate cable.

Connecting over a Telephone Line

The internal or external modem always has an outlet for a *UTP* cable. This is the same kind of cable used in an ordinary telephone cable. There are telephone plugs (also known as *RJ-11* plugs) on both ends. You plug one end of the telephone cable into the modem:

A UTP cable with telephone plugs

The UTP outlet on the modem

Plug the other end of the cable into the telephone jack on your wall:

The telephone plug

The telephone jack

If you want to connect your telephone to this same telephone jack, you can use a splitter. Some splitters fit directly into the phone jack. Others allow you to place it wherever you like, and connect it to the wall jack with another regular telephone cable:

A telephone splitter you can place anywhere

A splitter that connects directly to the phone jack

If you need a longer cable because your computer is too far from the phone jack, you can buy one in a variety of lengths at most appliance stores. Remember, all you need is a regular telephone cable.

Tips

 Tip

Sometimes you can do something quickly without having to use the mouse.
Do you see a dotted rectangle on a button?

Then this button is selected. Now you can press the Enter key instead of clicking on the button with the mouse pointer.

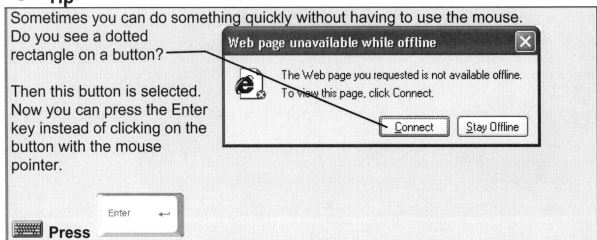

Web page unavailable while offline

The Web page you requested is not available offline.
To view this page, click Connect.

Connect   Stay Offline

 Press   Enter ⏎

 Tip

Starting *Internet Explorer*
Did you know there's another way to start *Internet Explorer*?
Find this icon on the *Desktop*:

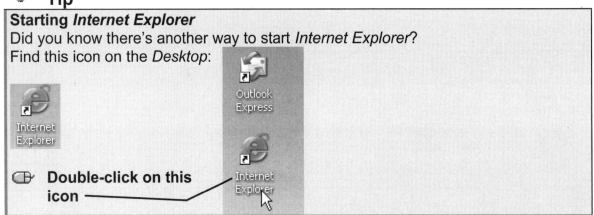

Outlook Express

Internet Explorer

🖰 **Double-click on this icon**

Internet Explorer

Tip

An Extension Reel
Make sure the telephone cable is neatly stored against the wall so you can't trip over it. Buy an extension cord if you need one. There are also telephone extension reels, with one or more telephone jacks on the reel and a telephone plug on the end of the cable. These allow you to keep your telephone cable at just the right length.

 Tip

A Busy Signal
Is your Internet connection made through your telephone line?
If you're connected to the Internet and someone tries to call you, they'll get a busy signal. If you're expecting a call, you should wait to connect to the Internet.
Is your Internet connection made through an ISDN line?
Then you can connect to the Internet and call or be called at the same time.
Is your Internet connection made through a DSL line?
Then you can connect to the Internet and call or be called at the same time.
Is your Internet connection made through the cable TV line?
Then, of course, you can always call or be called.

Tip

Block or Allow Pop-up Windows?
The ability to block pop-up windows is built into *Windows XP Service Pack 2 (SP2)*. A *pop-up* is a small window that automatically appears when you visit a particular website. The pop-up opens on top of the regular web page. Pop-ups often contain advertisements, but not always. You can set *Internet Explorer* to show or block these pop-ups.

☞ **Click on** Tools

☞ **Place the mouse pointer over** Pop-up Blocker **and keep it there**

The default setting is to block pop-ups. You see the following option in the menu: Turn Off Pop-up Blocker .

If you click on it, pop-ups will no longer be blocked.

☞ **Click on** Pop-up Blocker Settings...

In this window you can specify the websites for which you want to allow pop-ups:

Type the web address for an approved website here:

When you click on Add the web address will appear in this box:

You can specify how you want to be notified when a pop-up is blocked:

You can also set the filter level: high, medium, or low.

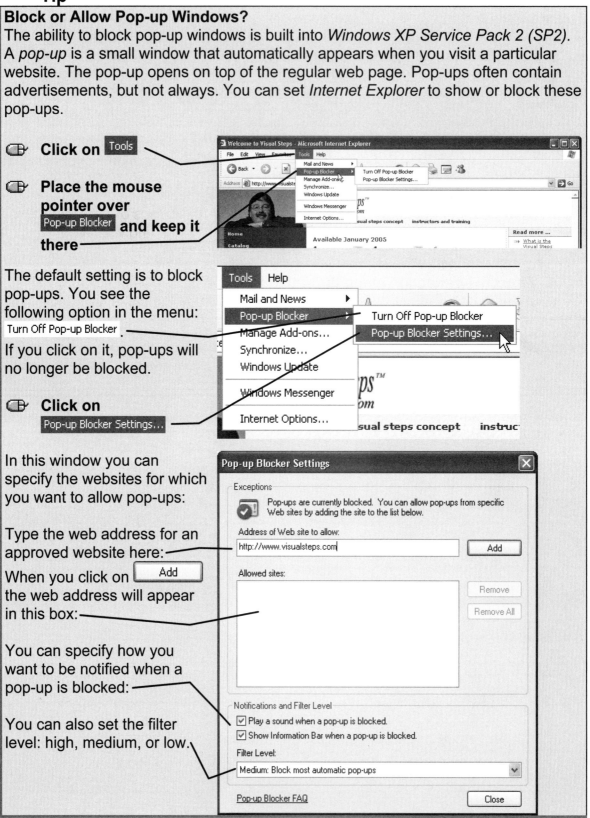

2. Navigating the Internet

Surfing the Internet is a fun and enjoyable activity. By clicking on various *hyperlinks*, you can visit many interesting websites and personal *homepages*. By *website* we mean an extensive system of web pages for a company or organization. A personal *homepage* may consist of only a few web pages. It usually belongs to an individual, or contains only a little commercial information about a company.

The *World Wide Web* is infinitely large and increases by thousands of websites daily. After surfing for a while, you'll no doubt want to revisit an interesting website from time to time. All those hyperlinks make it easy to lose your way, however. Fortunately, *Internet Explorer* has several built-in options for getting where you want to go. In this chapter, you'll learn how to use these convenient features, allowing you to "navigate" straight for your target: back to the web pages you visited earlier.

In this chapter, you'll learn how to:

- use the *History* button
- save a web address
- open a favorite
- organize your favorites
- use the address bar
- temporarily disconnect
- change the *Internet Explorer* home page
- give a website its own shortcut

Starting Internet Explorer

☞ **Turn on the computer**

Do you have an external modem?
☞ **Turn on the modem**

Now you can start *Internet Explorer*:

☞ **Start** 🅔 *Internet Explorer* 🖰¹

Internet Explorer starts, and you can connect to the Internet:

Are your username and password filled in?

👉 **Then click on**

Connect

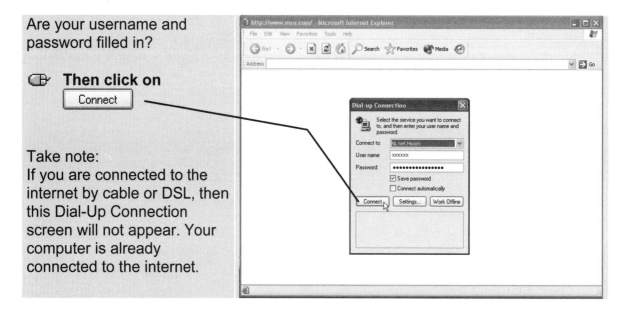

Take note:
If you are connected to the internet by cable or DSL, then this Dial-Up Connection screen will not appear. Your computer is already connected to the internet.

You see the home page as it is set up on your computer:

This page might be different on your computer.

The History Button

In the previous chapter, you visited several websites. You don't have to type in these addresses again. *Internet Explorer* remembers which websites you've previously visited. You can search for these addresses using the *History* button.

Click on

On the left-hand side, you see a separate frame with a chronological list:

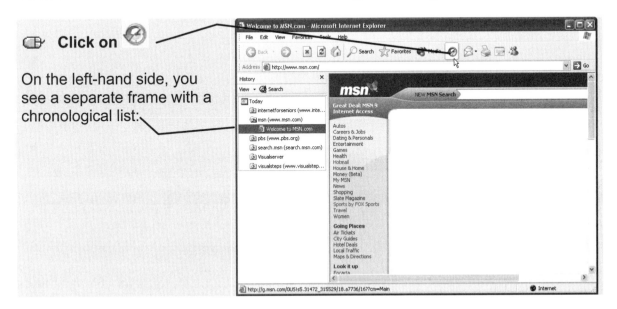

The websites are neatly organized under today, previous days, or previous weeks.

Today opens by default.

Under Today, you see the websites summarized:

Did you work through the previous chapter on a day other than today?

Then click on for the day that you worked through the previous chapter

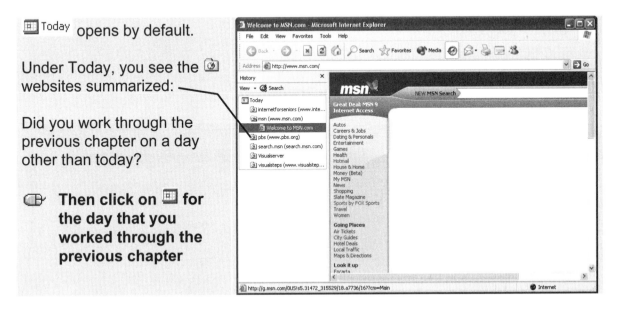

Click on the website
internetforseniors

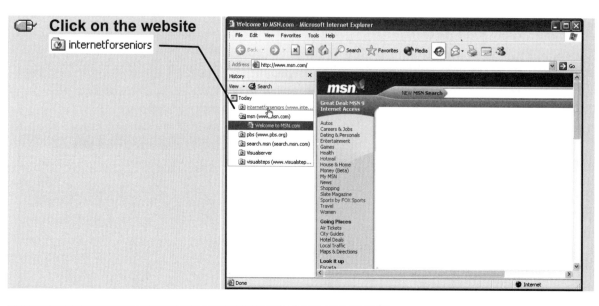

Now you see the web pages you've visited:

If you place the mouse pointer over the name, you'll see the page's web address in a little box.

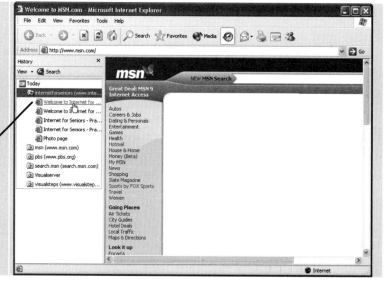

Click on
Welcome to Internet for ...

After a short time, you see the home page for the website for this book:

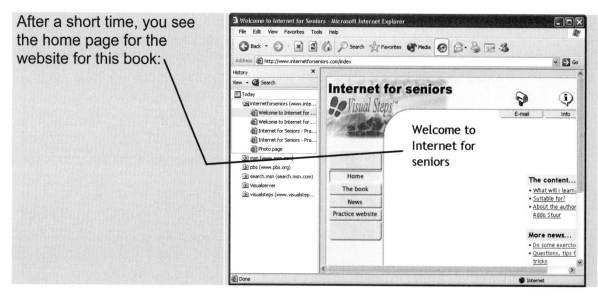

You can close the *History* frame now:

Click on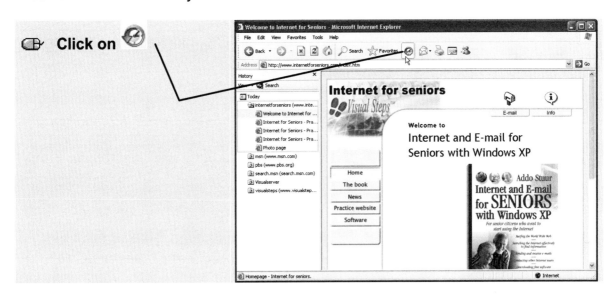

The web page fills the entire window again.

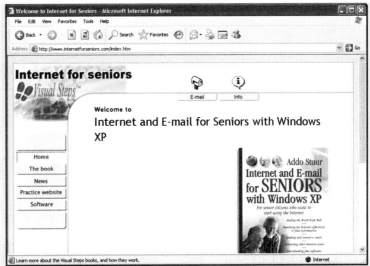

Returning to a website with the *History* button is only useful if you know when you last visited it. If you're on the Internet daily, however, and you visit a lot of websites, this method isn't as useful. That's why there are other options for saving and organizing web addresses.

Saving a Web Address

Once you've found an interesting website, you can save its address. From then on, you can quickly reopen this website anytime without typing in the web address. Saved websites are called **favorites** in *Internet Explorer*.

 Please note:

You can only save a web address when the associated website is displayed in the *Internet Explorer* window.

In this case, you see the *Internet for Seniors* website:

Click on Favorites

Click on Add to Favorites...

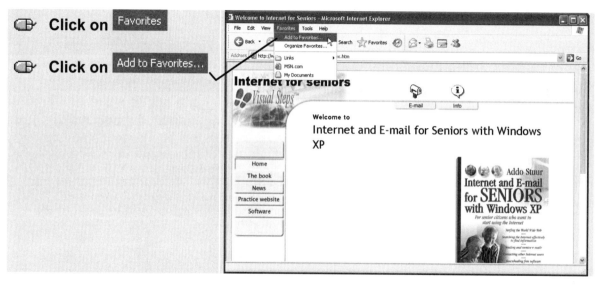

Now you see a small window in which the name *Welcome to Internet for Seniors* has already been filled in:

Click on OK

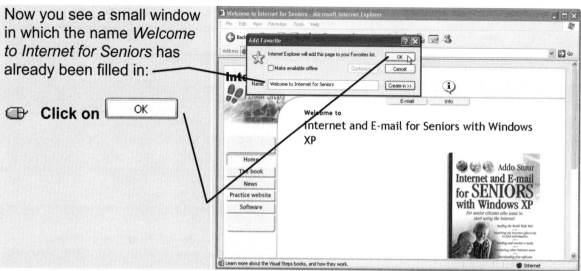

Later, you'll see how to quickly reopen this favorite website. To see how a favorite works, you first need to go to a different website.

You can go to the special website for seniors, *SeniorNet*, for example:

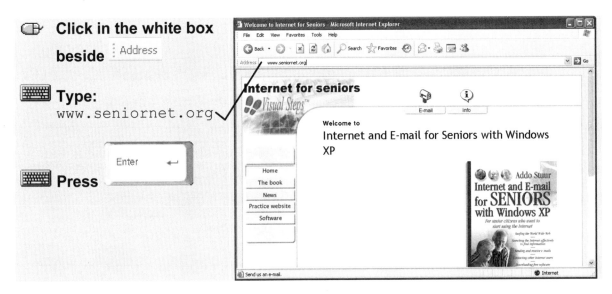

☞ **Click in the white box beside** Address

⌨ **Type:**
www.seniornet.org

⌨ **Press** Enter

You see the *SeniorNet* home page:

Now you can open the favorite you just saved.

Opening a Favorite

You can quickly open your favorite websites this way:

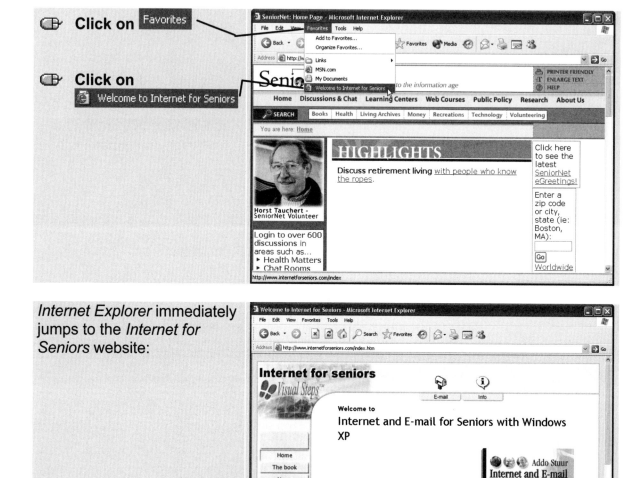

Click on Favorites

Click on Welcome to Internet for Seniors

Internet Explorer immediately jumps to the *Internet for Seniors* website:

Internet Explorer remembers your *Favorites* even after you've closed the program. This allows you to create an entire collection of websites you'd like to visit again later.

Organizing Your Favorites

You can save all your favorite websites in one long list, but in the long term that isn't very practical. Instead, you can organize them in separate folders. You can save websites according to subject, for example.
You can also use folders to separate your own favorites from those of other users on the same computer.

For practice, you're going to create a folder for websites related to this book.

Click on Favorites

Click on
Organize Favorites...

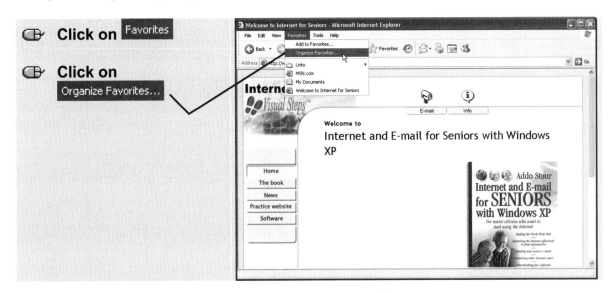

Now you see this small window. Usually there are already a few ☐ folders, which you can see on the right-hand side in the white box: ⎯⎯⎯⎯⎯⎯

Click on Create Folder

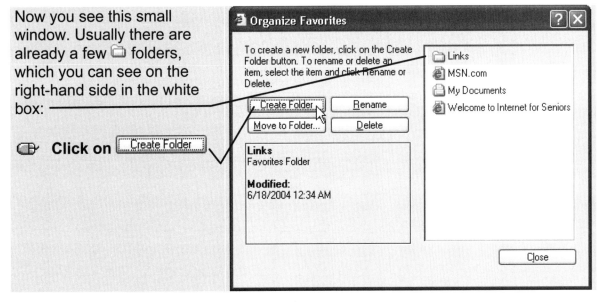

A new 🗀 folder appears at the bottom of the list, and you can immediately type in a name for it:

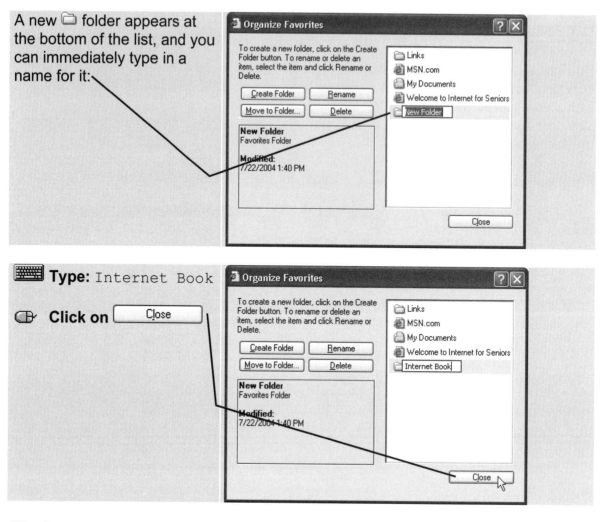

⌨ Type: Internet Book

☞ Click on `Close`

The folder has now been created. You can check this right away:

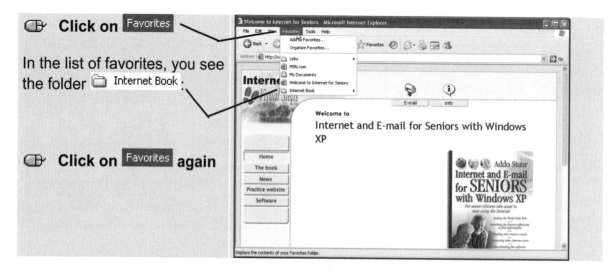

☞ Click on Favorites

In the list of favorites, you see the folder 🗀 Internet Book .

☞ Click on Favorites **again**

You've seen that the folder has been created. A little later on, you'll read how you can save all the websites related to this book in the folder.

Typing Part of a Web Address

Internet Explorer remembers all web addresses in a hidden list. Take a look at what happens if you type in just part of a web address:

Click in the white box beside : Address

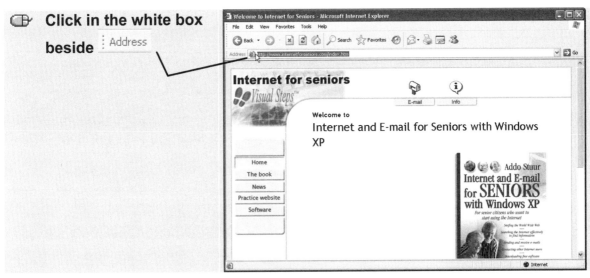

Type: `www.visu`

Under the address bar, you see a list of web addresses that begin with `www.visu`:

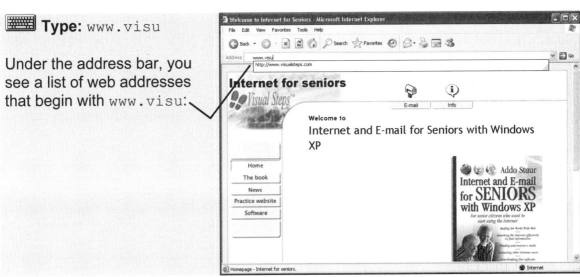

Now you just have to click on the desired web address in the list:

 Click on

http://www.visualsteps.com

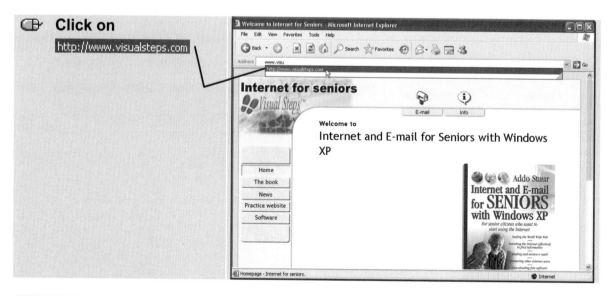

The website opens:

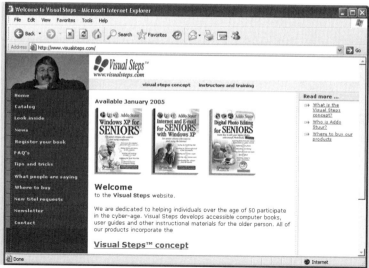

➡ **Please note:**

Pay attention to which address you click on – *Internet Explorer* also remembers incorrectly typed web addresses.

Saving a Web Address in a Folder

It's pretty easy to save a website in the new folder.

 Please note:

You can only save a web address when the associated website is displayed in the *Internet Explorer* window.

In this case, you see the *Visual Steps* website in the window. You can save it in the folder.

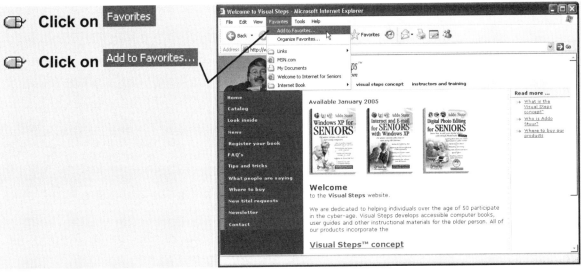

👆 **Click on** Favorites

👆 **Click on** Add to Favorites...

You see this little window again:

The name of the *Visual Steps* website has already been filled in:

Now you have to open the folder where you want to save this favorite:

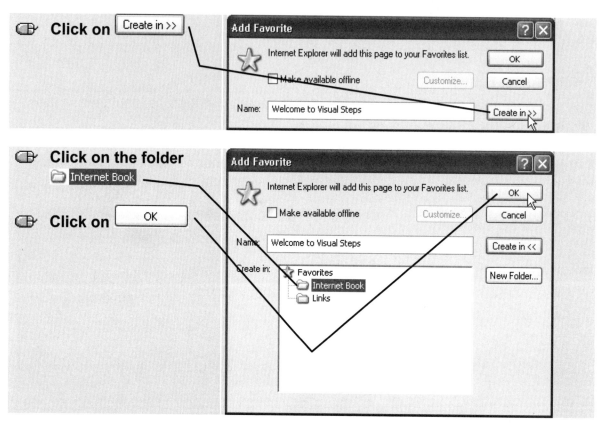

You can check later to see if the website has been saved in the folder. In order to do that, first go to another website, for example the AAA website:

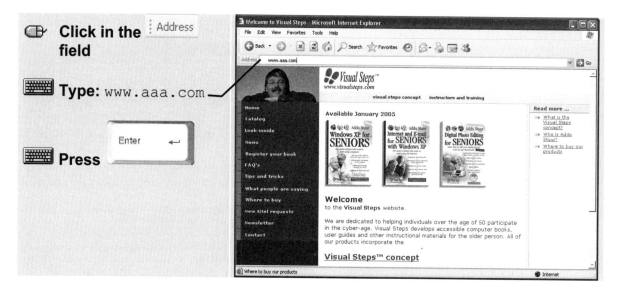

Now you see the home page for the *AAA*:

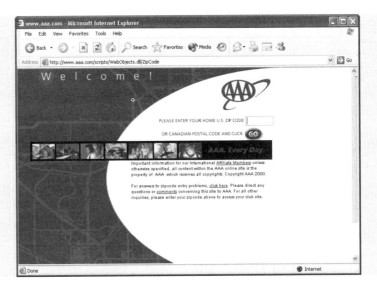

Now you can try the *Favorites* command:

👉 **Click on** Favorites

👉 **Click on the folder**
📁 Internet Book

👉 **Click on**
Welcome to Visual Steps

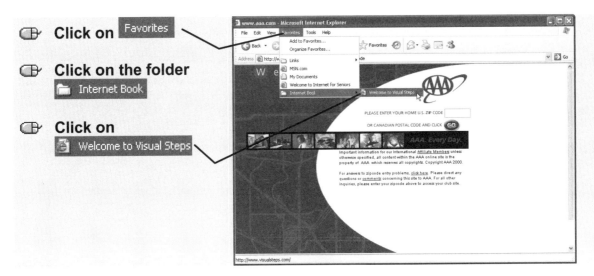

Now you see the *Visual Steps* home page:

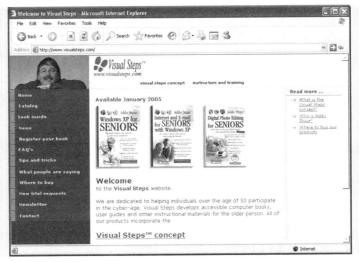

The Address Bar

Internet Explorer has another useful feature on the address bar that you can sometimes use. The address bar is the bar containing the white box where you type a web address.

Click on ⌄ **after the**
⌨ Address **field**

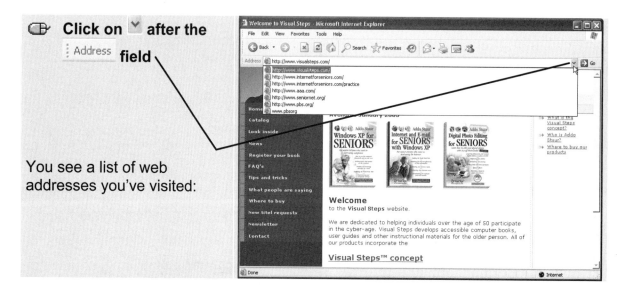

You see a list of web addresses you've visited:

You can click on one of these addresses to open it again:

Click on
⌨ http://www.internetforseniors.com/

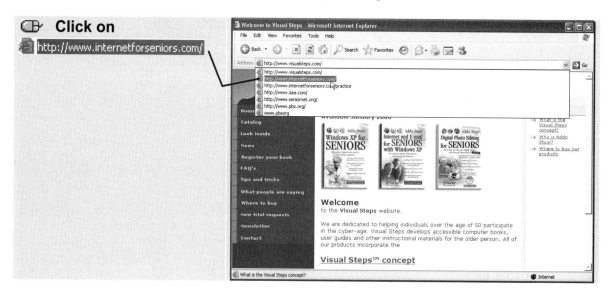

The website for this book will be opened.

Temporarily Disconnecting

At some point, you'll probably want to disconnect from the Internet for a short while. For example, you might want to do something else, or a web page might take a long time to read. This way you can free up your telephone line in case someone wants to call you. You don't have to close *Internet Explorer* to do so:

Double-click on the right-hand side of the taskbar on

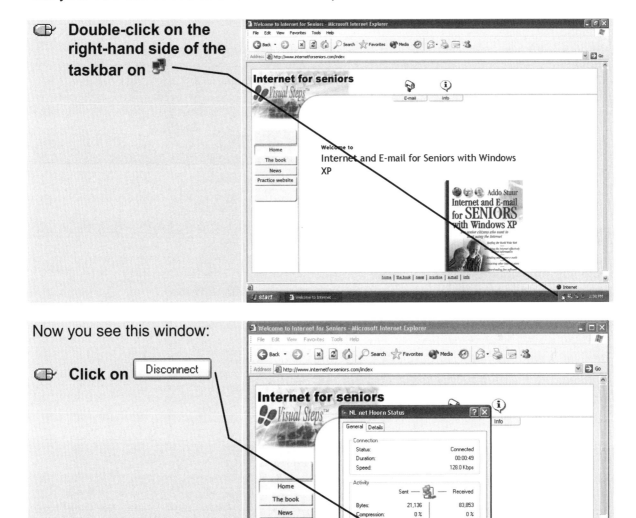

Now you see this window:

Click on Disconnect

The connection is broken.

The little computers have disappeared from the taskbar:

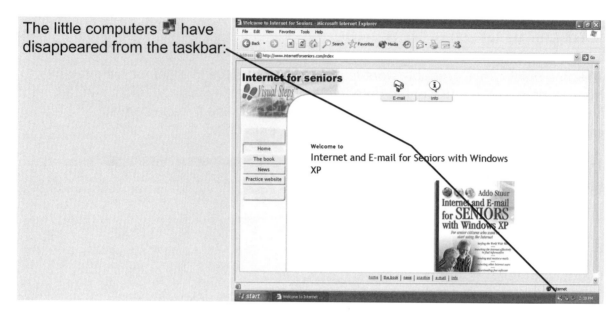

To reconnect, do the following:

☞ **Click on**

Now you see this window for the dial-up connection:

☞ **Click on** Connect

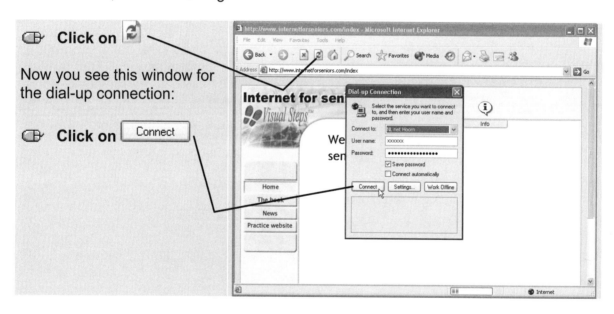

The connection to the Internet is re-established.

Changing the Home Page

Internet Explorer always starts up with a particular web page, called the *home page*. You can make your favorite page the home page.

 Please note:

You can make a page your home page when it is displayed in the *Internet Explorer* window.

You can make the *Internet for Seniors* web page your home page:

Click on Tools

Click on Internet Options...

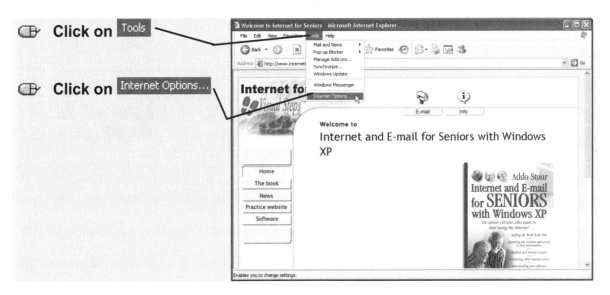

Now you see this window:

Click on Use Current

Click on OK

Internet for Seniors has now been stored as the home page.

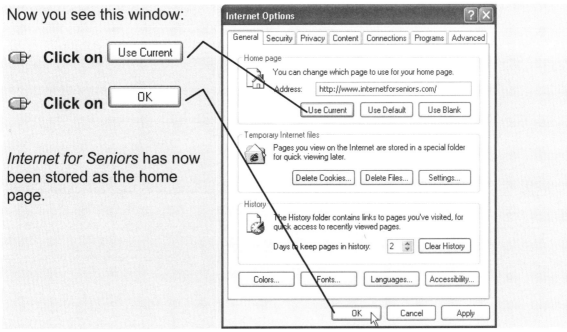

Favorites on Display

You can also keep your favorites permanently visible. This can be useful when you want to go from one favorite website to another. Here's how you do it:

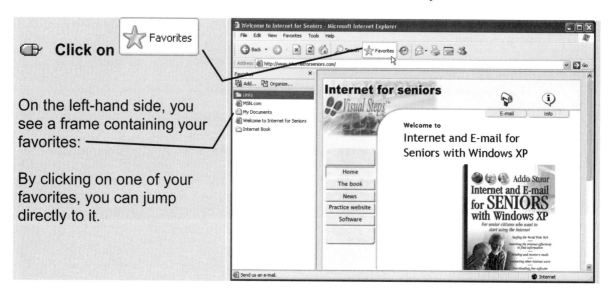

☞ **Click on**

On the left-hand side, you see a frame containing your favorites:

By clicking on one of your favorites, you can jump directly to it.

You can close this frame. You can do this by clicking on the ✕, but you can also just click on the *Favorites* button again:

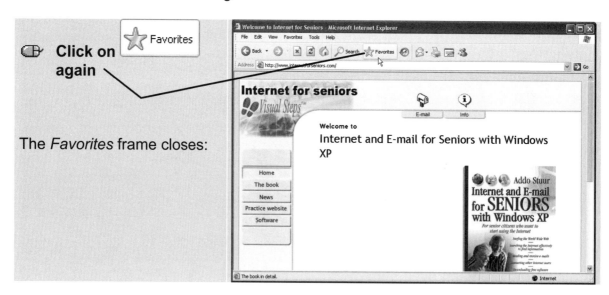

☞ **Click on again**

The *Favorites* frame closes:

Shortcuts

You can also put an icon called a *shortcut* for your favorite website on the *desktop*. Once you've started *Windows*, you just have to double-click on this icon to view the website. For practice, you can make a shortcut for the *Internet for Seniors* website. This is how:

☞ **Click on** File

☞ **Click on** Send

☞ **Click on** Shortcut to Desktop

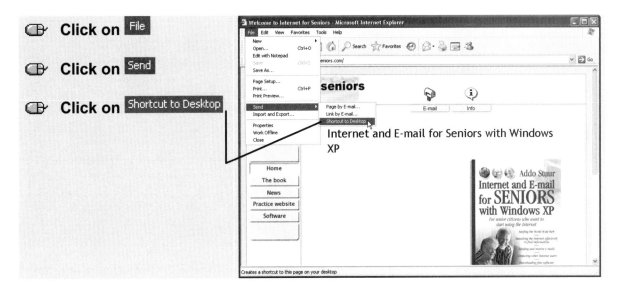

To see the result, minimize the *Internet Explorer* window:

☞ **Click on** ▬

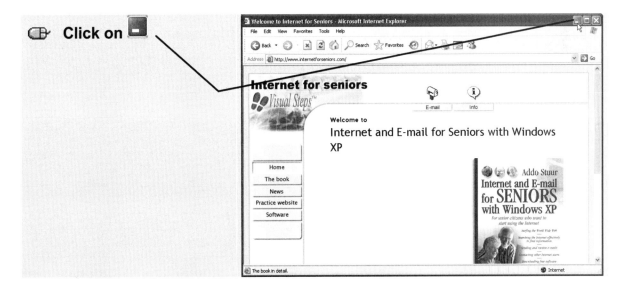

When all the windows are minimized, you see the *Windows* background. This is called the *desktop.*

You see the shortcut on the desktop:

By double-clicking on this icon, you can open the *Internet for Seniors* website without first having to start *Internet Explorer*. That happens automatically.

Now you know several ways to navigate effectively on the Internet, and to find your way back and forth between websites.

You can practice these techniques now in the following exercises.

 **Please note:**

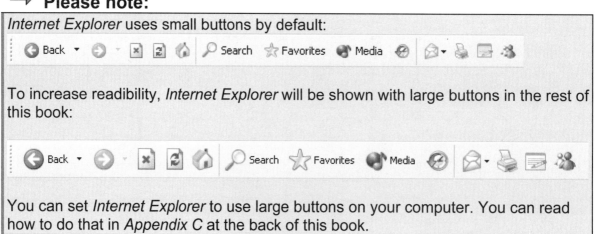

Internet Explorer uses small buttons by default:

To increase readibility, *Internet Explorer* will be shown with large buttons in the rest of this book:

You can set *Internet Explorer* to use large buttons on your computer. You can read how to do that in *Appendix C* at the back of this book.

Exercises

The following exercises will help you master what you've just learned. Have you forgotten how to perform a particular action? Use the number beside the footsteps to look it up in the appendix *How Do I Do That Again?*

Exercise: The SeniorNet Favorite

In this exercise, you'll open the websites for *SeniorNet* and *AAA* and add them to your favorites.

✓ Start *Internet Explorer.* $\ell\ell^1$

✓ Connect to the Internet. $\ell\ell^3$

✓ Use *History* to open: www.seniornet.org $\ell\ell^{14}$

✓ Make the address for *SeniorNet* a favorite. $\ell\ell^{15}$

✓ Use *History* to open: www.aaa.com $\ell\ell^{14}$

✓ Make the address for *AAA* a favorite. $\ell\ell^{15}$

✓ Temporarily disconnect from the Internet. $\ell\ell^{16}$

✓ Reconnect to the Internet. $\ell\ell^{48}$

✓ Open the favorite *SeniorNet.* $\ell\ell^{17}$

✓ Open the favorite *AAA.* $\ell\ell^{17}$

✓ Close *Internet Explorer.* $\ell\ell^2$

✓ Disconnect from the Internet if necessary. $\ell\ell^5$

Exercise: A New Favorite

In this exercise, you'll open the *National Geographic* website and add it to your favorites in the folder related to this book.

☑   Start *Internet Explorer.* 👣¹

☑   Connect to the Internet. 👣³

☑   Type the address: www.nationalgeographic.com 👣⁴

☑   Now you see this website:

☑   Make the address for *National Geographic* a favorite in the folder 📁 Internet Book . 👣18

☑   Open the favorite *AAA.* 👣17

☑   Open the favorite *SeniorNet.* 👣17

☑   Open the favorite *National Geographic.* 👣19

☑   Close *Internet Explorer.* 👣²

☑   Disconnect from the Internet if necessary. 👣⁵

Background Information

Why do I have to wait so long sometimes?
Once in a while, it might take a very long time before a page you want to see is displayed on your screen. The length of time it takes depends on a number of factors.

- There are slow and fast modems. The faster the modem, the faster the text and images can be sent. The speed of the connection is also important. At present, a modem connected to the standard telephone line is the slowest kind of connection. Other kinds, such as ISDN, DSL and cable Internet, are considerably faster.

- Some websites contain more images than others. Some pages have very many images or various graphic effects. All those fancy things have to be sent over the telephone line. Images in particular take a lot of time to receive. The more efficient the design of a web page, the sooner it will be on your screen.

- Sometimes it's very busy on the Internet. It can be so busy sometimes, with so many people working over the Internet at the same time, that a traffic jam occurs. At times like this, you have to wait longer than usual.

What can I do about it?

- You don't always have to wait until all the images on a page have been received.
  Sometimes you can immediately see which subject you want to visit.
  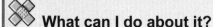
  Then you can click right away on a link to another page.

- Sometimes you'll see words like *Text Only* or *Low Graphics Version* on a website's home page.
  If you click on this, then only the text will be sent, without the images (or with a few very simple images). That will go much faster.

- Or you might see *skip intro* or *html only*.
  If you click on one of these, sophisticated film clips will be skipped. That will also go noticeably faster.

How does the WWW work?

The *World Wide Web* (WWW) is one of the more recent and most popular Internet applications. The idea for the web was developed in 1989 by Tim Berners Lee and Robert Cailliau at CERN (the European Organization for Nuclear Research) in Geneva, Switzerland.
The information on the WWW comes to us in the form of *hypermedia*. The word hypermedia is derived from *hypertext*.
A hypertext is a text containing *jump text* (or *hyperlinks*). The words in a *hyperlink* refer to the address of a different web page. By clicking on the jump text, you tell *Internet Explorer* to open that other web page. This page might be on any Internet-connected computer in the world, even one on the other side of the world. Words aren't the only things that can be used as a *hyperlink*. Drawings and photos can also be used. Web pages usually contain not only text, but also images, sound and moving images (*multimedia*). That's why you hear the term *hypermedia* these days; it's a contraction of the words *hyper*text and multi*media*.

How does the Internet system always find the right page? The WWW contains millions of pages. Each page has its own unique address, called an *URL* (Uniform Resource Allocator).
An example of an URL is: **http://www.internetforseniors.com**.
You can read this as follows:

http	HyperText Transfer Protocol
www	World Wide Web
internetforseniors	The domain name or "brand name" of the organization
com	A commercial website (as opposed to e.g. educational)

Based upon the URL, your ISP's computer knows on which computer the website is stored. In order to make communication between computers possible, every computer receives a unique address, the *Internet Protocol Number* (IP number or IP address). You won't use this number in daily practice. Instead, people use the URL, for example www.internetforseniors.com. When computers communicate with one another, this name is automatically converted to the numeric IP address. Sometimes you'll see these numbers displayed at the bottom of the *Internet Explorer* window.

HTML

Web pages are written in a special language. This makes it possible for the pages to look the same on completely different computers. *Internet Explorer* translates this language into a readable page for you. This language is called *HTML* or *HyperText Markup Language*.

Every HTML page looks the same in its simplest form.

<HTML>
    <HEAD>
        <TITLE>Internet for Seniors</TITLE>
    </head>

    <BODY>
        This will be the text.
    </body>
</HTML>

This language is fairly complicated, and therefore not very practical to use. Fortunately, we don't have to wrestle with all these unintelligible codes any more. Software companies like *Microsoft* have created special programs that make it possible to write web pages without the need to know a single word of HTML.
We call this kind of program an *editor*. One example of an editor is *FrontPage*. An editor works just like a text-editing program such as *MS Word*. You type in text, add images, and make sure that everything looks nice. The editor translates all your work into HTML. It couldn't be easier.

Bandwidth

In the early days of telecommunications, telephone lines were only used for speech. Now that the arrival of the Internet has appropriated these lines for other purposes in recent years – such as sending text, images, audio and video – it's become apparent that the bandwidth of these lines is too limited.

What do we mean by bandwidth?

The term can best be compared to a hallway between two rooms. Imagine that a hundred people are standing in one room. The time it will take for all these people to move to the other room depends primarily on how wide the hallway is. The wider the hallway, the better the flow. People have been searching for years for techniques to increase bandwidth for the Internet.

ISDN

One of these techniques is ISDN (Integrated Services Digital Network). ISDN allows much more information to be sent on the same copper wire in a given amount of time (up to 64 Kilobits per second). It's also possible to send different signals at the same time. That's how ISDN makes it possible to call someone on the phone and use the Internet at the same time. ISDN does have special requirements, however, such as a special modem and a different telephone subscription.

DSL

DSL (Digital Subscriber Line) is another technique for making broadband Internet possible. Here, the connection is split in two: an *upstream* channel (for sending information) and a *downstream* channel (for receiving information). Just as with ISDN, it's possible to call on the phone and use the Internet at the same time. Like ISDN, DSL has special equipment requirements. It also has a unique feature. With DSL, the user has a private line between two modems: one at home and the other at the exchange. This makes the channel secure. Your data goes over your own private line, in contrast to other techniques in which the line is shared with other users. Because you have your own line to the exchange, its speed is not affected by other users.

Cable

Fast Internet connections are also available over the television cable. This connection, however, becomes faster or slower depending on how many other people are using the same cable.

Tips

 Tip

Clearing the History
You might not like the fact that all the websites you visit are stored in a list. Another user on your computer could easily view your surfing behavior.
Fortunately, you can also clear your surfing history. Chapter 9 will show you how.

 Tip

The Home Button

If you click on the *Home* button, your default home page will be displayed.

 Tip

Removing Favorites
You might want to remove some of your favorites from time to time. Here's how you do it:

Click on Favorites

Click on Organize Favorites...

You see this window:

With the [Delete] button, you can remove a favorite:

You can do more "maintenance" on your favorites in this window. For example, you can use the [Move to Folder...] button to move a favorite to a different folder.

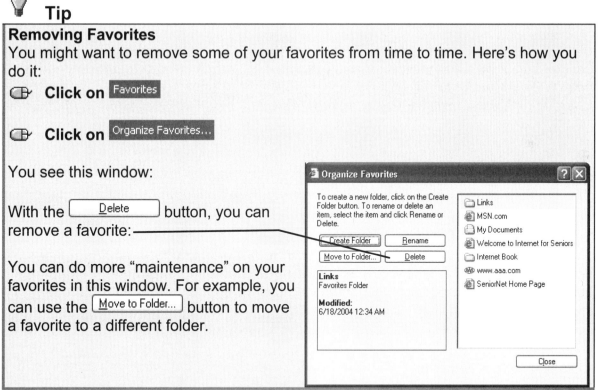

Tip

Keyboard Shortcuts
Just as with all *Windows* programs, you can also use the keyboard to operate *Internet Explorer*.
The list below gives a summary of the most important keys and their functions.

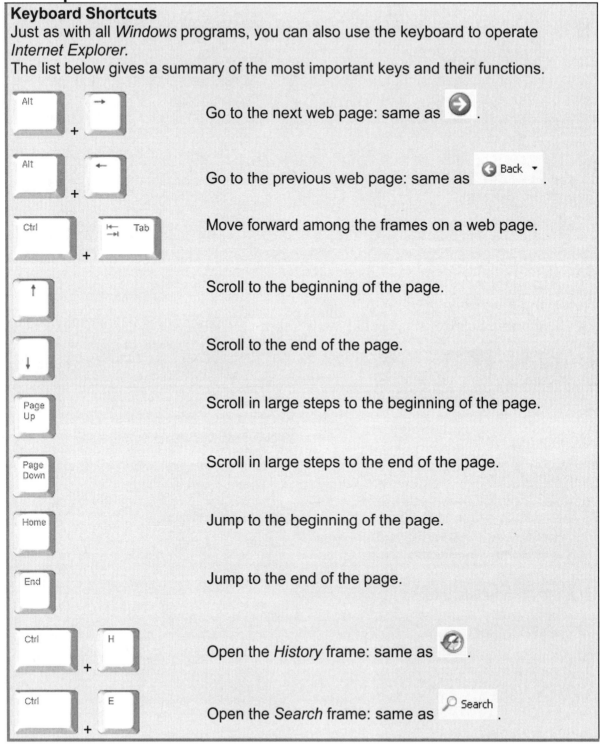

Go to the next web page: same as [→].

Go to the previous web page: same as [Back ▾].

Move forward among the frames on a web page.

Scroll to the beginning of the page.

Scroll to the end of the page.

Scroll in large steps to the beginning of the page.

Scroll in large steps to the end of the page.

Jump to the beginning of the page.

Jump to the end of the page.

Open the *History* frame: same as [icon].

Open the *Search* frame: same as [Search].

3. Searching and Finding on the Internet

The Internet is sometimes compared to a large library full of information on all kinds of subjects. Unfortunately, this library has no librarian. The books in this library are all jumbled up together. This comparison is a pretty good one. There is indeed no supervisory organization that organizes the information on the Internet. Everyone can place his own information on the Internet, which is immediately available to everyone else. This doesn't make searching on the Internet any easier.

There are a large number of companies and organizations that try to assist Internet users by organizing this enormous mountain of information. This occurs in several ways. The first way is via a *search engine*. This is a computer that is constantly busy indexing web pages. You can use the search engine's web page to search for all the web pages that contain certain words you type in, called *search terms*.

A second method for organizing information on the Internet is the *directory*. In this case, a company has already selected a large number of web pages and categorized them according to subject.

Despite these various resources, searching on the Internet can still be frustrating at times: You know, for example, that information on a particular subject must be out there somewhere, and yet you can't find the web page in question. That's where this chapter comes in. It covers the topic of searching on the Internet in great detail. You'll learn various techniques for searching for information and, hopefully, finding it. As with so many things, however, the more you practice, the better you'll get.

In this chapter, you'll learn how to:

- use the *Search* button
- put various search engines to work for you
- specify your search terms
- consult *AltaVista*
- use directories
- search within a web page

Starting Internet Explorer

☞ **Turn on the computer**

Do you have an external modem?
☞ **Turn on the modem**

Now you can start *Internet Explorer*:

☞ **Start 🎮 *Internet Explorer* 🦶1**

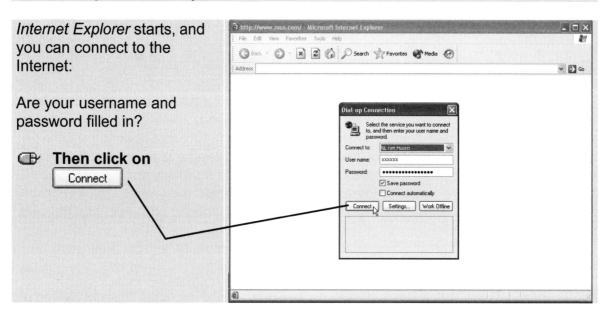

Internet Explorer starts, and you can connect to the Internet:

Are your username and password filled in?

🖱 **Then click on**
[Connect]

You see the home page as it is set up on your computer:

In the previous chapter, you set the website for this book as your home page.

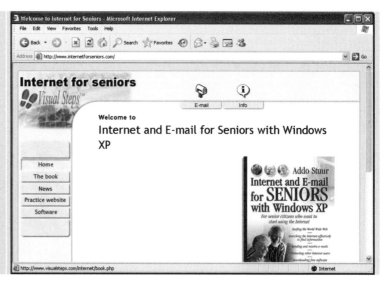

The Search Button

Internet Explorer offers direct access to several search engines. You can make use of this feature by clicking on the *Search* button:

Click on Search

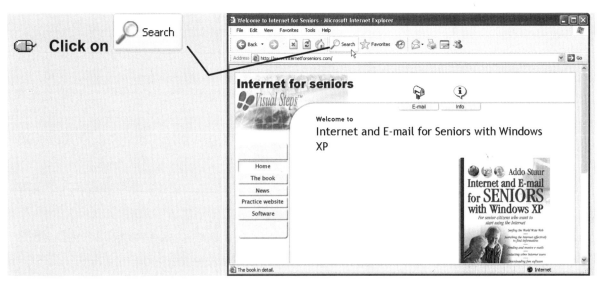

You see the *Search* frame:

Naturally *Microsoft*, the maker of *Internet Explorer,* has made sure that they're in first place, so the first search engine listed will probably be *Microsoft Network (MSN)*:

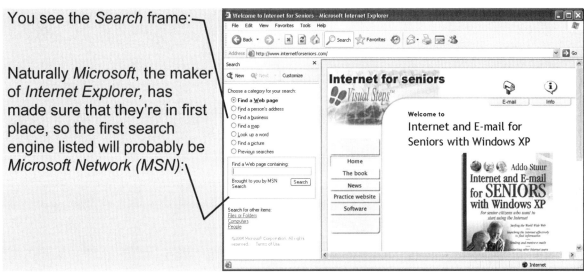

HELP! MSN Search isn't in the *Search* frame.

☞ **Click on**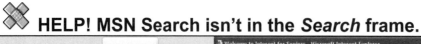

Now you see this window:

☞ **Click on** MSN Search

☞ **Click on** ⏷ **until** MSN Search **is listed at the top**

☞ **Click on** OK

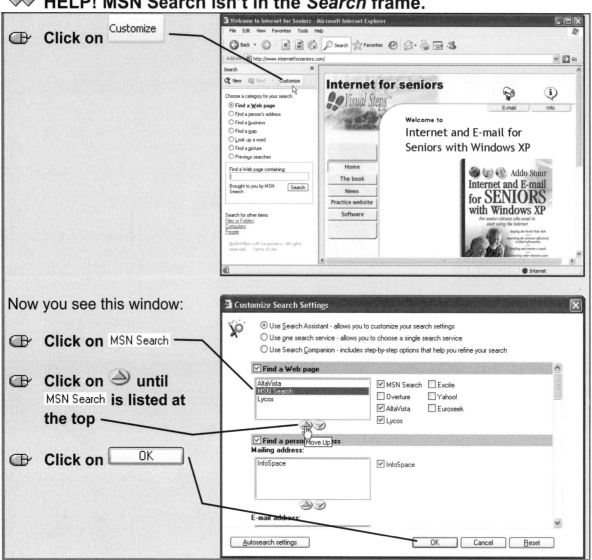

You begin a new search like this:

**Click on the circle in
front of**
○ Find a **W**eb page

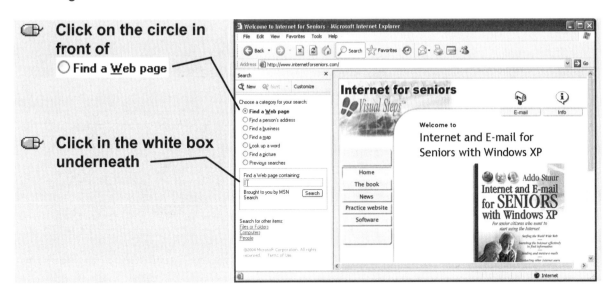

**Click in the white box
underneath**

In this box, you can type in a search term, for example the word *highway*.

Type: highway

Click on Search

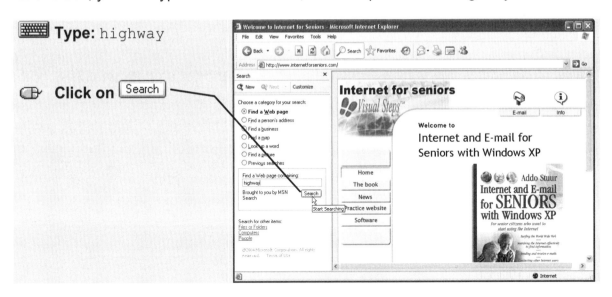

The search engine goes to work. You'll have to wait a bit.

On the left-hand side in the *Search* frame, you see *MSN Search*:

Various website names are listed below it: ——

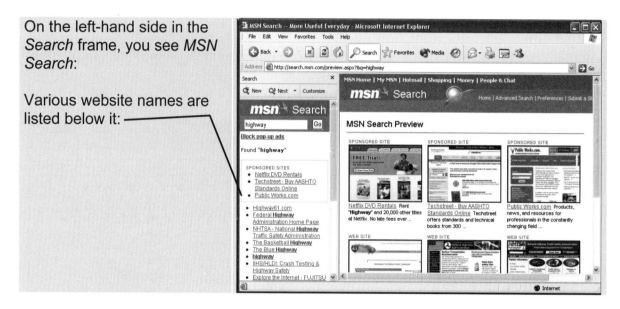

These names are references, or *links*. By clicking on a link in the *Search* frame, that website will be opened.

☞ **Click on the link for the *Federal Highway Administration***

The *Federal Highway Administration* website opens in the right-hand frame:

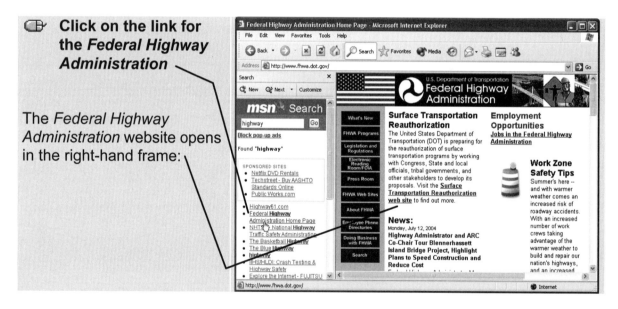

A Website in a New Window

You can also open a website in its own window. Later you'll see that this can sometimes be useful. Here's how you do it:

Press 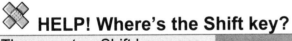 **and hold it down**

Click on a second web address, for example, the _NTHSA_

Release Shift

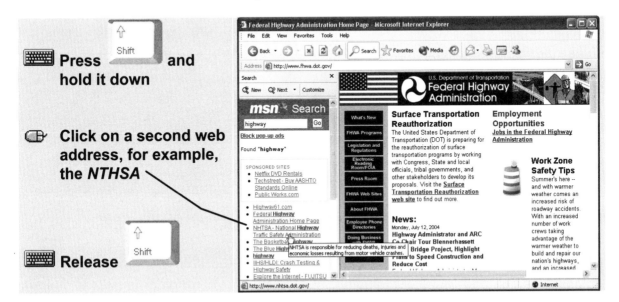

HELP! Where's the Shift key?

There are two Shift keys, one at each end of the bottom row of letters:

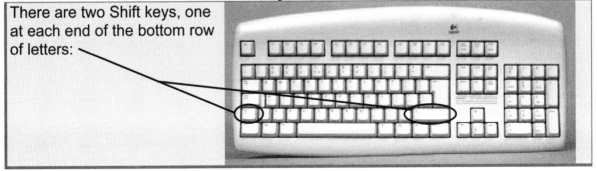

You see that a second window containing the *NTHSA* web page opens on top of the first:

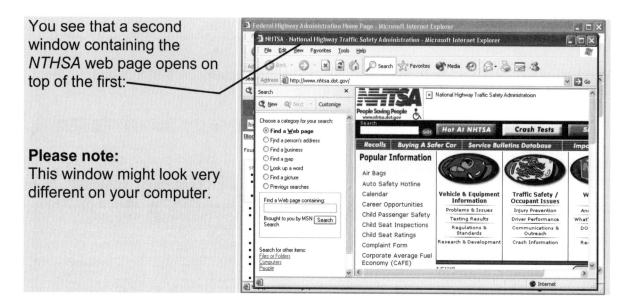

Please note:
This window might look very different on your computer.

You can close the *Search* frame to get a better view of the whole web page:

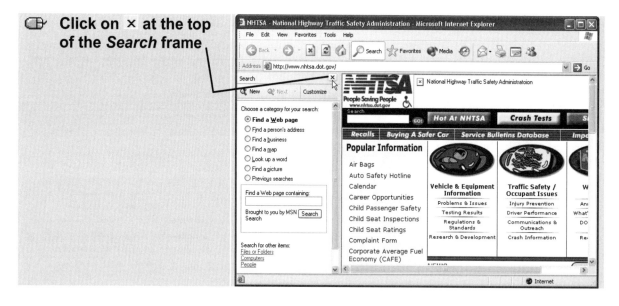

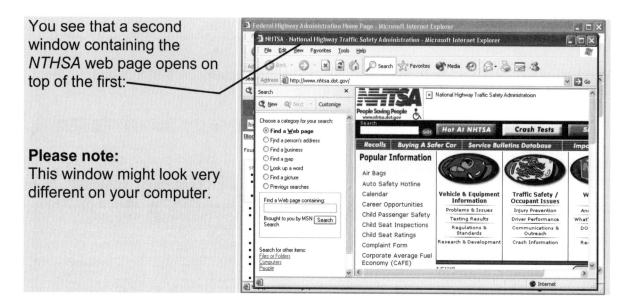 **Click on × at the top of the *Search* frame**

The web page now fills the whole window. When you're finished looking at the page, you can close this second window containing *NTHSA*:

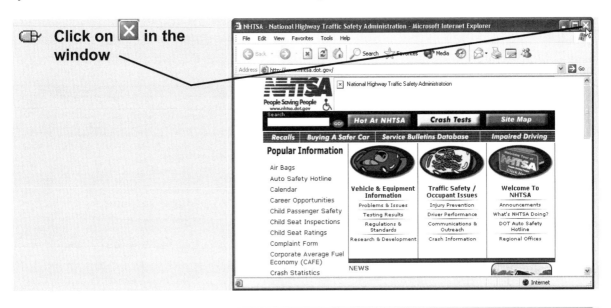

☞ **Click on** ⊠ **in the window**

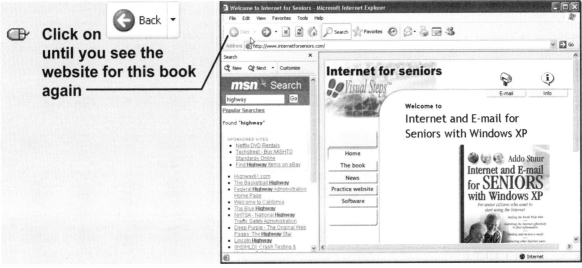

☞ **Click on** [← Back ▾] **until you see the website for this book again**

The Search Frame

It's a good idea to take a look at the other features of the *Search* frame.
There's more information at the bottom of the page. To see it, move down the page with the scrollbar:

☞ Drag the scrollbar all the way to the bottom

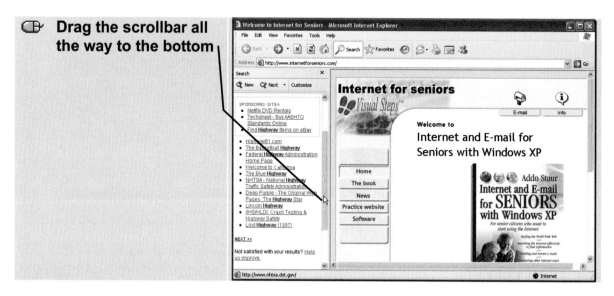

Now you can see the bottom of the *Search* frame.

At the bottom you see NEXT >> :

☞ Click on NEXT >>

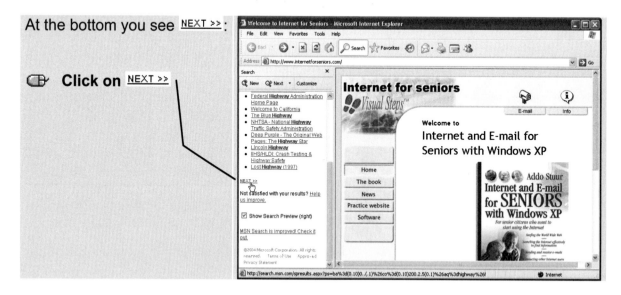

The next batch of websites that were found appear in the frame:

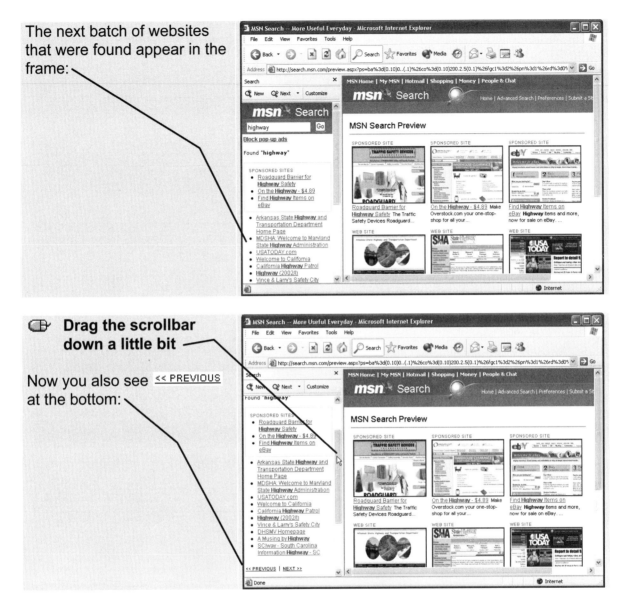

Drag the scrollbar down a little bit

Now you also see << PREVIOUS at the bottom:

You can use the << PREVIOUS and NEXT >> commands to browse through all the results.

When you move the mouse pointer over one of the websites, you see a short summary. This gives you a better idea whether the website actually contains the information you're searching for:

Move the mouse pointer onto one of the addresses

Now you see a short summary of this website:

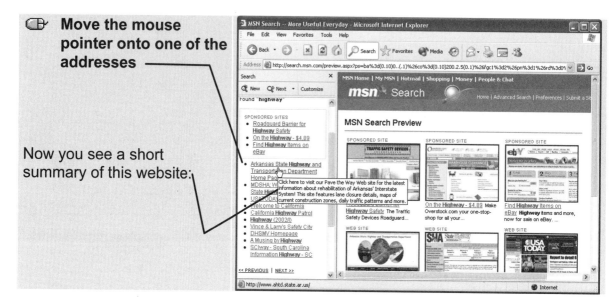

You can also widen the *Search* frame. You do that by dragging with the mouse:

Place the mouse pointer on the right-hand edge of the frame

The mouse pointer turns into a double arrow ↔:

Press the left mouse button and keep it pressed

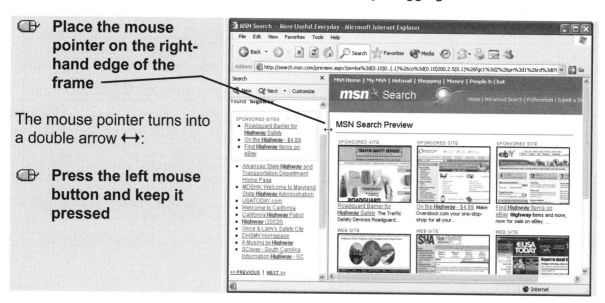

Drag the edge to the right

Release the mouse button

The frame is now wider:

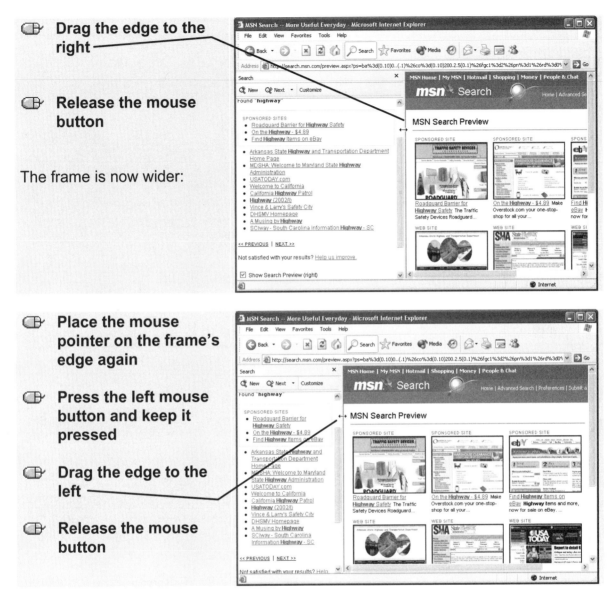

Place the mouse pointer on the frame's edge again

Press the left mouse button and keep it pressed

Drag the edge to the left

Release the mouse button

The *Search* frame is narrower again.

Tip

MSN Search Preview

After you've entered in a search command, you're immediately given a preview of the pages that were found. Sometimes this can be useful, but it can also become annoying. You can easily turn off this preview. Here's how you do it:

 Slide the scrollbar all the way to the bottom

☞ **Click on the check mark in front of**
Show Search Preview (right)

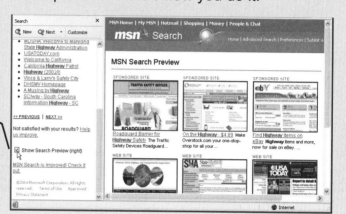

The check mark disappears, and the *MSN Search Preview* window is no longer displayed.

How does a search engine work?

Search engines are programs that are busy indexing web pages around the clock. This creates an enormous index of search terms. Search engines differ in the method they use to do this. That's why the results from different search engines are often very different. Some search engines index as many words as possible on a web page. Others only use search terms found in the titles of web pages. There are also search engines that primarily use key words on web pages. These hidden key words are put in by the web page designer. Sometimes this feature is abused, and particular key words are used intentionally because these words are frequently typed into searches. This can be the reason why you sometimes see web pages in your search results that have very little to do with your search term.

Search engines work like a kind of robot and are therefore fairly limited. No editing or selection is performed on the pages. This limitation becomes particularly evident when you search for words that have multiple meanings. An editor would be able to separate out the web pages based upon their content.

All the well-known search engine companies also have a department where editing does take place, and hundreds of websites have been organized by subject or category.

There are also websites that specialize in this. These are called *directories* or *portals*. Later in this book you'll learn more about these too.

Usually a website has to be submitted to a search engine in order to be included in its index. Websites that haven't been submitted can't be found by the search engine. That might be a reason why you can't find the particular website you were looking for.

How to Get the Most out of Search Engines

Searching with search engines can sometimes lead to disappointment. The search engine goes about its business in a fairly limited way, listing all imaginable pages that might possibly relate to your search. Often you miss finding just the information you need.
The most common problems and ways to solve them are listed below.

Too few results	Sometimes you don't get enough results. In that case, try: • a different search engine: The various search engines often give very different results; • a more general search term.
Too many results	Often you get far too many pages. In that case, try: • narrowing your search by using multiple search terms or more specific terms; • using a directory instead of a search engine. Particularly if you're searching for a general search term, such as *animals*, you're better off searching for the category *animals* than using a general search engine. You'll read more about this later in this book.
The wrong pages	This occurs because no editing or selection takes place. It happens frequently when a word has multiple meanings, such as *fine* (you pay for speeding) and *fine* (very delicate). In that case, try: • using a different word or idea for your search term; • using a directory.

Narrowing Your Search

One of the problems in using search engines is that they find too many websites containing the search term. Some search engines, for example, will list thousands – even millions – of references for the word *retirement*. You can use multiple search terms to find the right information, for example, *retirement* and *planning*.

➡ **Please note:**

The screen images shown here may be different from what you see. The Internet is a dynamic medium, and *MSN Search* changes its appearance regularly. The basic functions will remain the same for the most part, however, and you'll be able to work through this chapter. For more information, see: **www.internetforseniors.com**

 Click on 🔍 New

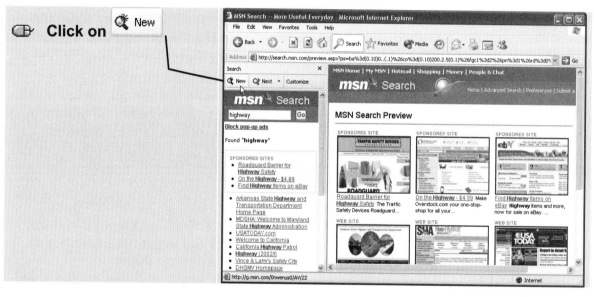

⌨ **Type:** retirement planning

 Click on Search

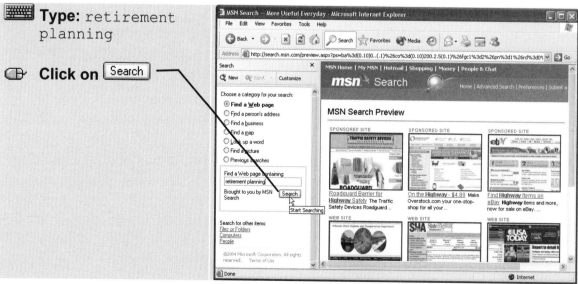

The first ten results for web pages containing *retirement* or *planning* are listed here:

You can be more specific about what kind of web pages you want to see. The options vary among different search engines. Here's how to select different options using *MSN Search*:

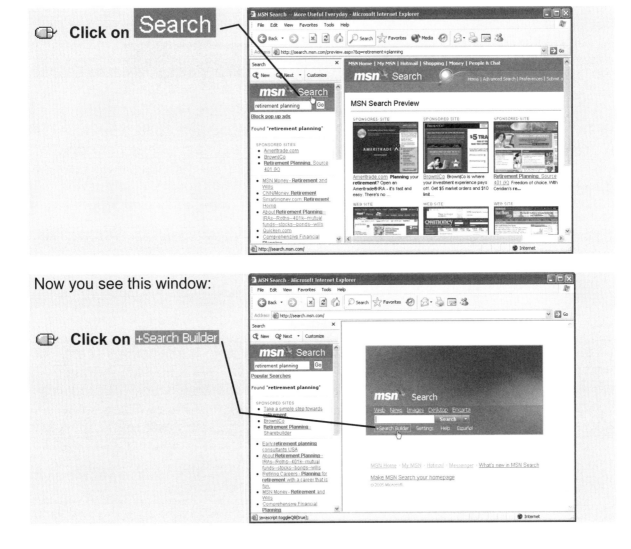

Click on Search

Click on +Search Builder

Now you see this window:

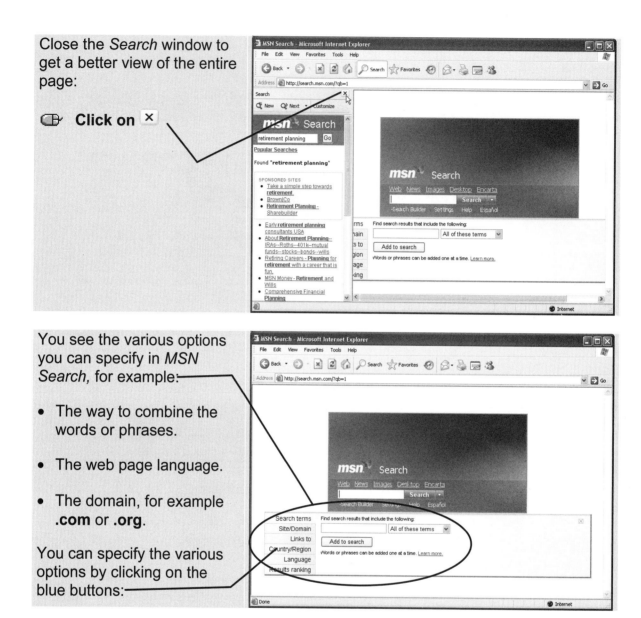

Close the *Search* window to get a better view of the entire page:

☞ **Click on** ⊠

You see the various options you can specify in *MSN Search,* for example:

- The way to combine the words or phrases.

- The web page language.

- The domain, for example **.com** or **.org**.

You can specify the various options by clicking on the blue buttons:

When using multiple search terms, it is important to pay attention to how you combine these search words.

⇨ **Please note:**

> If you use multiple words, such as *Frank Sinatra*, many search engines will search for web pages in which the words *Frank* and *Sinatra* appear. This is how *MSN Search* works. However, this search method will not guarantee that the pages found, actually concern the singer *Frank Sinatra*. Pages about *Anne Frank* or *Nancy Sinatra* may also appear. To get a better result, treat the words *Frank Sinatra* as a unit.

You can see here the effects of combining words to pinpoint specific information. The more specific your terms are, the more specific your results will be.

Searching for an Exact Phrase

All search engines give you the opportunity to indicate whether multiple search terms should be treated as a unit. Most search engines call this an "exact phrase". An example of an exact phrase is *Frank Sinatra*. Here's how to use an exact phrase with *MSN Search*:

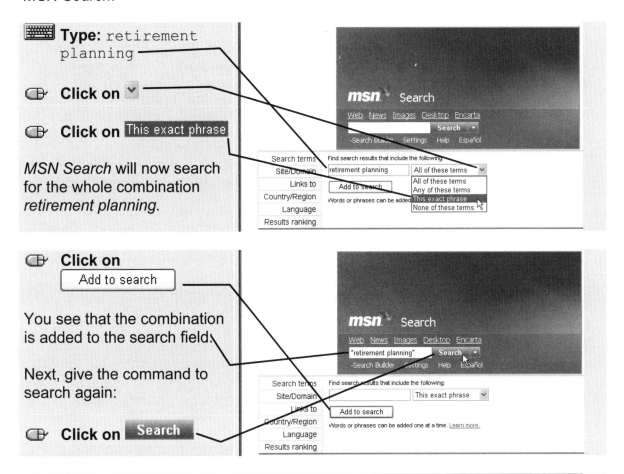

Type: retirement planning

Click on ⌄

Click on `This exact phrase`

MSN Search will now search for the whole combination *retirement planning*.

Click on

`Add to search`

You see that the combination is added to the search field.

Next, give the command to search again:

Click on `Search`

MSN Search now shows the references it's found:

⇒ **Please note:**

There are also search engines that will look for pages containing any one of the words: either *Frank* or *Sinatra* (or both). You may get a lot of web pages with other *Frank*s and other *Sinatra*s. If you only want to see pages containing *Frank Sinatra* as a unit, you will need to indicate this.

The best thing to do is to read the Help by the search engine to see how it performs a search when you have indicated multiple search terms:

○   *Frank* **and** *Sinatra* on **one** web page

or

○   *Frank* **or** *Sinatra* on **one** web page

You can open the *Search* window again:

☞ **Click on** 🔍 Search

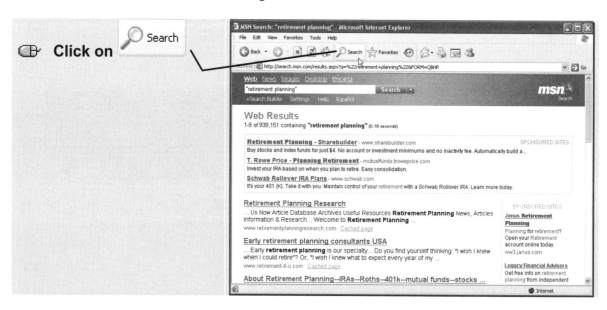

☞ **Click on** ← Back ▾
until you see the
website for this book
again

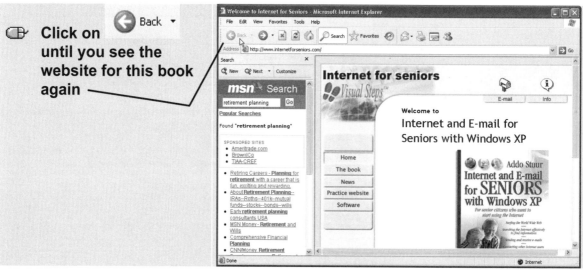

Previous Searches

Sometimes you might want to repeat a search. For example, you might not have had time to look at all the results of a search, and you want to continue looking at them later. Or you might want to see the results of a particular search at a later time; some subjects are very topical and the information changes quickly.
In such a case, it's useful to return to a previously formulated search:

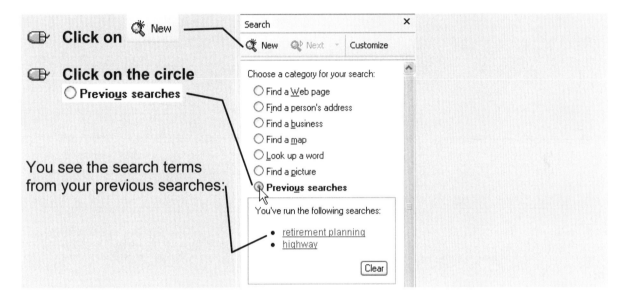

Click on ⚲ New

Click on the circle
○ **Previous searches**

You see the search terms from your previous searches:

You can repeat one of these searches by clicking on it:

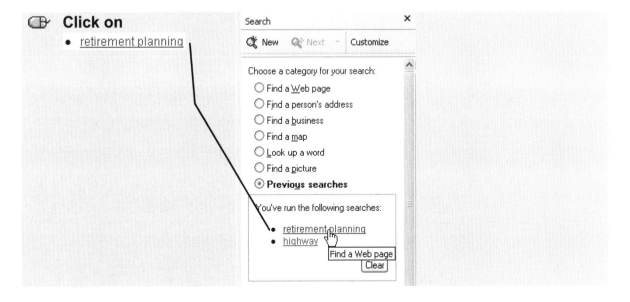

Click on
• retirement planning

The search is now repeated:

You can clear the list of searches. Here's how you do it:

Click on 🔍 New

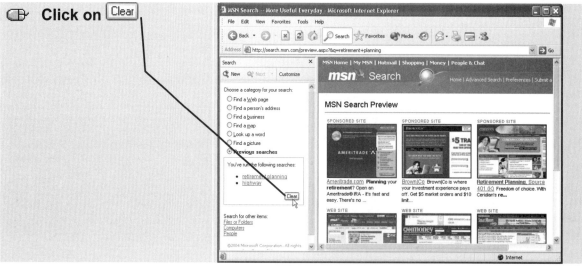

Click on [Clear]

Consulting Other Search Engines

There are a multitude of search engines you can use on the Internet. You don't have to limit yourself to *MSN Search* and the other search engines in *Internet Explorer*. According to the experts, these aren't even the best search engines that exist.
On the website for this book, you can find the most important search engines listed on one page:

☞ **Close the Search frame** 𝓁𝓁 **32**

☞ **Go back to the website for this book** 𝓁𝓁 **6**

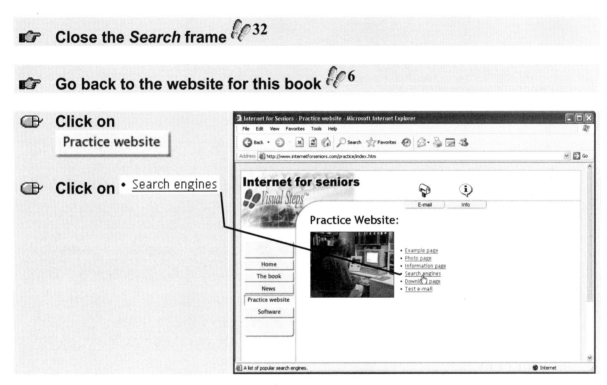

☞ **Click on**
Practice website

☞ **Click on** • Search engines

The addresses for several search engines have been gathered on this page.

You see this page:

☞ **Drag the scrollbar all the way to the bottom**

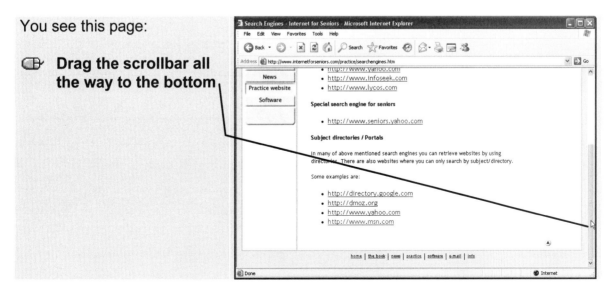

Now you see the part of the page containing various *directories*:

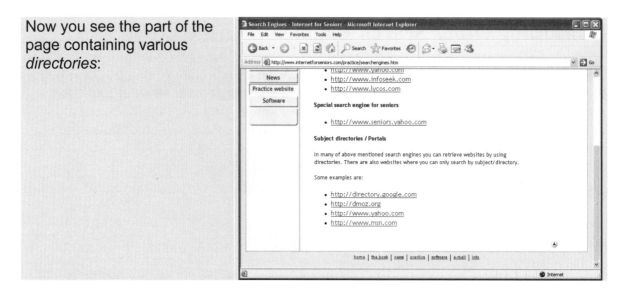

A *directory* is a website containing a large number of web addresses categorized by subject. This categorizing is done by a large editorial staff, and this staff also regularly checks the content of the web pages. Another name for a directory is a *portal*. A portal is a useful gateway to the Internet, because you can see in one glance which websites offer what kind of information. America's most extensive portal website is www.dmoz.org. You'll take a look at this later.

Now you can go back to the top of the page.

☞ **Click on**

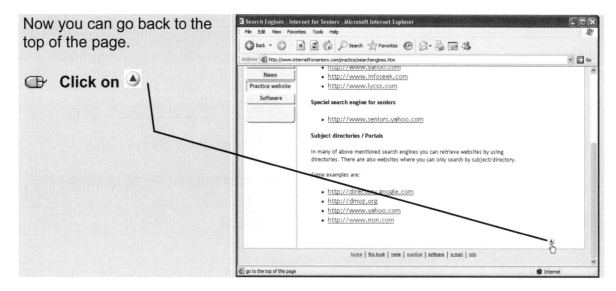

You see the list of search engines again:

For practice, you can try out the well-known *AltaVista* search engine.

 Tip

Visit this page regularly. If important new search features are developed for the Internet, they will most certainly be included on this page.

A Closer Look at AltaVista

You can open *AltaVista* by clicking on the web address:

Click on
- http://www.altavista.com

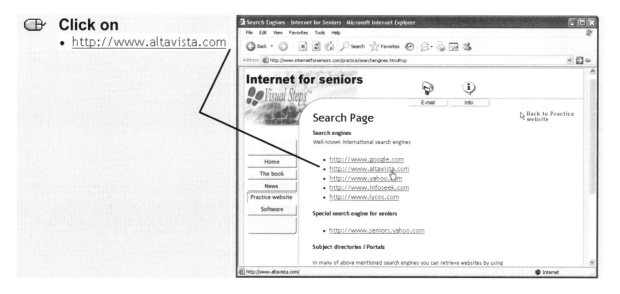

You see the home page for
AltaVista in a separate
window:

You see several sections.

This is the search area,
where you can type in your
search terms:

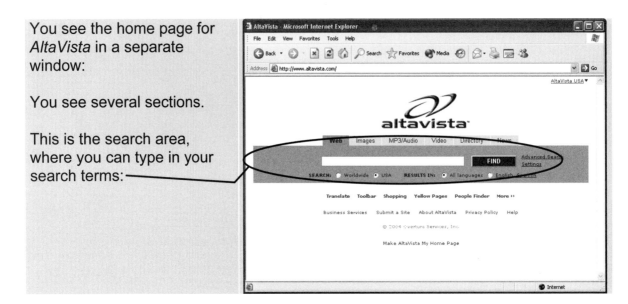

➡ **Please note:**

Search engines also change regularly, not only in terms of appearance, but
sometimes also in terms of the way they work. Consult the website for this book if
this description of *AltaVista* isn't right. We'll list any changes that may have been
made there.

You see that *AltaVista*
provides a large number of
categories:

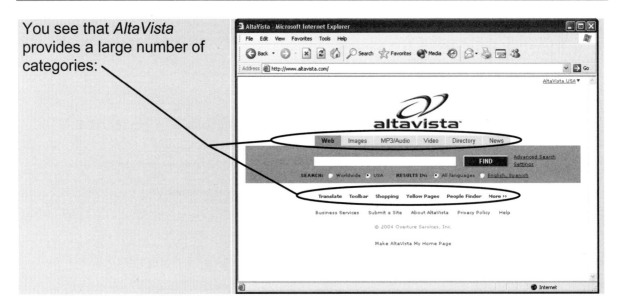

For practice, you're going to search for the famous Dutch painter *Karel Appel*. In the
process, we'll cover a number of important tips.

Please note:

> **Capital Letters**
> The search engine pays attention to the use of capital letters. If you type only small letters: *karel appel*, it will search for pages containing *Karel*, *karel*, *KAREL*, *appel*, *APPEL* and *Appel*.
> If you use initial capitals, however: *Karel Appel*, it will only search for *Karel* and *Appel* and not for *karel*, *KAREL, APPEL* and *appel*.

 ## Please note:

> **Words That Belong Together**
> Are you searching for two words that belong together such as *Karel Appel*? Then type quotation marks around them: *"Karel Appel"*. The *AltaVista* search engine will then look for the exact phrase and not for *Karel* on one line and *Appel* e.g. two lines further down.

Click in the search field

Type: "Karel Appel"

By default, it will only search for American websites:

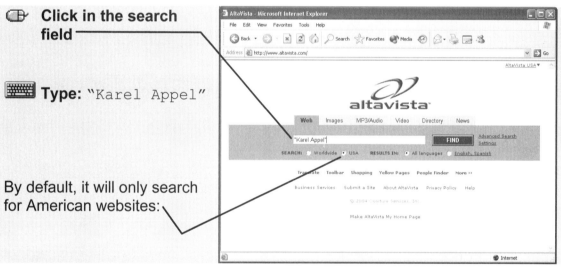

You can also choose to search for websites in other languages:

Now you can give the search command:

Click on [FIND]

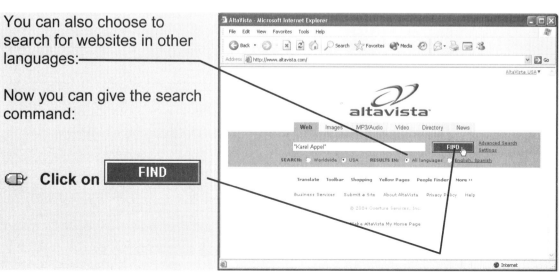

After a while, the results will be displayed:

You see that a large number of web pages have been found:

At the bottom of the page, you'll see a list of websites.

☞ **Scroll all the way to the bottom**

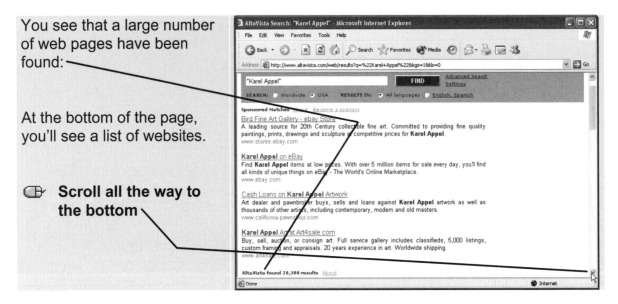

AltaVista displays the results in sets of ten. You can see the sets of results at the bottom of the page.

At the bottom of the list you see a row of numbers and

Next >>:

If you click on this, you can view the next ten results.

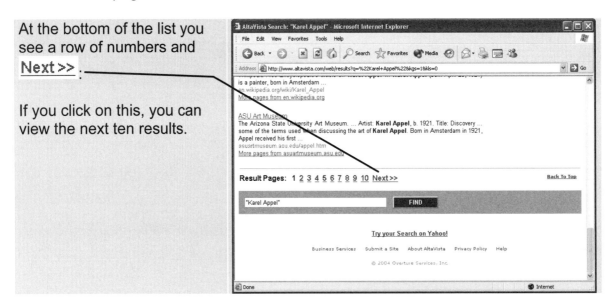

Now you can take a look at what the results are if you don't use quotation marks or capital letters. It should find very many more pages, for example, Dutch pages about the fruit *appel* (apple).

 Tip

You can use the Home button to quickly return to the top of the web page:

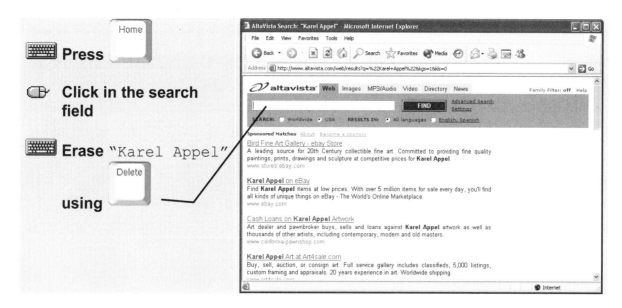

Now you can type *karel appel* in the search field:

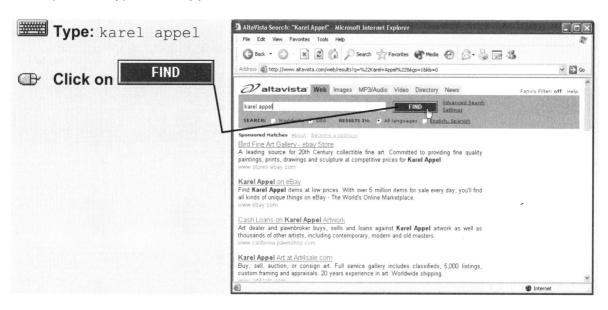

If the theory checks out, many more websites will be found this time:

The number of websites found is indeed much larger:

You can close the *AltaVista* window.

☞ **Click on** ⊠

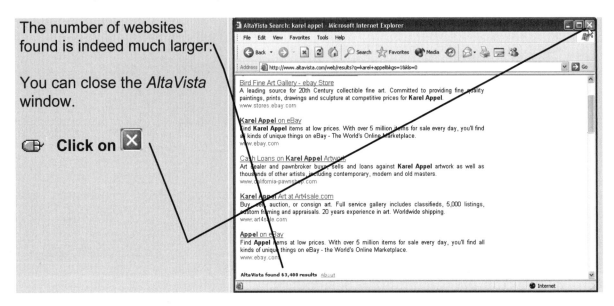

Now you've become acquainted with the *AltaVista* search machine. There are a number of refinements you can make when searching with *AltaVista*. These are described in detail at the end of this chapter.
The *AltaVista* page also offers access to other kinds of search systems, such as those for images, audio and video.

You see the Search Page for this book again:

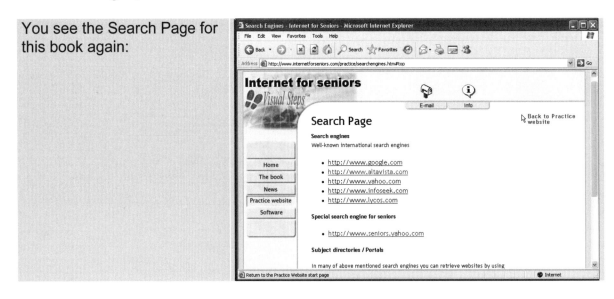

You can now try another search method: using directories. These are listed at the bottom of the Search Page:

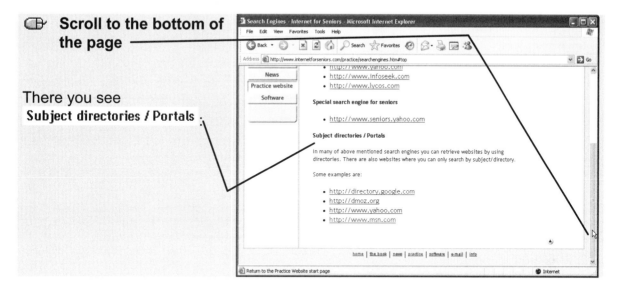

Directories

In practice, search engines aren't always the fastest way to find information about a particular subject. Sometimes, in fact, it's a downright roundabout method, due to the immense number of pages found. The reason is simple: the searching is done by computers, not people.

Directories are becoming more and more popular. A whole team of people works on a directory by organizing, evaluating and checking websites. This results in a useful summary. That's why many people use this kind of page as their *Internet Explorer* home page.

One very popular directory has a very simple name: The Open Directory Project at **www.dmoz.org**.

Click on
- http://www.dmoz.org

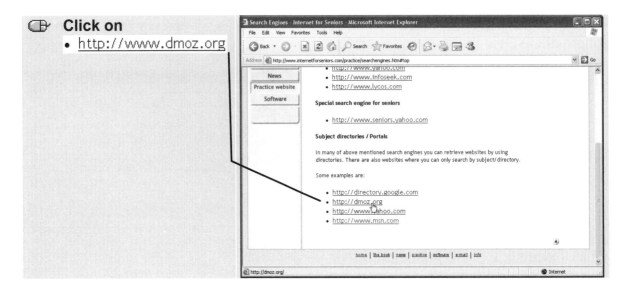

The Open Directory Project page opens. Here's how you can use the search function on this website:

Click in the text box

Type: Bonaire

Click on Search

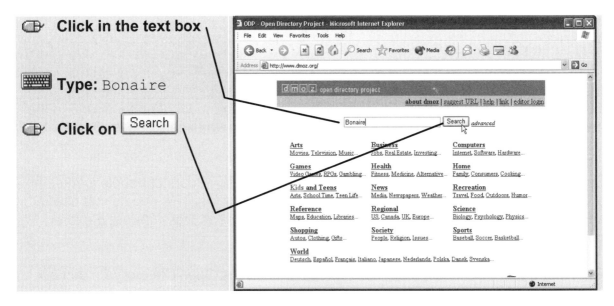

Now it will search for pages containing *Bonaire*.

You see a window with a list of website categories:

👆 **Click on**
  1. <u>Regional: Caribbean:</u>

Now you see a page with more categories about Bonaire:

👆 **Click on the category**
  - <u>Travel and Tourism</u>

Now you see a page with various subjects under the category *Travel and Tourism*:

👆 **Click on**
  - <u>Restaurants and Bars</u>

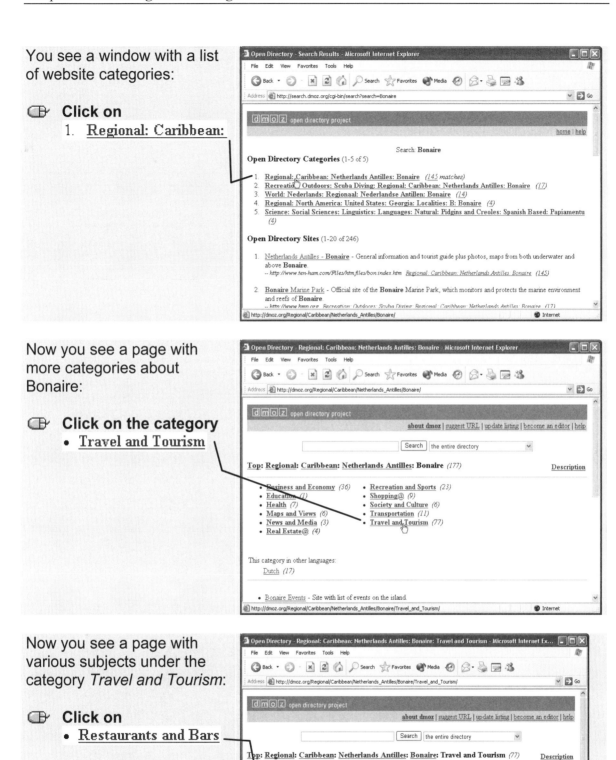

Now you see a page with
several restaurants in
Bonaire:

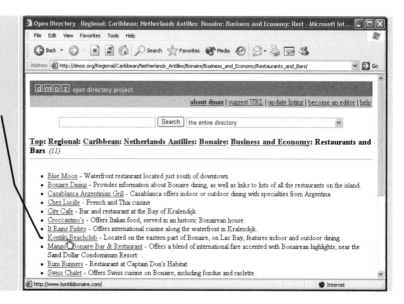

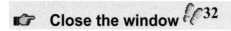 **Click on a restaurant**

The page for the restaurant
opens:

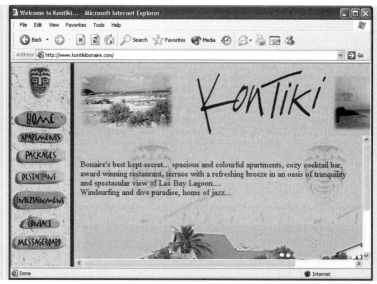

You can close this window now.

☞ **Close the window** ℓℓ³²

You see the Search Page for this book again:

☞ **Drag the scrollbar all the way to the top**

☞ **Click on** Practice website

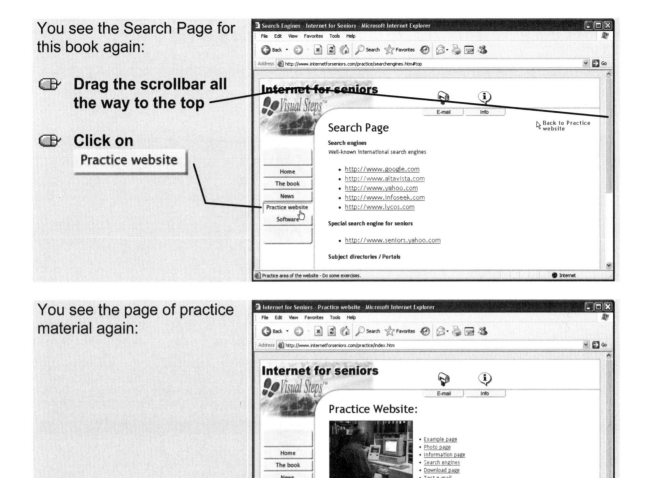

You see the page of practice material again:

You've seen how to search using a directory. In addition to *www.dmoz.org*, there are several other directory websites.

There are a few more handy tricks in *Internet Explorer* that you can use when you want to search for something on the Internet.

Searching Within a Page in Internet Explorer

Sometimes a web page has so much text that you can't find your search term. In that case, you can make use of a handy trick. *Internet Explorer* lets you search the text in a window for a particular word or phrase. Here's how you do it:

Click on
- Information page

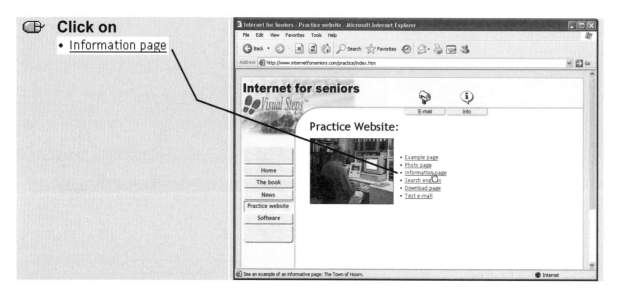

You see a text in the window which describes the town of Hoorn in Holland.

👆 **Click on** `Edit`

👆 **Click on**
`Find (on This Page)...`

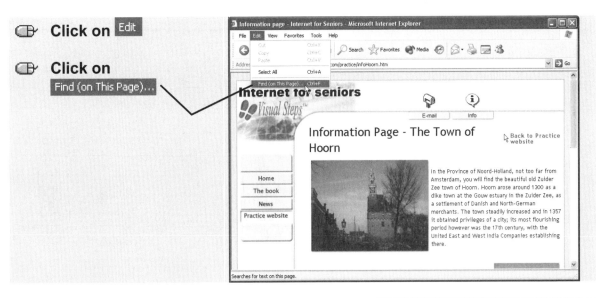

Now you see a small *Find* window where you can type in your search word:

⌨ **Type:** `Fries`

👆 **Click on** `Find Next`

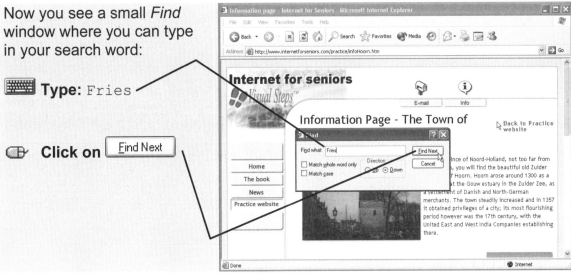

If the word is found, it will be highlighted in the text:

Now you can continue searching to see if the word occurs again:

👆 **Click on** `Find Next` **again**

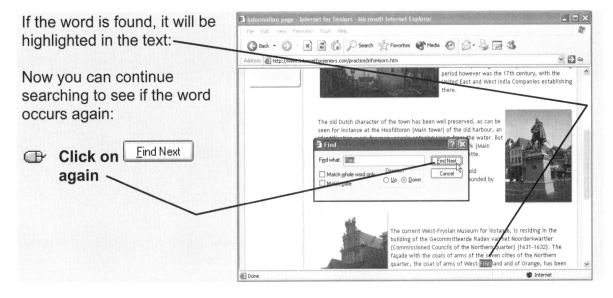

If the word isn't found again,
you see this little window:

☞ **Click on** ☐ OK ☐

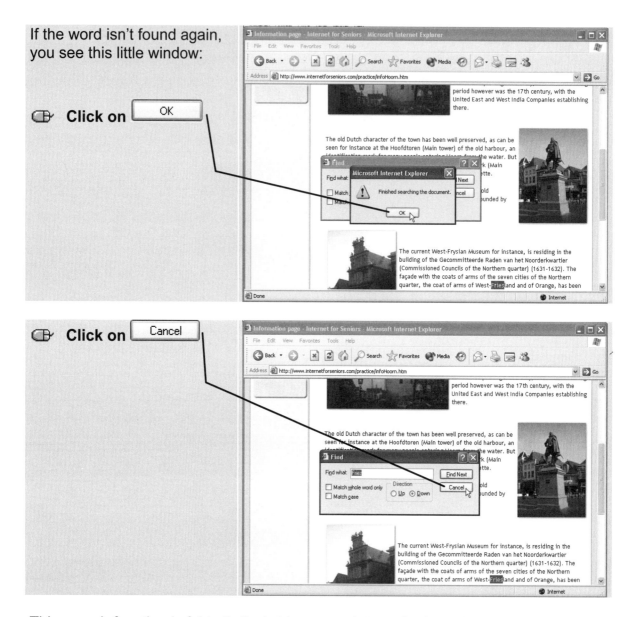

☞ **Click on** ☐ Cancel ☐

This search function is fairly limited. At some point, you're bound to search for a word that you know must occur somewhere on a web page, but the Find window can't find it. When that happens, pay attention to the following things:

- Always click first at the top of the page – the search proceeds from top to bottom.
- Check to see if the word is hidden underneath the Find window.

Read the following tips for using the Find window. There are a number of settings you can use to avoid disappointment.

Tip

Using the Find Window

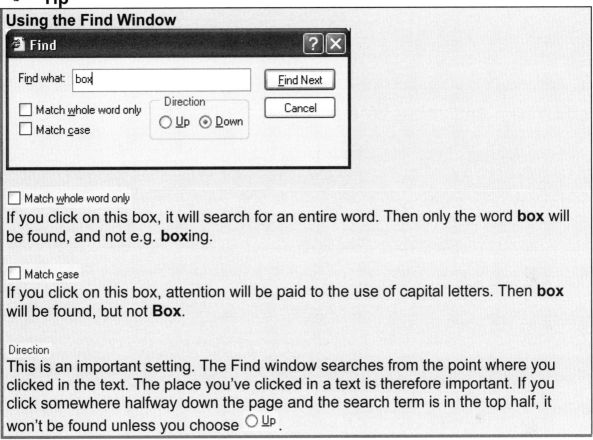

☐ Match whole word only
If you click on this box, it will search for an entire word. Then only the word **box** will be found, and not e.g. **box**ing.

☐ Match case
If you click on this box, attention will be paid to the use of capital letters. Then **box** will be found, but not **Box**.

Direction
This is an important setting. The Find window searches from the point where you clicked in the text. The place you've clicked in a text is therefore important. If you click somewhere halfway down the page and the search term is in the top half, it won't be found unless you choose ○ Up .

 Tip

Didn't find the search term?
The Find window sometimes covers the word you're looking for. To check this, you have to drag the window away. Here's how you do it:

☞ **Place the mouse pointer on the title bar**

☞ **Drag the window away with the mouse**

Exercises

Have you forgotten how to perform a particular action? Use the number beside the footsteps to look it up in the appendix *How Do I Do That Again?*

Exercise: Searching with Internet Explorer

In this exercise, you'll practice searching for information.

✔ Start *Internet Explorer.* [1]

✔ Connect to the Internet. [3]

✔ Open the search frame for *MSN Search.* [20]

✔ Search for the word *bridge.* [21]

✔ Take a look at a couple of the websites that were found. [23]

✔ Begin a new search. [22]

✔ Search for *Vincent van Gogh.* [21]

✔ Take a look at a couple of the websites that were found. [23]

✔ Close the search frame for *MSN Search.* [24]

Exercise: AltaVista

In this exercise, you'll practice searching with the *AltaVista* search engine.

✔ Open from History: *www.altavista.com* [14]

✔ Search for *Elvis Presley.* [21]

✔ Take a look at a couple of the websites that were found. [23]

✓ Search for the car *Ford* 🦶**22**

✓ Take a look at a couple of the websites that were found. 🦶**23**

Exercise: A Different Search Engine

In this exercise, you'll use a different search engine, namely *Lycos*.

✓ Open the favorite: *Internet for seniors.* 🦶**17**

✓ Click on Practice website .

✓ Click on • Search engines .

✓ Click on • http://www.lycos.com .

✓ Search for the word *butterflies.* 🦶**21**

✓ Take a look at a couple of the websites that were found. 🦶**23**

✓ Search for *Empire State Building.* 🦶**21**

✓ Take a look at a couple of the websites that were found. 🦶**23**

✓ Close *Internet Explorer.* 🦶**2**

✓ Disconnect from the Internet if necessary. 🦶**5**

Background Information

Advanced Searching
Would you like to search for two or more words that belong together, for example, a name like *James Brown*?
Usually all web pages containing *James Brown* will be found, but also pages with only *James* or only *Brown*.
If you only want to find pages containing the name *James Brown*, you'll have to use *Boolean searching*. This means the use of words such as *and*, *not*, *or* and *near*.

If you type: James **and** Brown
The search engine will search for web pages containing both *James* **and** *Brown*.

If you type: James **or** Brown
The search engine will search for web pages containing either *James* **or** *Brown*.

If you type: James **and not** Brown
The search engine will search for web pages containing *James* **but not** *Brown*.

If you type: James **near** Brown
The search engine will search for web pages where *James* is **near** *Brown* on the page.

Using Special Symbols

You can also use various symbols in your search, such as **+**, **-**, ``, *****

If you type: **+**James **+**Brown
The search engine will search for web pages containing both *James* **and** *Brown*.

If you type: James **–**Brown
The search engine will search for web pages containing *James* **but not** *Brown*.

If you type quotation marks around the words: **"James Brown"**
The search engine will search for web pages containing the phrase *James Brown*.

If you type a star ***** next to a word, for example: Brown*****
This means that any symbol(s) at all can come at the end of the word, and the search engine will find Brown, Browning, Brownies, Brownbag etcetera.
If you search for James Brown*****, then you might for example find sites for the illustrator James Browne.

Paying over the Internet

Just as in the regular world, both customer and merchant on the Internet want security. The customer wants to be sure he gets what he's paid for. In turn, the merchant wants to be sure he gets paid. The merchant asks the customer for information. He wants to know where the order should be sent and where he can recover his losses if something goes wrong with the payment.

To help consumers, a company called *ShopSafe* has developed online directories that list companies worldwide that practice "safe shopping". ShopSafe independently reviews the companies and lists only those that meet its criteria for safe shopping.

How can I pay online?

Credit Card or Bank Debit Card

You provide the online merchant with your credit or debit card data.

Check or Money Order

You place your order online, then send your paper check or money order by regular mail to the address listed on the merchant's website.

Electronic Funds Transfer or Electronic Check

You provide the online merchant with your bank account number and routing number, and authorize him to deduct the funds directly from your account.

PayPal

This is an increasingly popular alternative for individuals and small businesses accepting payments over the Internet.

C.O.D.

You place your order online and pay the delivery person at the door when you receive it. Many merchants no longer accept this kind of payment.

Internet Safety

Payments over the Internet are a fact, but the system isn't foolproof yet. It's such a complicated system that it may be a while before maximum security can be guaranteed. This lack of security has to do with two problems.

First, it isn't yet possible to send your data – name, address, and e.g. credit card number – so that a third party cannot intercept it. Great strides forward have been made in this area, but it's still not 100% secure. Second, the degree to which your data are secure varies greatly from one Internet merchant to another. Reports circulate regularly over hackers (computer fanatics that break into networks in which confidential information is stored) who've gained access to thousands of credit card numbers. We shouldn't blow these stories out of proportion, however; most fraud still occurs in the "real world". Nonetheless, it's a good idea not to give out your name and address in combination with your e-mail address unless necessary. Your e-mail address by itself offers a degree of anonymity. Once you reveal all your data, however, you run the risk of being swamped with advertisements from all sides.

Windows XP and Service Pack 2

In the second half of 2004, *Microsoft* issued an important update for the *Windows XP* operating system, called *Service Pack 2* (*SP2*). This extensive update adds more powerful security settings that help in the fight against viruses, hackers, and worms. In addition, *SP2* contains new security functions you can use to protect your PC more easily. For owners of the "old" *Windows XP*, the most obvious change after installing *SP2* is the presence of the *Windows Security Center*.

This *Security Center* shows you all your computer's security settings at a glance, and tells you which items you still need to check. A number of security functions are automatically activated under *SP2*, such as *Automatic Updates* and the *Firewall*. *SP2* also monitors the status of your computer's virus protection.

A number of security functions are automatically activated under *SP2*, such as *Automatic Updates* and the *Firewall*. *SP2* also monitors the status of your computer's virus protection. Automatically updating *Windows* remains very important, because small new updates that repair newly discovered leaks and bugs appear regularly. The *Windows Firewall* protects your computer against unsolicited incoming traffic. You can find more information about *Service Pack* 2 on the Microsoft website: You can find more information about *Service Pack* 2 on the Microsoft website:

www.microsoft.com

Tips

 Tip

Using Search Engines

- First, get a lot of practice using a particular search engine such as *AltaVista*. Thoroughly investigate all its search options.
  What settings can you specify?
  How does the search engine handle multiple search terms?
  You can find all this information on the search engine's Help pages.
- Once you have some experience, try out some other search engines.
  You'll discover through experience which search engines you like best.
- Always begin with the most specific search possible. For example, if you want to know something about the *Epson Stylus 740* printer, then use this whole phrase as your search term. If you don't get enough results, then try *Epson Stylus*. As a last resort, type just the word *Epson*.

 Tip

Searching Directly on Name

You don't always have to use a search engine to find a particular web address. You can find many websites by typing in a name. Brand names and companies are generally easy to find.

For example, if you want to visit the website of the car manufacturer *Ford*, you can type in **www.ford.com**

Tip

Searching with Start
Once *Windows* has started, you can begin searching right away without having to open *Internet Explorer* first. This is how:

👆 **Click on** 🪟 **start**

👆 **Click on** 🔍 Search

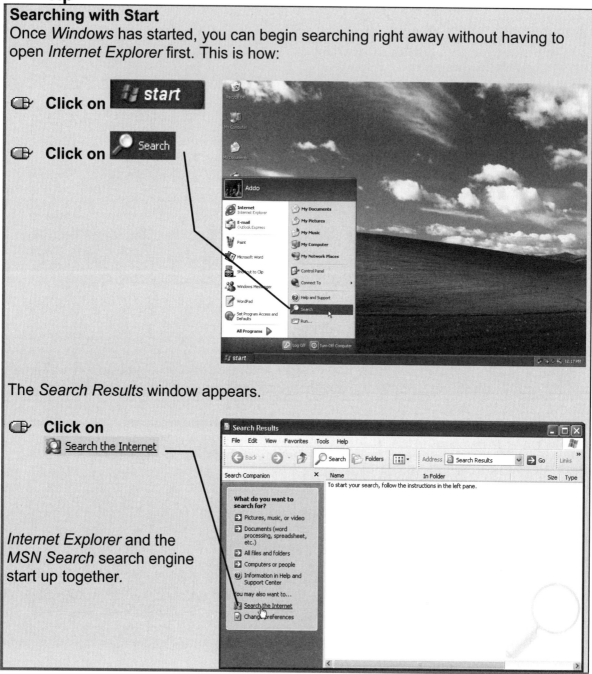

The *Search Results* window appears.

👆 **Click on**
🔍 Search the Internet

Internet Explorer and the
MSN Search search engine
start up together.

Tip

Searching in the Address Bar
Internet Explorer has a built-in way to quickly search for something. You usually search for information based on a search term; for example, the word *bike*:

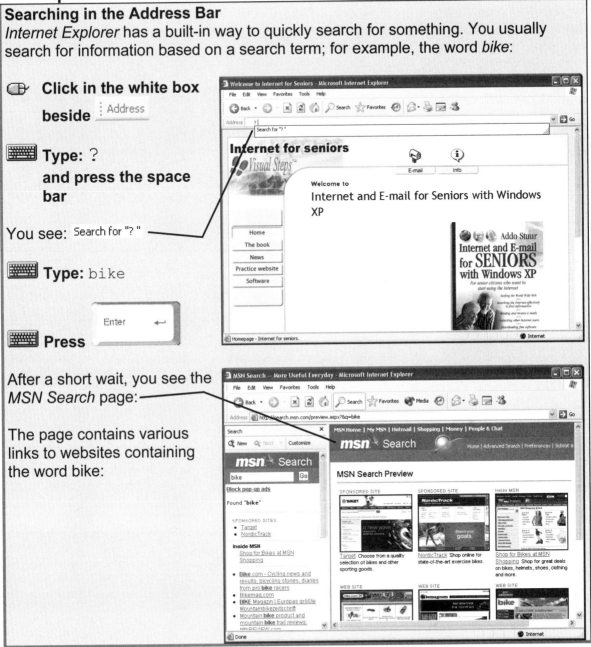

Click in the white box beside Address

Type: ?
and press the space bar

You see: Search for "? "

Type: bike

Press Enter

After a short wait, you see the *MSN Search* page:

The page contains various links to websites containing the word bike:

 Tip

Does your computer behave differently than described in this book? Then your computer has been set up differently. This is easy to change. See Appendix B in the back of this book.

Tip

Searching with *Google*

Google is a search engine that has recently gained enormous popularity. *Google* is so popular because it's a search engine without any frills. In addition, it's very fast and easy to use. You can find *Google* at the address: **www.google.com**

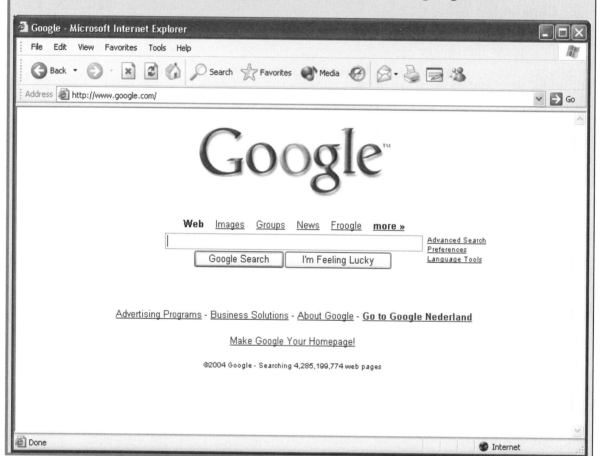

4. Internet, Your Source of Information

The Internet can be viewed as an enormous library containing all kinds of information: text, photos, drawings, video and music. The most amazing thing is that everything on the Internet that you see on your screen can be printed out or saved on your computer's hard drive. Later on, you can use the stored information again, for example in your work or for a hobby.

You can copy texts and re-use or edit them in a text-editing program. You can open and edit photos with a photo-editing or drawing program. In this way, the Internet serves as an enormous source of information. In this chapter, you'll learn the basic techniques for saving and re-using text and photos on your own computer.

In this chapter, you'll learn how to:

- print a page
- select text
- copy and paste text
- copy and paste images
- save an image
- save a web page
- open a web page in *Internet Explorer*

Visiting the Practice Page

First, start *Internet Explorer.*

Do you have an external modem?
☞ **Turn on the modem**

☞ **Start *Internet Explorer*** 🐾¹

☞ **Connect to the Internet** 🐾³

☞ **Open the *Internet for Seniors* website** 🐾⁵²

There's a practice page for this chapter on the website. You can open it now.

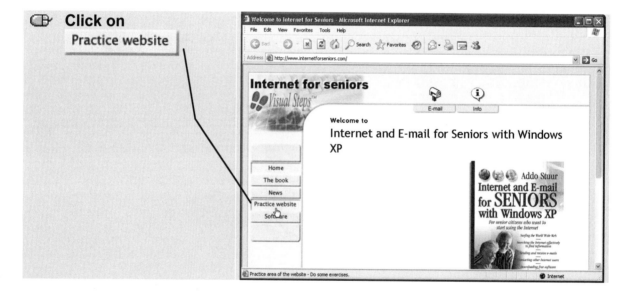

Click on

• <u>Information page</u>

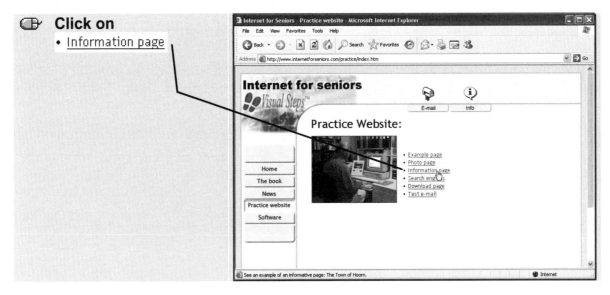

Now you see this Information Page with text and a photo which you can use for practice:

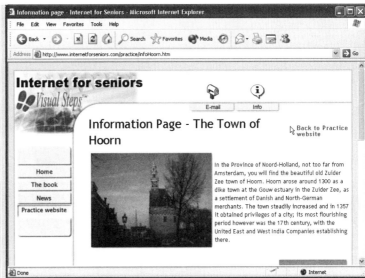

Do you want to disconnect from the Internet so you can receive calls?

☞ **Wait until the entire page has been loaded**

☞ **Disconnect from the Internet** 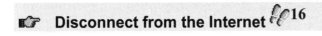¹⁶

Now you can take all the time you'd like to work through the rest of this chapter.

Printing a Page

It isn't always easy to read a web page on the screen, particularly if it contains a lot of text.

If you have a printer, you can print the page if you'd like, so you can read through it on paper at your own pace later.

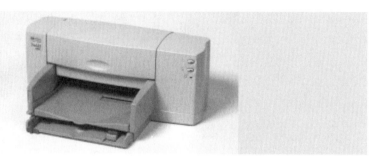

 HELP! I don't have a printer.

Then you can simply skip this section.

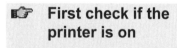 **First check if the printer is on**

Many web pages contain multiple *frames*. You must first specify which frame you want to print. In this case, you only want to print the right-hand frame containing the information text. You need to click somewhere in this frame before you give the command to print.

➡ **Please note:**

Always click first in the frame you want to print.

 Click in the right-hand frame

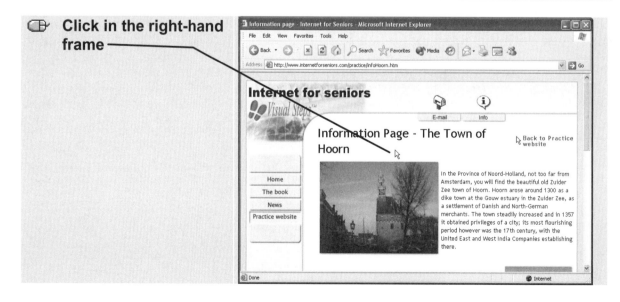

Now you can give the command to print the page:

☞ **Click on** File

☞ **Click on** Print...

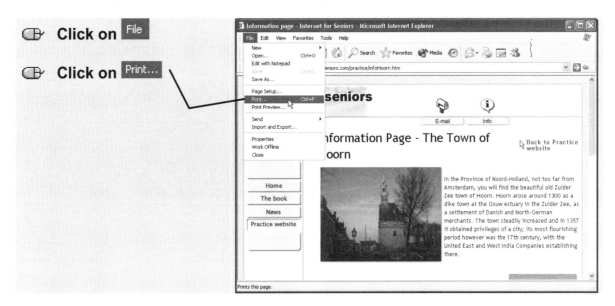

In the next window, you specify how the page should be printed.

You see the *Print* window:

☞ **Click on** Options

On this tab, you can choose
how the various frames on
the page should be printed. In
this case, you don't have a
choice:

☞ **Click on** Print

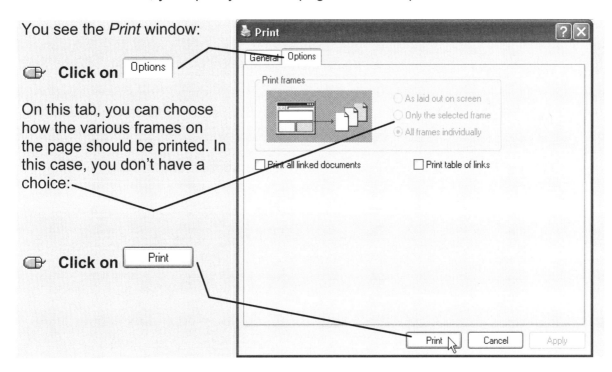

A little later, the text and photos on the information page will be printed by your printer:

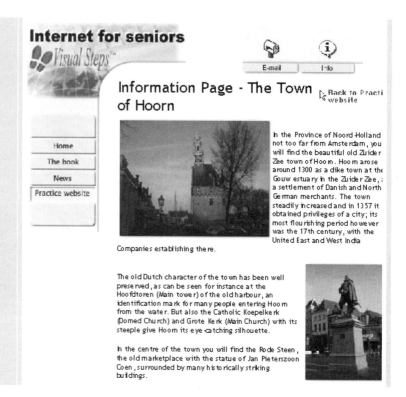

Selecting Text

You can save a text you've read on the Internet to your computer and edit it later, perhaps using it in a text of your own. For example, you could copy information and use it in a club newsletter.
To do this, you copy the text and paste it into another (text-editing) program.

For practice, you're going to copy a section of text and paste it into the *WordPad* program.
Before you can copy something, you have to *select* it first. In *Windows*, you do this by *dragging* the mouse.

 HELP! I don't know how to drag.
Read page 42 to find out how to drag.

Place the mouse pointer in front of In

 Press the left mouse button and keep it pressed

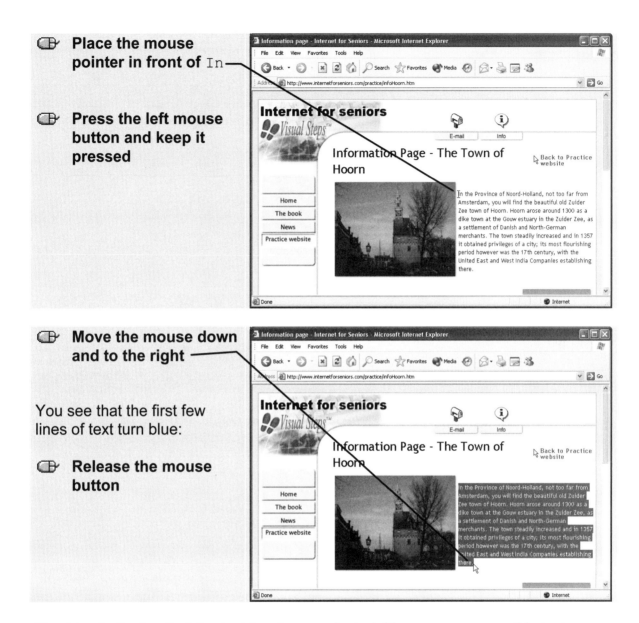

 Move the mouse down and to the right

You see that the first few lines of text turn blue:

 Release the mouse button

The blue indicates that the text has been selected. Now you can copy this text.

HELP!

Having trouble selecting exactly the right text? It doesn't matter for this exercise. The important thing is that some part of the text has been selected.

Copying Text

Once the text has been selected, you can copy it:

👆 **Click on** Edit

👆 **Click on** Copy

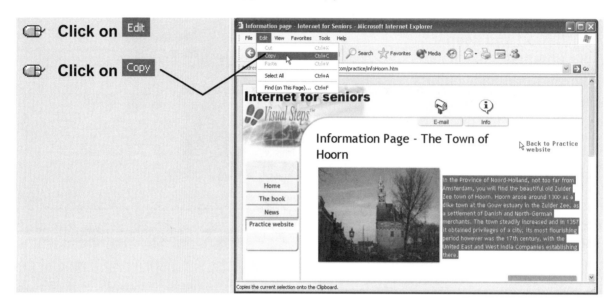

Although you don't see anything happening, the text has indeed been copied, and now you can paste it into another program. You can paste it into a text-editing program such as *WordPad* or *MS Word*, an e-mail message, or a drawing program.

Pasting Text into WordPad

For practice, you're going to paste the copied text into the text editor *WordPad*. *WordPad* is a simple text-editing program that comes standard with *Windows*. This is how to open it:

👆 **Click on** start

👆 **Click on** All Programs

👆 **Click on** Accessories

👆 **Click on** WordPad

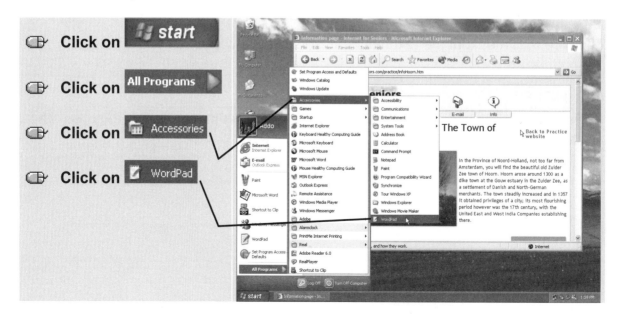

You see the *WordPad* window:

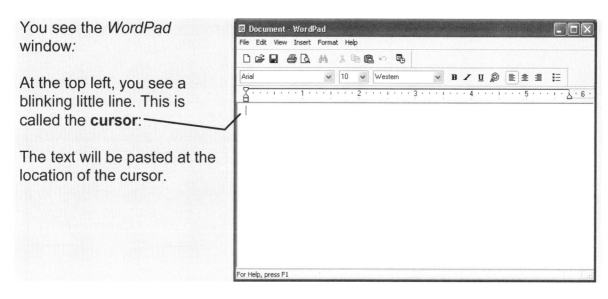

At the top left, you see a blinking little line. This is called the **cursor**:

The text will be pasted at the location of the cursor.

 HELP! I don't have *WordPad*.

You don't see the folder [Accessories] or the program [WordPad]?
Then it hasn't been installed on your computer.
Read *Appendix A* to find out how you can install it.

Now you can give the command to paste the text:

Click on Edit

Click on Paste

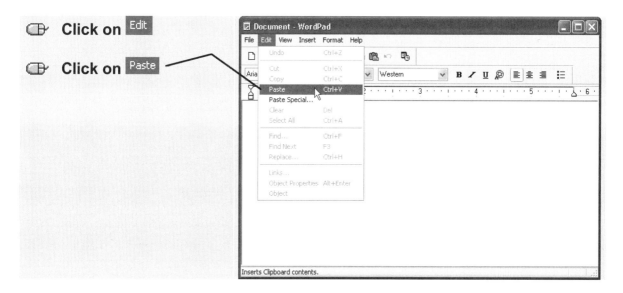

The copied text about Hoorn is pasted:

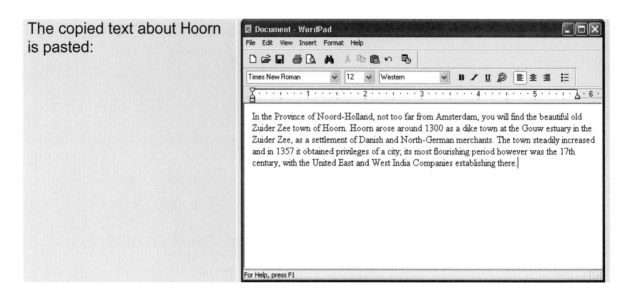

In this way, you can copy any text on the Internet and use it in another program. You can edit and save this text on your computer just like any other text.

You can also select all the text on a web page at one time and then paste it. To see how, first minimize the *WordPad* window:

Click on ☐

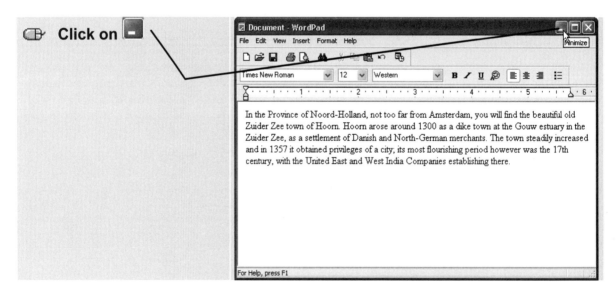

You see the *Internet Explorer* window containing the information page again:

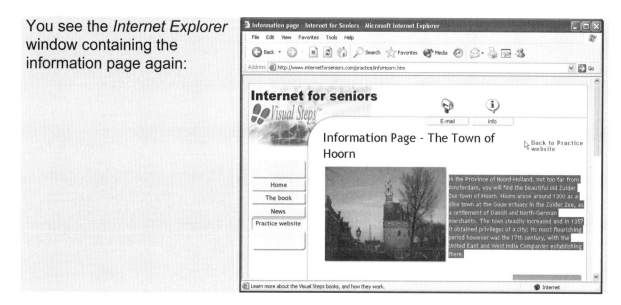

It isn't always practical to select a text by dragging the mouse. There is another method you can use.

Select All

You can select all the text and images on a web page with a single command. This is useful if you want to work quickly while you're surfing. Here's how you do it:

☞ **Click on** Edit

☞ **Click on** Select All

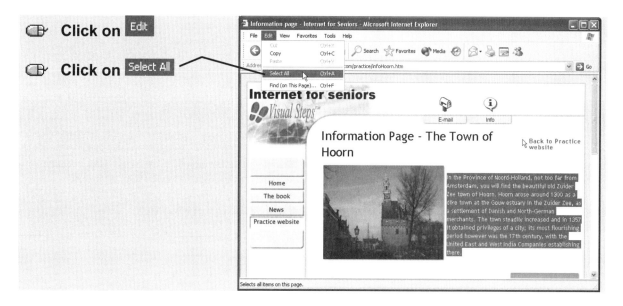

You see that not only all the
text, but also the photos have
been selected:

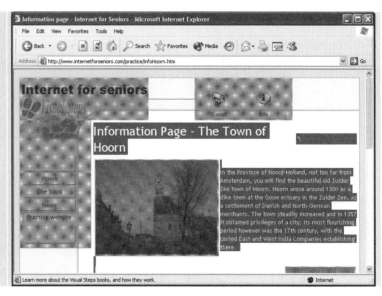

You can copy the text and pictures:

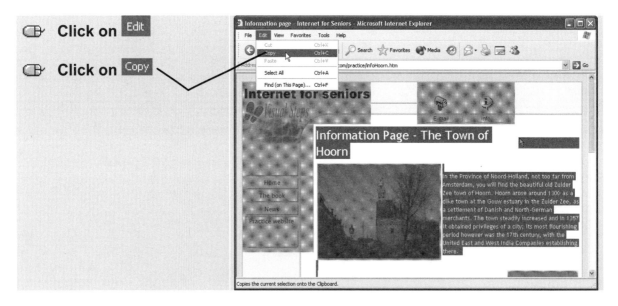

The entire page has been copied, and now you can open the *WordPad* window
again.

Click on 🖱

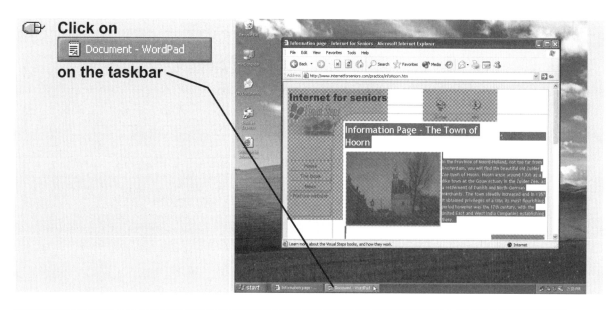

on the taskbar

You see the *WordPad* window again:

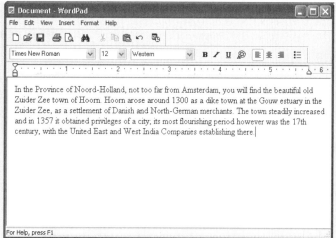

Now you want to put the cursor (the blinking line) at the very top. Then the text will be pasted there:

🖱 **Click before the first line**

The cursor is now in front of the first line.

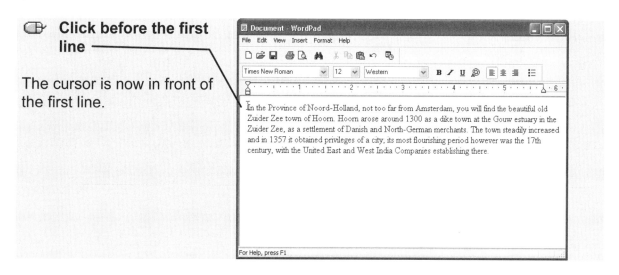

Now you can paste the text:

 Click on Edit

Click on Paste

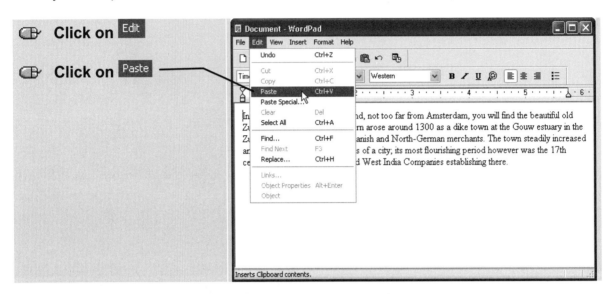

You see that the text has been pasted:

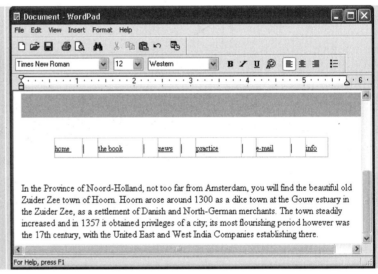

HELP! I don't see any pictures.

Unfortunately, not all versions of the *WordPad* program display the picture.

If you paste this web page into *MS Word* or into an e-mail message in *Outlook Express*, however, it does work properly. The technique for doing this using one of these programs is exactly the same as described above.

Closing WordPad

Now you can close *WordPad*. You don't need to save the text. This is how:

👈 **Click on** `File`

👈 **Click on** `Exit`

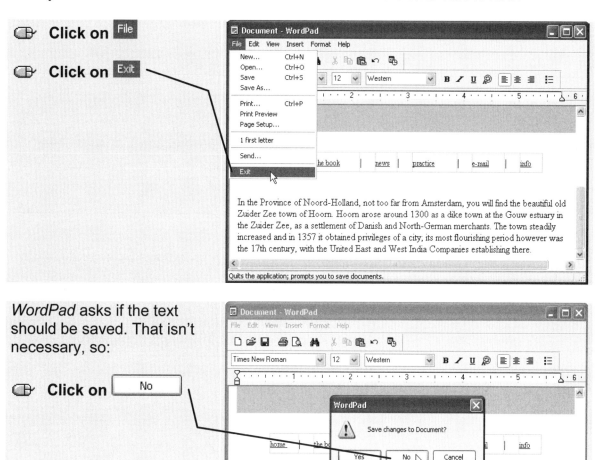

WordPad asks if the text should be saved. That isn't necessary, so:

👈 **Click on** `No`

💡 **Tip**

Text or Image?
Some text on the Internet is in fact an image. For example, the text on the button is an image. You can't copy the text on an image like this and paste it into a text-editing program or an e-mail program. You can, however, copy and paste the entire image. You'll read how to do that later on in this chapter.

"Grabbing" Images from the Screen

Maybe you see an interesting photo, image or drawing on the Internet that you'd like to save or even print. You can copy and save almost all the graphic material that appears on your screen, to use or print at a later time.

You can manipulate an image by right-clicking on it. Here's how you right-click:

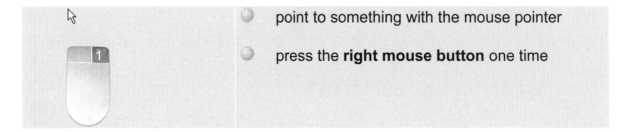

○ point to something with the mouse pointer

○ press the **right mouse button** one time

This mouse action is the same as regular clicking, except with the right mouse button instead of the left. The right mouse button has an entirely different function, however, as you'll see.

First you have to select the photo, like this:

☞ **Click on the photo with the left mouse button**

☞ **Then click on the photo with the right mouse button**

Now you see a menu with various commands:

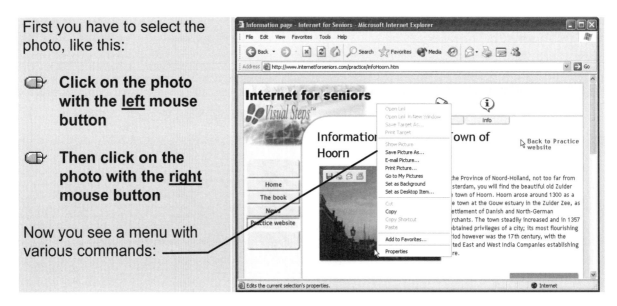

You can choose one of these commands. Use the left mouse button again to do that.

Copying an Image

First you're going to copy the image. Then you can use it another program, such as a drawing program.

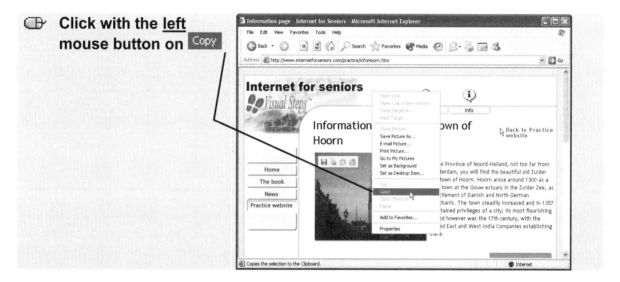

Click with the <u>left</u> mouse button on Copy

You don't see anything happen, but rest assured that the image has indeed been copied.

Pasting an Image into Paint

You can paste the image not only into a text-editing program like *WordPad* or *MS Word*, but also into a program for photo editing or a drawing program.
For practice, you're going to paste the image into the drawing program *Paint*. *Paint* is a simple drawing program that comes standard with *Windows*.
Here's how you start this program:

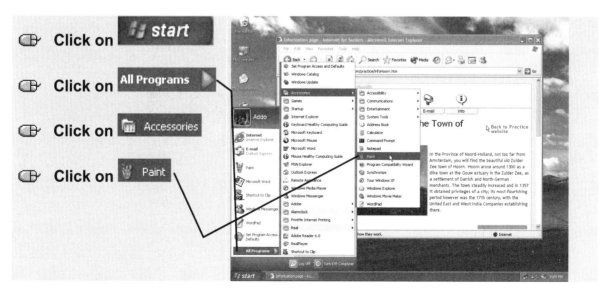

Click on start

Click on All Programs

Click on Accessories

Click on Paint

Now you see the *Paint* window:

There's a vertical bar containing all kinds of tools on the left-hand side:

At the bottom, you see a bar containing colors:

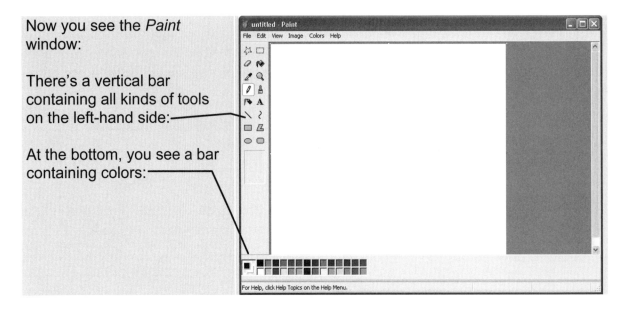

There's a large white surface in the middle of the page on which you can draw. This is the piece of paper, so to speak. You can paste the image onto it.

 HELP! I don't have Paint.

You don't see ![Accessories] or the program ![Paint] ?
Then it hasn't been installed on your computer.
Read *Appendix A* to find out how you can install it.

☞ **Click on** Edit

☞ **Click on** Paste

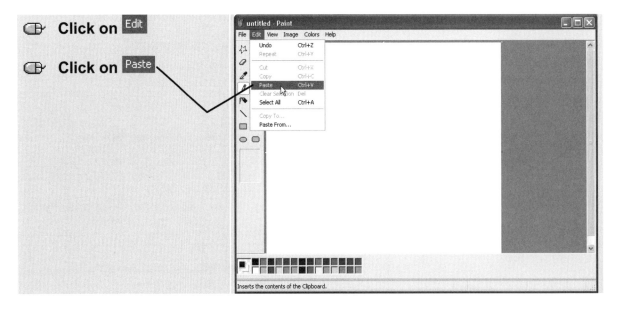

You see that the photo of Hoorn has been pasted:

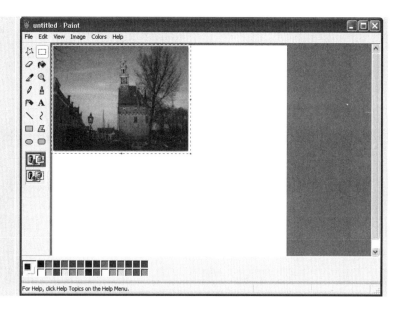

You can use *Paint* to edit, save, or print the photo, or to add text to it.

 Tip

Want to know more?
Would you like to know more about the *Paint* program, for example how to edit and save drawings? You can read about that in the book *Windows XP for Seniors*.
Have a look at: **www.visualsteps.com/winxp**

Now you can close the *Paint* program. You don't have to save the photo:

☞ **Click on** `File`

☞ **Click on** `Exit`

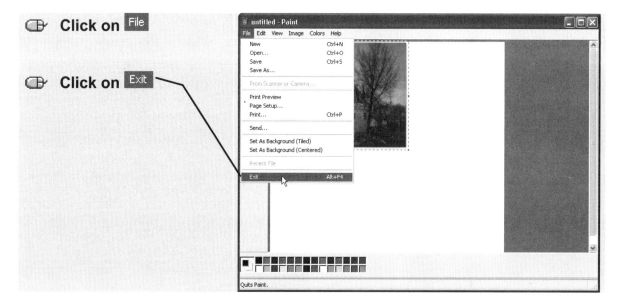

Paint asks if the photo should be saved. That isn't necessary, so:

 Click on No

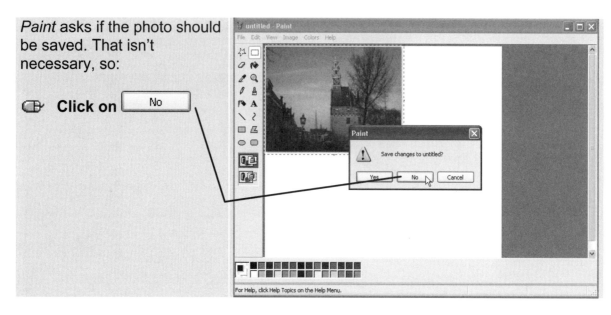

💡 Tip

You can use this method to paste an image into e.g. an *MS Word* document or an e-mail message in *Outlook Express*. In fact, you can paste it into a document in almost any program.

Saving an Image

You can also save an image directly to your computer, without first pasting it into a drawing program. Then you can use your favorite program to open it later.
This is how:

 Click with the right mouse button on the photo of Hoorn

You see the menu again:

 Click with the left mouse button on Save Picture As...

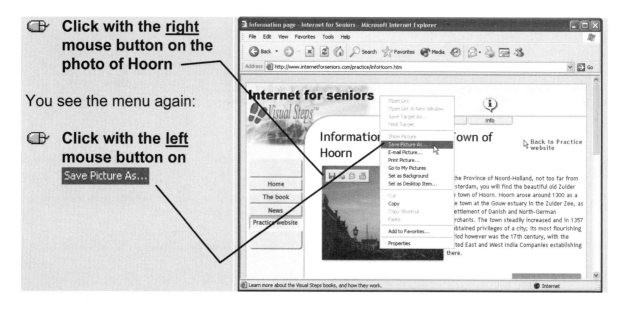

Now you have to specify the folder on your hard drive where you'd like to save the photo.

You see this window.

The photo already has a name: *Tower_Hoorn*:

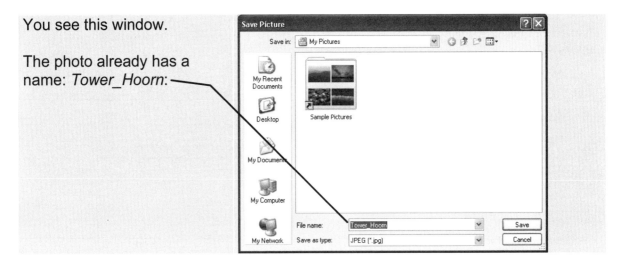

You can give this photo a different name if you'd like. For example, you can choose a name that tells you this is a photo.

Type: Photo Hoorn

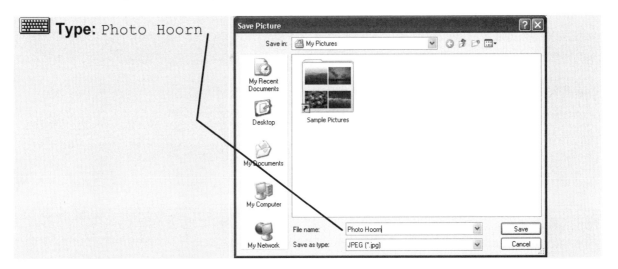

Now the photo has a name. It's time to specify in which folder on your hard drive you'd like to save the photo.

Where to Save?

It's important to pay attention to where you save the photo. It's a good idea to always save to the same folder. That makes it easier to find things later and helps keep you from forgetting where things are.

By default, images in *Windows XP* are saved in the folder 📟 My Pictures . You can find this folder in the folder 📟 My Documents .

Here you see that the folder 📟 My Pictures has been opened;

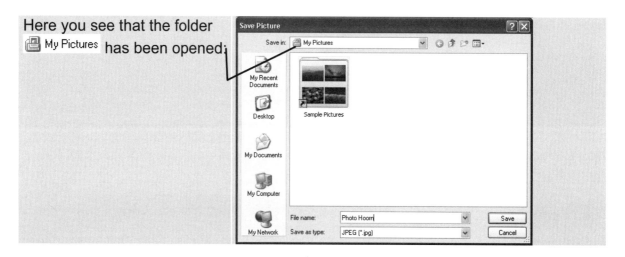

The folder 📟 My Pictures is intended for saving your work. That might be drawings or photos. You can save the photo of Hoorn in this folder 📟 My Pictures .

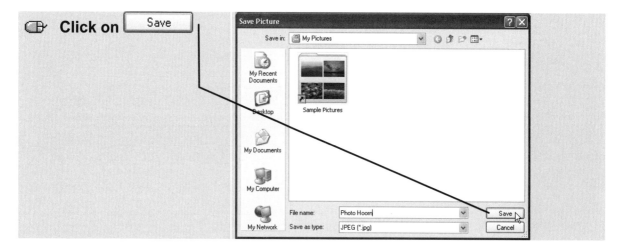

The photo has now been permanently stored on your hard drive. You can open it again later and use it in a different program, or perhaps send it to someone in an e-mail.

Saving a Web Page

You can also save an entire web page, including all its text and images. The page will be saved as a web page on your hard drive. You can open it again later in *Internet Explorer*. This can be useful, for example, if you find an interesting web page and want to look at it again later at your convenience without having to connect to the Internet.

Here's how you save a web page:

Click on File

Click on Save As...

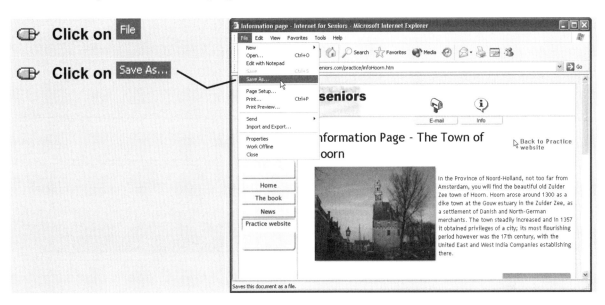

The page will be saved in the folder My Documents :

The web page already has a name, *Internet for Seniors*:

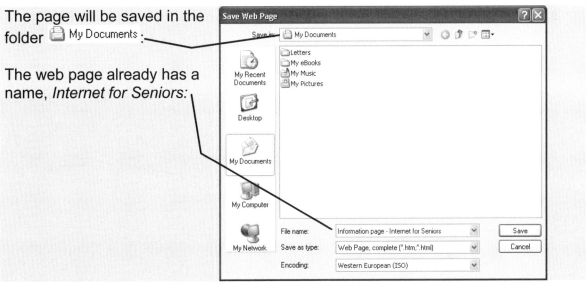

It's a good idea to choose another name – one that better describes the content:

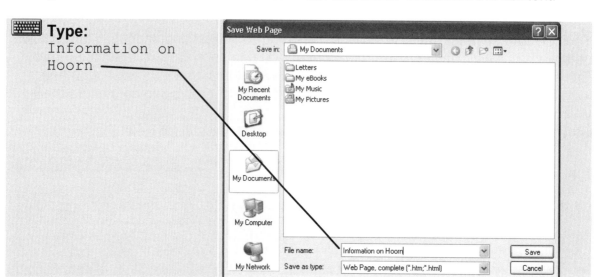

Type:
Information on
Hoorn

Now you need to make sure the whole web page will be saved. Then you can save the web page:

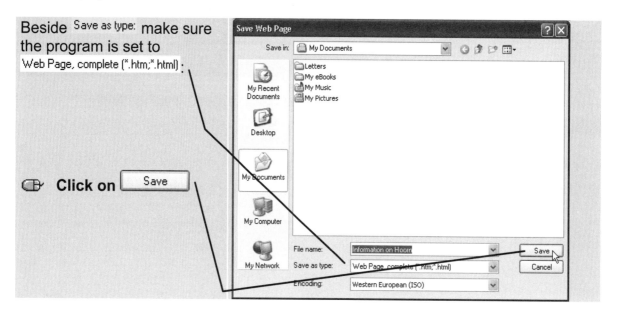

Beside Save as type: make sure
the program is set to
Web Page, complete (*.htm;*.html) :

Click on Save

The web page has now been saved to your hard drive in the folder 📁 My Documents .
You can open the page again any time you like.

Let's close *Internet Explorer* now. You can do that using a window button:

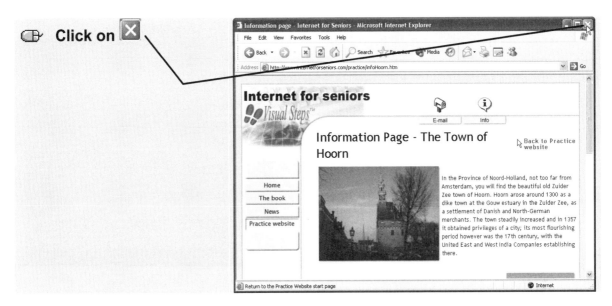

In the following section, you'll start the program *Internet Explorer* again.

Internet Explorer Offline

You're going to start *Internet Explorer* again, but this time you won't connect to the Internet. This is called *working offline*.

☞ **Start** *Internet Explorer* 1

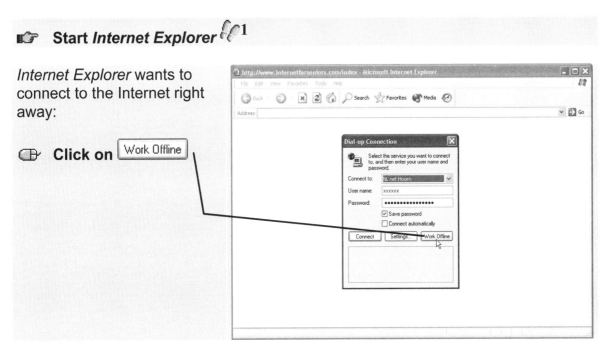

On the taskbar you can tell that there is no Internet connection by the fact that the little computers 🖥 are missing:

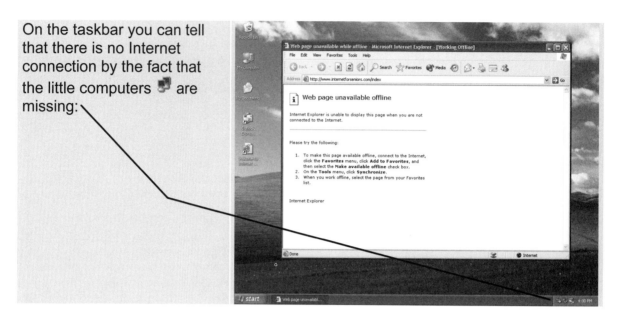

Now you've started *Internet Explorer* in offline mode, and you can open the page you saved.

Opening the Web Page

The web page has been saved to your computer's hard drive, and you can open it up again like this:

🖰 **Click on** File

🖰 **Click on** Open...

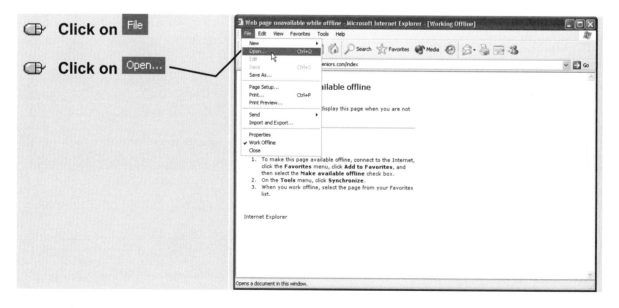

First you have to find the folder where you saved the web page. You do this by "browsing" through the folders on your hard drive.

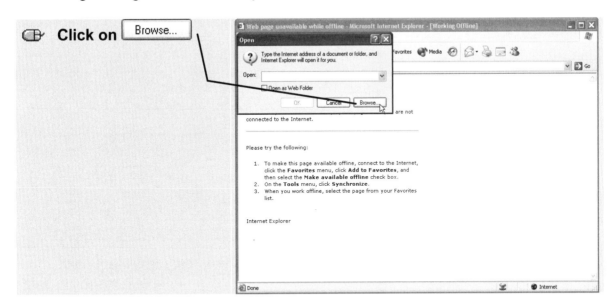

☞ **Click on** `Browse...`

You see this window:

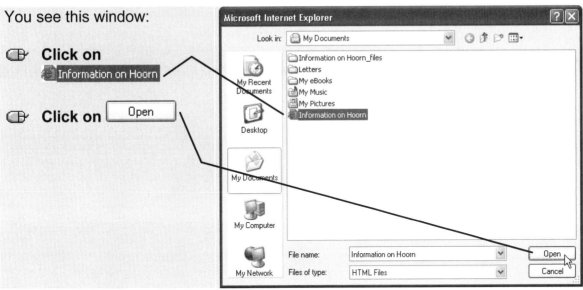

☞ **Click on** `Information on Hoorn`

☞ **Click on** `Open`

Now you see a small window
that already contains the
name of the 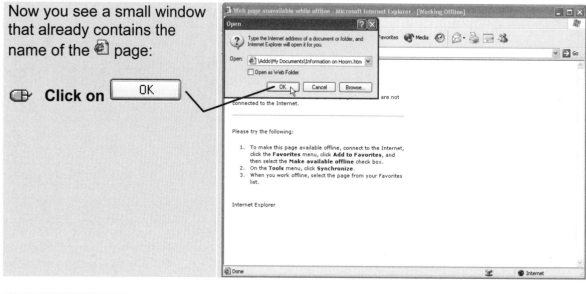 page:

☞ **Click on** [OK]

You see the web page:

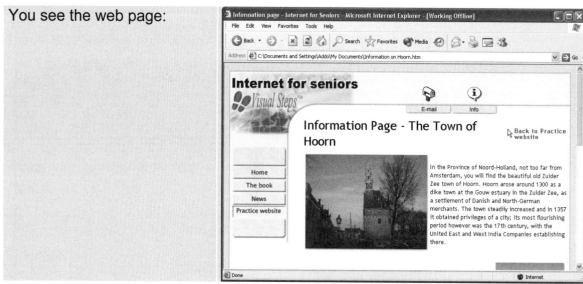

You can practice what you've learned in the following exercises.

Exercises

Have you forgotten how to perform a particular action? Use the number beside the footsteps to look it up in the appendix *How Do I Do That Again?*

Exercise: Copying Text

In this exercise, you'll practice at copying text again.
You don't need to open the information page on the Internet again, because you've saved this web page.

✔ Start *Internet Explorer,* but stay offline. 🦶25

✔ Open the web page *Information on Hoorn.* 🦶26

✔ Go to the last line of the text. 🦶9

✔ Select the last line of the text. 🦶27

✔ Copy the text. 🦶28

✔ Minimize the *Internet Explorer* window. 🦶11

✔ Start *WordPad.* 🦶29

✔ Paste the text. 🦶30

✔ Close the *WordPad* window without saving the text. 🦶31

Exercise: Saving an Image

In this exercise, you'll practice saving an image.

☑   Open the *Internet Explorer* window on the taskbar. 🐾 **12**

☑   Click with the right mouse button on the photo of *Jan Pieterszoon Coen*:

☑   Save the photo. 🐾 **33**

☑   Give the photo the name *Jan Pieterszoon Coen*. 🐾 **34**

☑   Close *Internet Explorer*. 🐾 **2**

Exercise: Saving a Page

☑   Start *Internet Explorer*. 🐾 **1**

☑   Connect to the Internet. 🐾 **3**

☑   Open the favorite: *Internet for Seniors*. 🐾 **17**

☑   Click on ⎹ Practice website ⎹ .

☑   Click on • Search engines .

☑   Save this page. 🐾 **53**

☑   Close *Internet Explorer*. 🐾 **2**

☑   Disconnect from the Internet if necessary. 🐾 **5**

Background Information

Photos
You might be wondering how to get a photo onto a computer. There are different ways of doing this.

You can copy a printed photo with a **scanner**.

The photo is placed in the scanner, which is then closed. The computer then "scans" the picture. This is also called *digitizing*.

It's also possible to scan photo negatives with a special kind of scanner, or to have a camera store place your photos directly onto a CD when you have them developed.

Scanner

The newest way to get photos onto a computer is by taking them without film rolls or paper. The image is immediately stored digitally. This is done with a **digital camera**.
The camera connects to the computer over a cable and the pictures are transferred to the computer. The photos can also be stored inside the camera on a small memory card. This card can then be "read" by the computer.

Digital camera

Photo Editing Programs

Paint is a very simple drawing program that also provides a few photo-editing techniques. Special photo-editing programs contain many more features. In these programs, you can increase and decrease a photo's size, or crop it into a particular shape. You can also change the colors or sharpen the contrast. You have access to a complete digital darkroom.

Many programs also have options for framing your photos or placing them in albums. Sometimes you can even create special web pages that you can place on the Internet. In short, you can enjoy endless possibilities of using your computer with digital photography.

On the *Internet for Seniors* website, you'll find a web page of recommended software. Some interesting drawing and photo-editing programs are listed there.

Paint Shop Pro is a very well-known program with a free trial version you can download from the Internet. It's an inexpensive alternative to expensive professional programs. Like every professional program, however, it's a program you have to learn how to use because it has many extensive features.

Paint Shop Pro with an extensive set of tools on the left

Photo-editing Programs and the Internet

Photo-editing programs are increasingly being specialized for Internet applications. Photos can be optimally edited for use on the Internet. Even with digital photos, the size, file type and color often have to be adjusted for the specific requirements of the Internet. Modern photo-editing programs offer a variety of tools for making these kinds of technical modifications.

With the help of one of these programs, you can also place your photos on the Internet and share them with others. You can make a family album, for example, that is immediately accessible to anyone in your family around the world.

Well-known examples of this kind of program are *ArcSoft PhotoStudio*, *Adobe Photo Deluxe* en *Microsoft Picture It!*

Easy photo editing and organizing in ArcSoft PhotoStudio

If you are considering buying a program like this, you might want to check and see what programs are already on your computer. Often a program of this type is included with a scanner or a digital camera.

Pixels

Computer images (drawings or photos) are made out of dots. These dots are called *pixels*. If you zoom in on one of these photos, you'll see the grid of colored dots:

In computer terminology, this grid is called a *bitmap*. You'll encounter this word in *Windows* from time to time.

The quality of a photo depends upon the number of pixels it contains. If the photo contains a lot of pixels, it will be sharp. As the number of pixels decreases, the photo becomes fuzzier. In addition, the quality is affected by the number of colors used. The more colors, the more realistic the photo. At present, 16 million colors are the standard on a normal PC. Much larger numbers are used for professional photos, however.

Copyright

By copyright, we mean the rights of the creator of an original work. That work might be a book, an article, a composition, a painting or a CD recording. Someone who has created one of these things is entitled to call it his or her "intellectual property". It's obvious that this person also has the right to a reasonable compensation. That's why the law forbids copying another person's "intellectual property". The symbol © is often used to indicate that a work is protected by copyright. Even if there's no © symbol, the work may not be copied without permission.

This law clearly extends to the Internet. A good rule of thumb is to assume that nothing may be copied unless clearly stated otherwise, and under what conditions. The Internet contains countless websites offering all kinds of material for free: images, photos, sounds, midi files (music), text, computer programs or complete music CDs.

On these websites, copying is permitted or even encouraged, sometimes on the condition that the source is identified – for example, if you copy a photo to put on your own website.

Sometimes website owners solicit material for which they don't own the copyright. In this case, both the offering and the copying are illegal activities strongly contested by the rightful copyright holders.

Making Your Own Website

Most Internet Service Providers allow you to put your own website on the Internet. They give you a certain amount of space (in MB) on their hard drive for this.

Creating web pages isn't all that terribly difficult, particularly if you use a special program. This kind of program is called a *web editor*.

Creating web pages is a lot like creating any kind of text: you write the text, add images and then add hyperlinks to your text. When your website is ready, you send the pages to your ISP's server. Your ISP gives you the web address where everyone can find your website.

Image Types

A computer screen is made out of small dots we call *pixels*. Depending on your monitor's settings, there may be 640 or more pixels horizontally and 480 or more pixels vertically. We call this the *screen resolution*. The larger the number of pixels, the more space there is on your screen.

Each pixel can have a different color. The more colors that are used, the more information that can be stored in the photo. This is called the *color depth*. The more information that has to be saved, the larger the file. The standard files are called *bitmap files* and are denoted by the file extension *.bmp*.

Color Depth	Number of Colors Possible	File Size BMP
1-bit	2 colors	59 kB
4-bit	16 colors	235 kB
8-bit	256 colors	470 kB
24-bit	millions of colors	1407 kB

BMP images with sizes like these are impractical for use on the Internet. They take far too long to load.

This is why two file types have been developed that give good results, but still maintain a reasonable file size.

The first file type, *GIF,* is often used for colorful images like drawings. GIF files have the extension*.gif*.

The other file type, *JPEG*, is mainly used for photos and is recognizable by the extension *.jpg*.

A photo with 256 colors and a file size of 470 kB as a BMP needs only 3 kB when converted to GIF format.

The Internet Keyboard

In recent years, the computer has been increasingly adapted for use with the Internet. One important component of this is the keyboard.

This keyboard has a number of buttons for starting Internet programs, surfing the Internet and answering your e-mail:

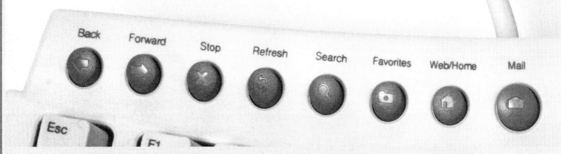

Here you see buttons for browsing a website, searching on the Internet and opening your favorites. There's also a button for opening your home page. Another button opens your e-mail program.

Tips

 Tip

Opening Other File Types

When you open a file in *Paint*, it shows you drawings and photos with the file type *BMP*.

You see these files in the file list: ——

Next to Files of type: you see that *BMP* has been selected: —

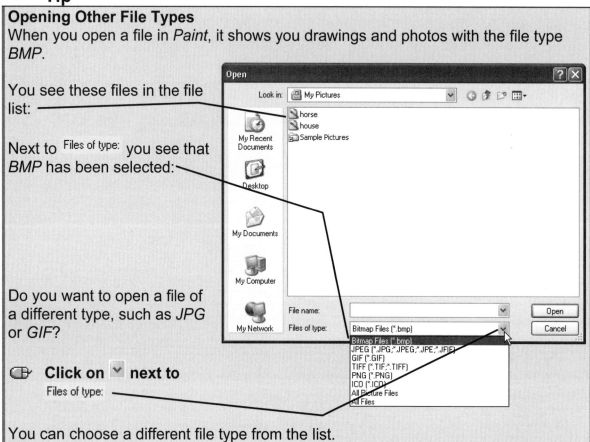

Do you want to open a file of a different type, such as *JPG* or *GIF*?

 Click on ⌄ **next to**
Files of type: ———

You can choose a different file type from the list.

 Tip

Want to know more?

Would you like to know more about the programs *WordPad* and *Paint*, for example: how to edit and format text or increase and decrease the size of images?
You can read about that in the book *Windows XP for Seniors*.
Have a look at **www.visualsteps.com/winxp**

Tip

Where can I find photos and drawings?
You can find an enormous number of drawings and pictures on the Internet that you can use. Well-known search engines like *Google* and *AltaVista* offer the option to search for images:

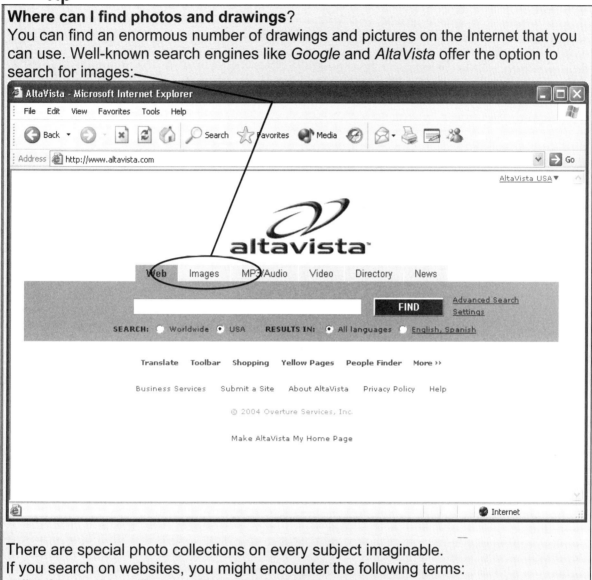

There are special photo collections on every subject imaginable.
If you search on websites, you might encounter the following terms:
collection, archive, library, stock, clip art, graphics, images, bitmaps

Tip

Zooming In

If you want to view the pixels in a photo in *Paint*, you have to zoom in:

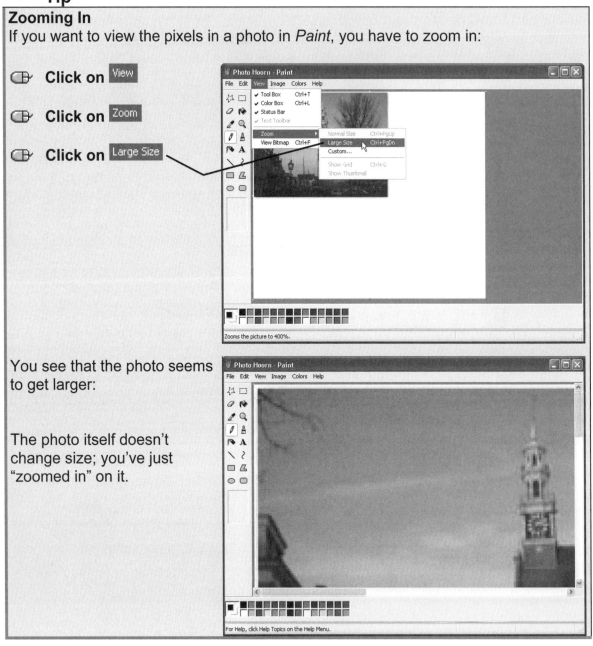

☜ **Click on** View

☜ **Click on** Zoom

☜ **Click on** Large Size

You see that the photo seems to get larger:

The photo itself doesn't change size; you've just "zoomed in" on it.

5. E-mail, Your Electronic Mail

One of the most widely-used Internet applications is electronic mail, or e-mail. No pens, paper, envelopes or stamps are involved. You type your message on the computer and send it through the Internet.

When you sign up with an Internet Service Provider, you automatically get an *e-mail address*. You can use this e-mail address to send and receive mail. Your ISP has a kind of post office for this, called a *mail server*. This electronic post office handles all the mail traffic.

Of course, the addressee must also have an e-mail address if you want to send him an e-mail. It doesn't matter where the addressee lives, however. It costs exactly the same to send an e-mail to China as it does to send one to your next-door neighbor. There are no costs to you for sending an e-mail other than your Internet service subscription. There is also no limit on the number of messages you may send or receive. Sending an e-mail takes only seconds.

E-mail is used a great deal by people who work with computers. It's fast: the message usually arrives at its destination within 60 seconds.

Windows has a program, *Outlook Express*, that you can use to simply and quickly send and receive electronic letters. You'll learn to use this program in this chapter.

In this chapter, you'll learn how to:

- start *Outlook Express*
- create an e-mail message
- send and receive e-mail
- read e-mail

 Please note:

In order to work through this chapter, you should have your own e-mail address, and your e-mail program must be set up correctly. If this is not the case, contact your Internet Service Provider for help.

Starting Outlook Express

Windows contains the program *Outlook Express*, which you can use to send and receive electronic mail. Here's how you start *Outlook Express*:

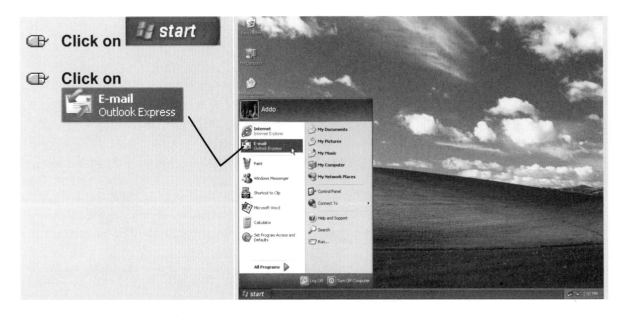

Connect Right Away, or Wait?

Outlook Express tries right away to connect to the Internet in order to check if there's any e-mail for you.

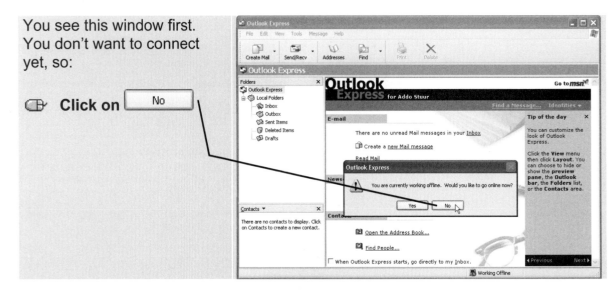

HELP! I don't see these windows.

You don't see the windows shown above about your connection?
Then *Outlook Express* has been set up differently on your computer and doesn't
automatically try to connect.

 ## Tip

Would you like to set up *Outlook Express* differently?
You can read how to do that in Chapter 9.

Outlook Express Has Started

After the dial-up window has closed, you see the *Outlook Express* welcome screen:

There's a frame containing
various folders on the left-
hand side:

You see an overview of the
program's options on the
right-hand side:

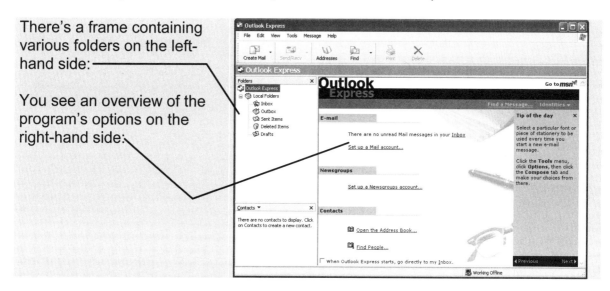

The E-mail Address

As practice, you're going to send an e-mail to yourself. This will show you how to send e-mail. What's more, the e-mail will be delivered immediately to you, so you can see how to receive e-mail.
Here's how you create a new e-mail message:

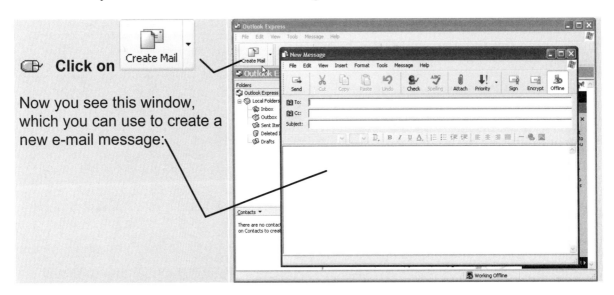

Click on Create Mail

Now you see this window, which you can use to create a new e-mail message:

Sending an e-mail is a lot like sending a regular letter.
First of all, the letter needs an address: the e-mail address.
Every e-mail address consists of a number of words with an "at" symbol (@) near the middle. For example:

name@provider.net

The name comes before the "at" symbol. Usually, the address of the ISP comes after the "at" symbol.

 Please note:

E-mail addresses may not contain spaces.
This is why names or words are sometimes separated by a period. These periods are very important. If you leave one out, the e-mail message will never arrive. The mail carrier on the street understands what you mean if an address isn't completely correct. A computer, however, won't.

The best way to test whether your electronic mail is working is to send a letter to yourself.

The e-mail address should be typed in the white box next to 📧 To: .

The cursor is already blinking in this field:

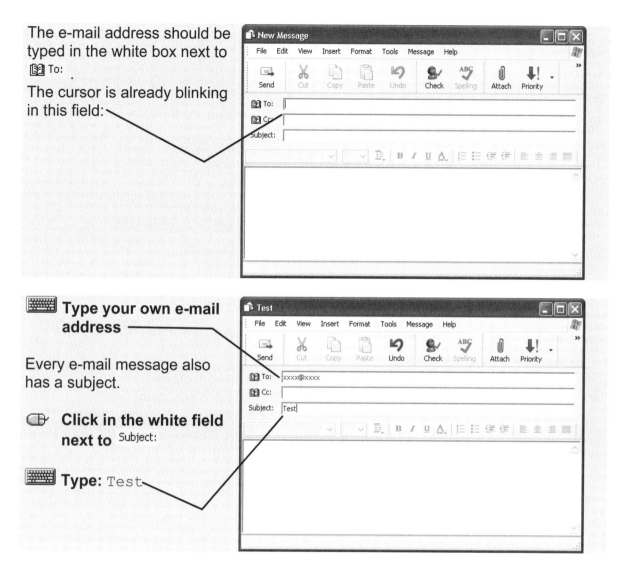

⌨ **Type your own e-mail address**

Every e-mail message also has a subject.

🖱 **Click in the white field next to** Subject:

⌨ **Type:** Test

Now you can type in the actual text of your message. You do this in the large white area.

🖱 **Click in the large white area**

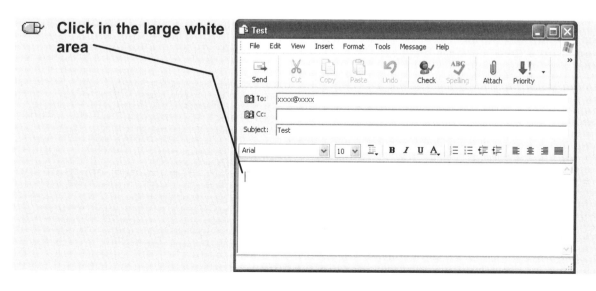

This text box works just the same way a text-editing program such as *WordPad*. All the buttons and icons have the same functions.

 Tip

Would you like to know more?
Would you like to know more about typing and formatting text in *Windows*?
Then read the *Visual Steps* book *Windows XP for Seniors*.
See **www.visualsteps.com/winxp** for more information.

The most important keys for editing and correcting text are shown below.

 Tip

The Keys for Typing Text

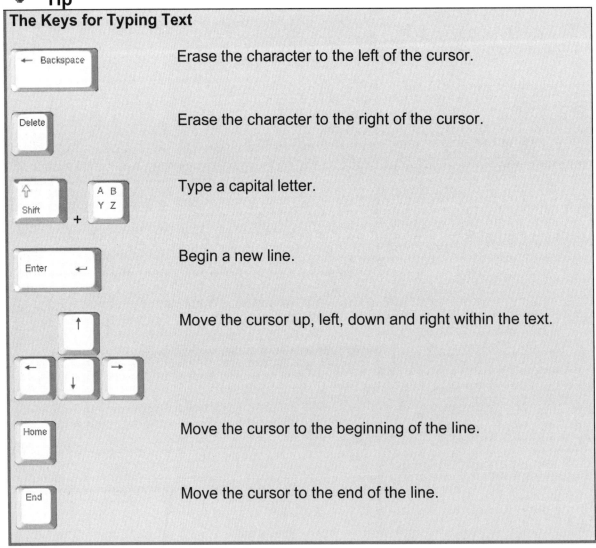

Erase the character to the left of the cursor.

Erase the character to the right of the cursor.

Type a capital letter.

Begin a new line.

Move the cursor up, left, down and right within the text.

Move the cursor to the beginning of the line.

Move the cursor to the end of the line.

Type:
This first e-mail
is a test.

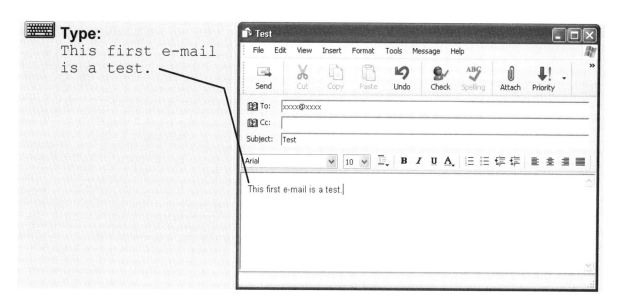

When the e-mail message is ready, you can send it.

Sending E-mail

Sending an e-mail usually occurs in two steps. First, the e-mail is placed in the *Outbox*. This is a separate folder where all the messages you write go first. After that, you connect to the Internet and all the messages in your *Outbox* are sent.
First, send the message to the *Outbox*:

Click at the top left on

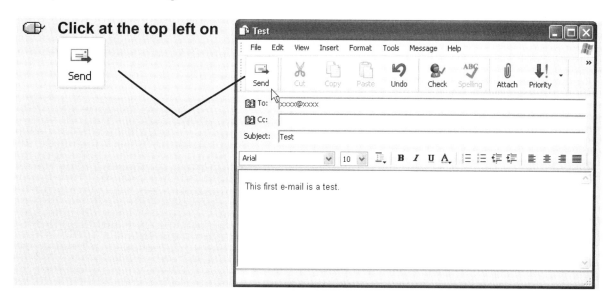

You're notified that your message will first be placed in the *Outbox*:

 Click on ☐ OK

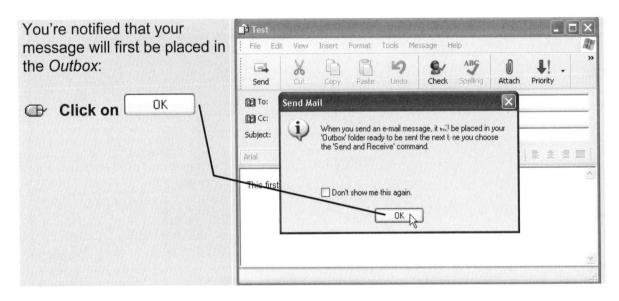

HELP! I don't see the window.

You don't see the above window about the *Outbox*?
Then your *Outlook Express* has been set up differently and your e-mail is sent immediately.
☞ **Skip the following section**
☞ **Continue reading at *Sending and Receiving***

The Outbox

All your e-mail messages are collected in the *Outbox*. Your messages will only be sent after you've connected to the Internet. This allows you to write all your e-mails first, then send them all at once.

You see the *Outlook Express* window again.

There is one message in 📁 **Outbox** (1). You can see this by the letters in bold and the number after the name:

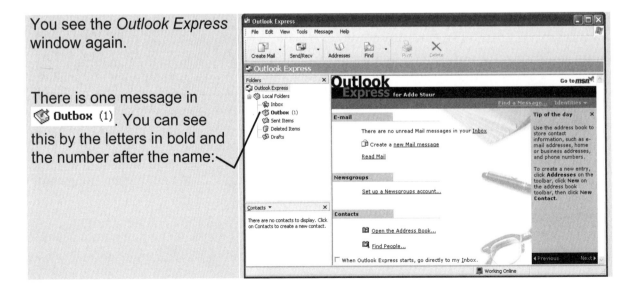

Sending and Receiving

Now you can send your message. To do this, the program will connect to the Internet.

Is your modem ready?
It's important to check that your modem is ready before you connect.

Do you have an external
    modem?
☞ **Turn the modem on**

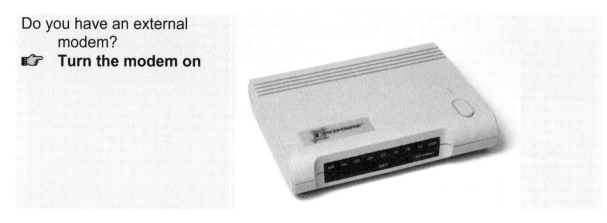

Do you have an internal modem?
☞ **Then you don't have to do anything**

Now you can have *Outlook Express* connect to the Internet.

☞ **Click on** Send/Recv

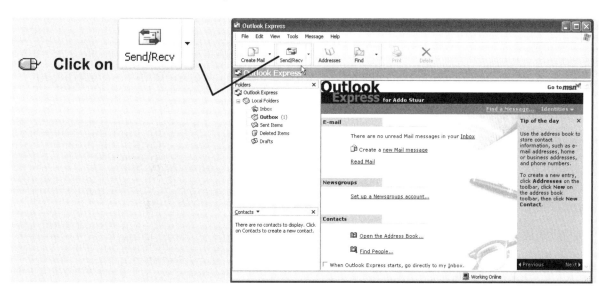

Outlook Express tells you that you're still working offline, and asks if you want to remain online. You have to be online to send a message, so:

☞ **Click on** ⬚ Yes ⬚

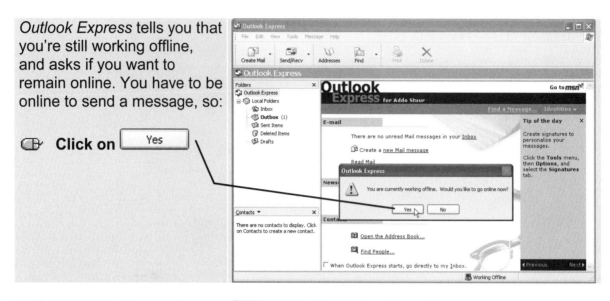

You see the window that will connect you:⎯

 Type in your password if necessary

☞ **Click on** ⬚ Connect ⬚

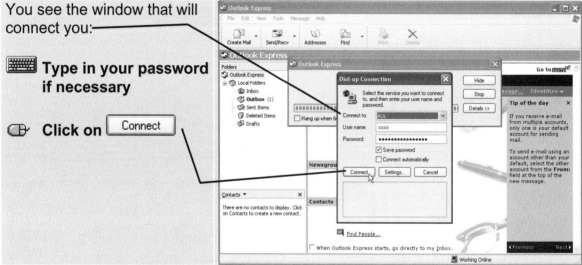

✖ HELP! I don't see the window.

You don't see the above window about the dial-up connection?
Then your *Outlook Express* has been set up differently and the program automatically connects when you click on the **Send** button.
☞ **Just keep reading**

Your computer will connect to your Internet Service Provider. Once this connection has been established, your e-mail message will be sent and *Outlook Express* will check to see if any e-mail has arrived for you.

You can follow the progress
of this process in this window:

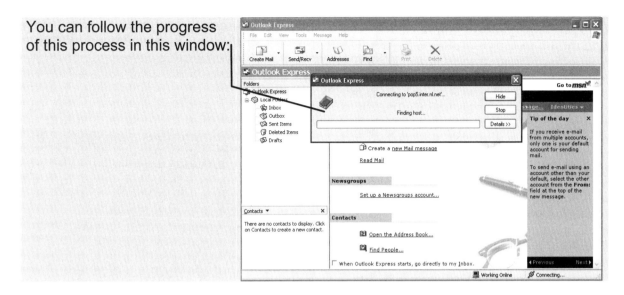

If everything's gone well, your test message has already been delivered to you. It will
be in the *Inbox*.

Reading an E-mail

All the e-mails you receive are stored in a separate folder called the *Inbox*.

Click on 🔖 **Inbox** (1)

You see your own message
on the right-hand side:

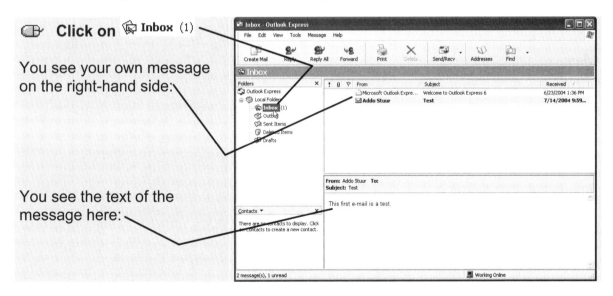

You see the text of the
message here:

 HELP! I don't have any mail.

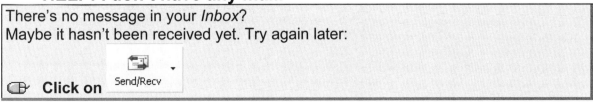

There's no message in your *Inbox*?
Maybe it hasn't been received yet. Try again later:

Click on Send/Recv

You can open the message in a larger window so you can read it better:

 Double-click on your message

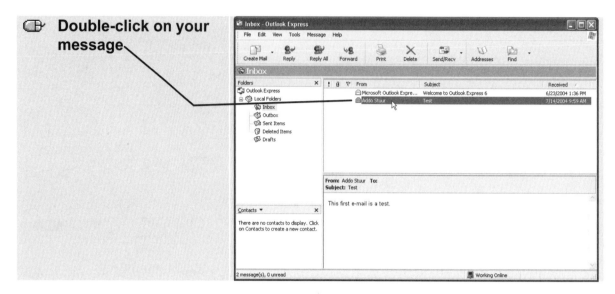

💡 Tip

Are you having trouble double-clicking?
You can also use the following trick:

 Click once on the message

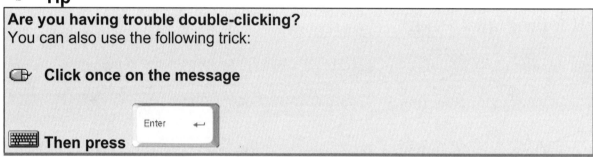

⌨ **Then press** `Enter ←`

The e-mail message is easier to read in a separate window:

Then you can close this window:

 Click on 🗙

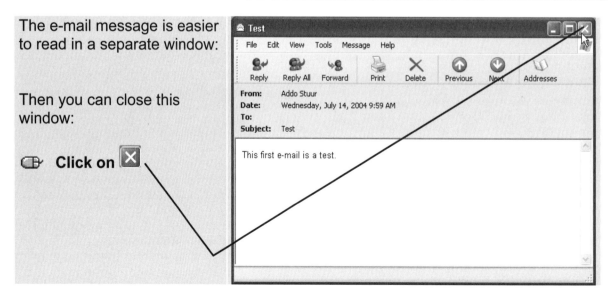

The Folders

Outlook Express has a sophisticated system of folders for organizing your e-mail messages. In addition to the **Inbox** and the **Outbox**, there are three other folders. *Outlook Express* saves all the e-mail messages you've sent in a separate folder called **Sent Items**.

You can delete messages you don't want to keep. These will be stored in the folder **Deleted Items**.

Last but not least, there's a folder for messages that are not yet finished. These are placed in the folder **Drafts**.

The ⓖ Sent Items folder
contains copies of the e-mails
you've sent:

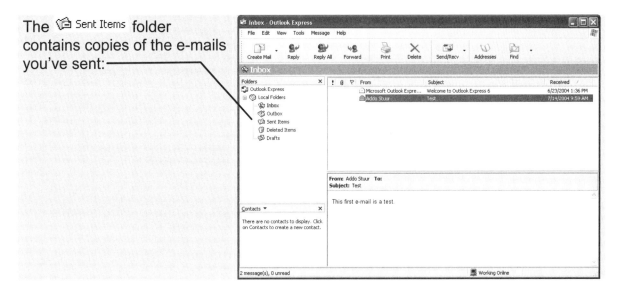

The message you just sent to yourself should be in there.

Click on ⓖ Sent Items

Your first e-mail is indeed in
this folder:

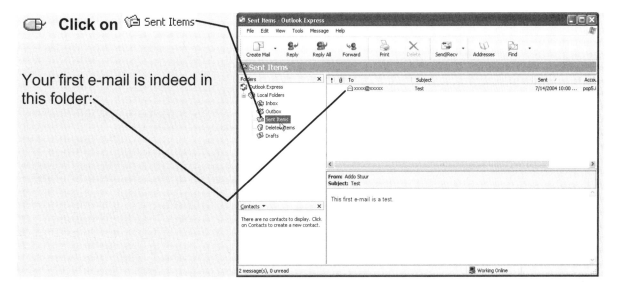

Now you can delete this e-mail message as a test.

Deleting E-mail Messages

Many people use the folders *Inbox* and *Sent Items* as a kind of archive. All your correspondence is stored together neatly, and you can easily retrieve your e-mail messages. There's no limit on the number of e-mail messages you can store. In practice however, you'll want to regularly delete unnecessary messages to keep your folders uncluttered. You can erase the test message now.

Before you can delete an e-mail, you have to select it:

☞ Click on the e-mail message

The message is now blue, meaning it has been selected:

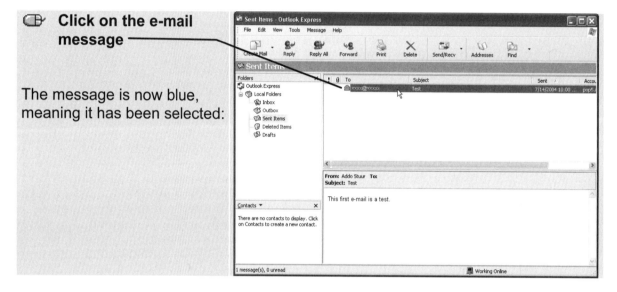

Now you can tell *Outlook Express* to delete the message.

☞ Click on [Delete]

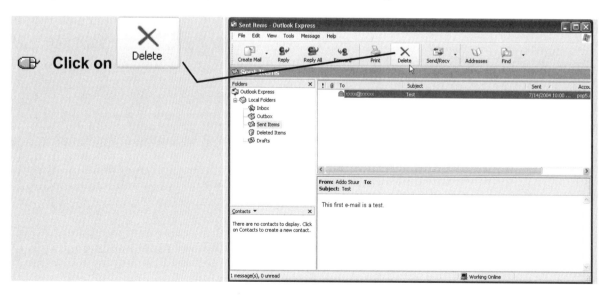

The folder 📬 Sent Items is now empty:

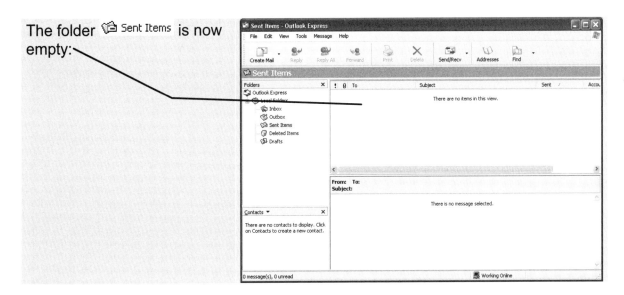

Outlook Express saves all the e-mail messages you've deleted in a separate folder.

👆 **Click on** 🗑 Deleted Items

Now you see your test mail here:

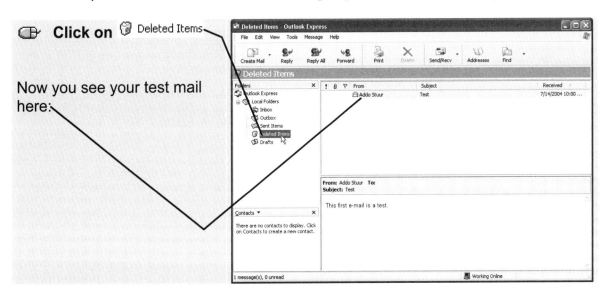

When you're ready to permanently delete e-mails, you can empty the 🗑 Deleted Items folder. This is how:

Click on Edit

Click on
Empty 'Deleted Items' Folder

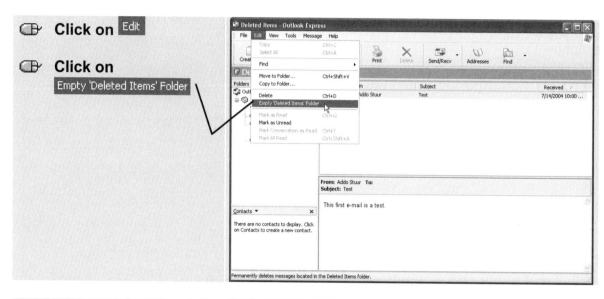

Outlook Express asks you to confirm, just to be sure:

Click on Yes

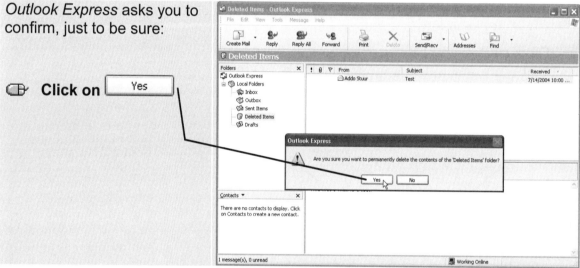

The whole folder is now empty:

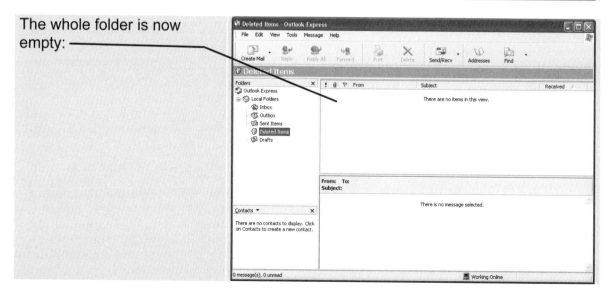

A Second Test Message

In order to practice receiving, answering and forwarding e-mails, you can send a test message to a special e-mail address. You'll get an automated e-mail reply back.

Start a new e-mail.

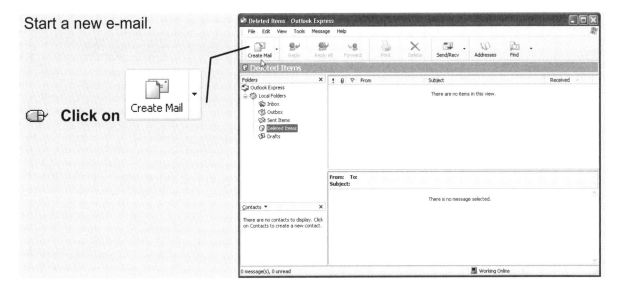

☞ **Click on** Create Mail

The e-mail address for the test message is: **test@visualsteps.com**

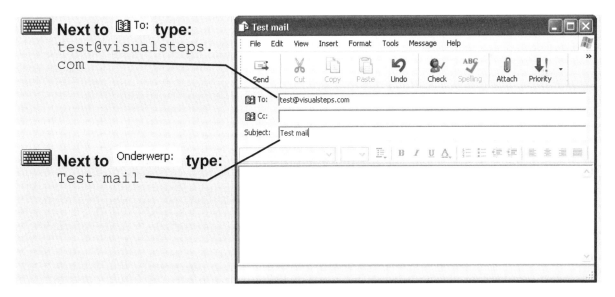

⌨ **Next to** 📖 To: **type:**
test@visualsteps.
com

⌨ **Next to** Onderwerp: **type:**
Test mail

The test message is ready. You're not going to send this message immediately; instead, you're going to save it in the 📁 Drafts folder first.

The Drafts Folder

Sometimes you won't want to send a message immediately, because you want to think about the content a little longer, for example. In that case, you can save the e-mail in the 📄 Drafts folder.

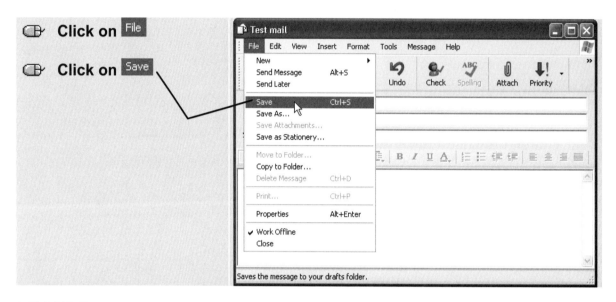

   👉 **Click on** File

   👉 **Click on** Save

Outlook Express tells you the e-mail has been saved in 📄 Drafts:

   👉 **Click on** OK

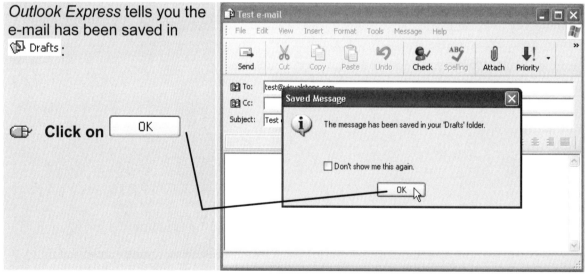

Now you can close the window containing the e-mail for a while.

Click on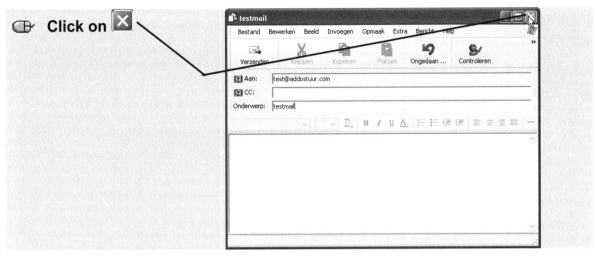

The letters in the word
Drafts (1) are in bold, and
the number 1 is displayed.
That means there's one
message in the folder:

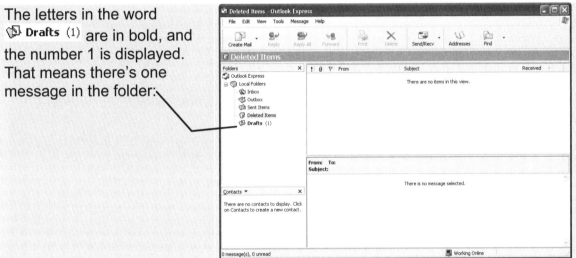

You can leave the message in this folder even if you close *Outlook Express.* Later
on, you can simply open this message back up and continue working with it:

Click on **Drafts** (1)

**Double-click on the
message**

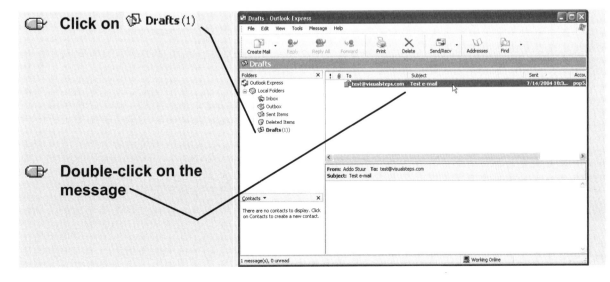

The message opens, and now you can send it to the *Outbox*:

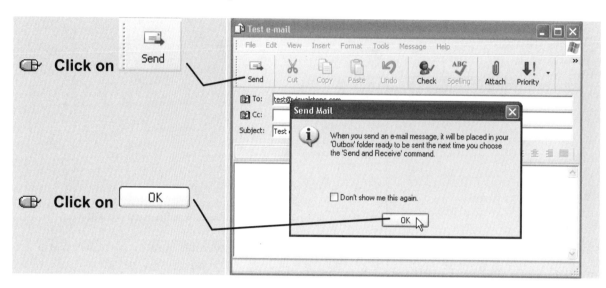

Now the message is in the *Outbox*.

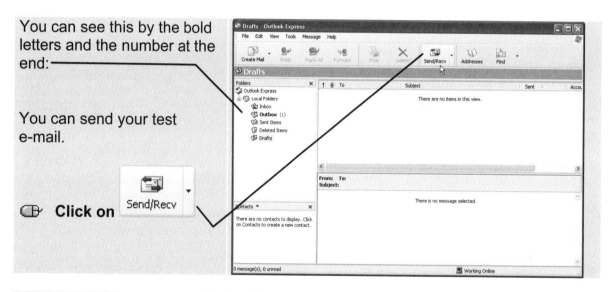

You can see this by the bold letters and the number at the end:

You can send your test e-mail.

Click on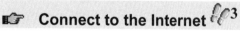

☞ **Connect to the Internet** 🦶³

Your message is sent, and *Outlook Express* immediately checks if you've received any mail.

⇨ **Please note:**

It might take a little while before you receive a reply to your test mail.
Wait about fifteen minutes and try again:

Click on

Replying to an E-mail

Have you gotten a response to your test mail?

Then you see a message with the subject *Response to test e-mail:*

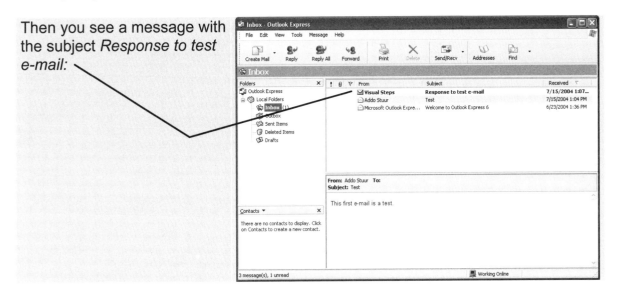

Outlook Express has a quick and handy option for answering e-mail messages. If you've received an e-mail, you don't have to type in the e-mail address again in order to reply to it. Give it a try:

Double-click on the e-mail message

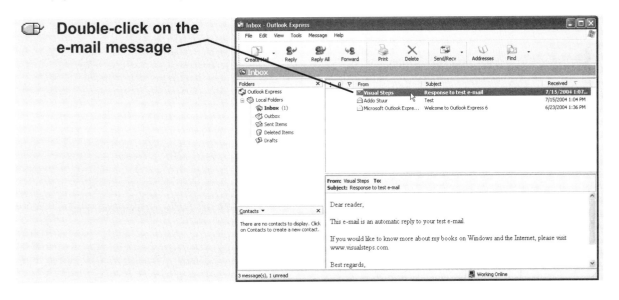

Now you see this window containing the response e-mail:

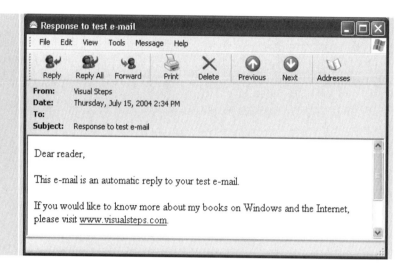

Outlook Express has various options for replying to this e-mail. There's a toolbar for this, containing the following buttons:

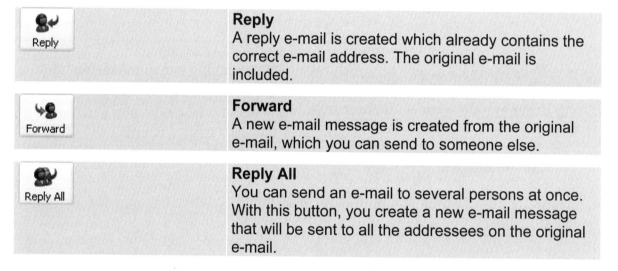

Reply
A reply e-mail is created which already contains the correct e-mail address. The original e-mail is included.

Forward
A new e-mail message is created from the original e-mail, which you can send to someone else.

Reply All
You can send an e-mail to several persons at once. With this button, you create a new e-mail message that will be sent to all the addressees on the original e-mail.

In most cases, you'll just want to reply to a message:

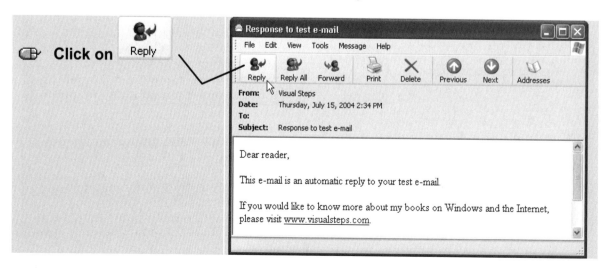

☞ **Click on**   Reply

Now you see this window:

The e-mail address has already been entered in the right place:

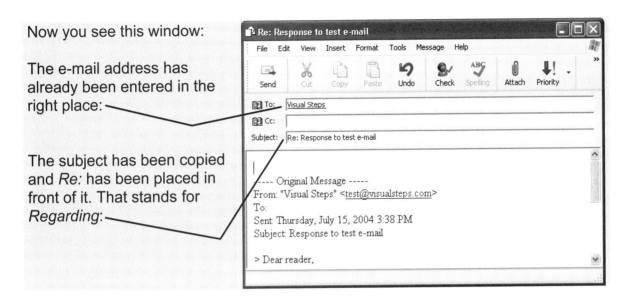

The subject has been copied and *Re:* has been placed in front of it. That stands for *Regarding*:

The text of the original message is automatically included in the reply message. You can see it under *---Original Message---*.
This is pretty useful: the person to whom you're replying can immediately see what the message was about. On the other hand, the message just gets longer and longer in an extended correspondence.

 Tip

Would you rather the original message wasn't included in the reply?
You can prevent its inclusion by:
  creating a new message instead of using the *Reply* button
  setting up *Outlook Express* differently; see Chapter 9

You can type your reply at the top of the message:

Type:
     This is my reply.

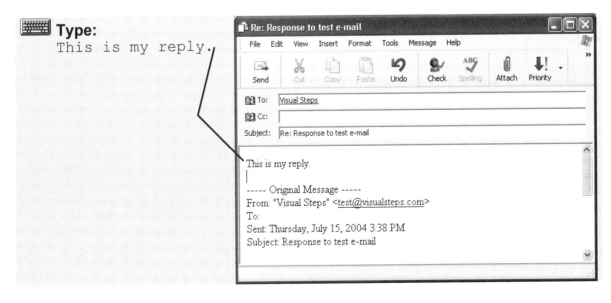

Please note:

You'll only get one reply a week to e-mail you send to test@visualsteps.com. The reply message is automatically sent by my ISP's computer. The limitation to one message per week has been made so that two computers don't fall into a vicious circle, endlessly sending automated messages back and forth.

Now you can send this message, but you won't get a reply to it.

☞ **Send the message to the *Outbox*** $\ell\ell^{37}$

☞ **Send the message** $\ell\ell^{39}$

In the following Exercises, you can practice sending and receiving e-mails.

Exercises

Have you forgotten how to perform a particular action? Use the number beside the footsteps to look it up in the appendix *How Do I Do That Again?*

Exercise: Creating an E-mail

In this exercise, you're going to write a new e-mail message.

✔ Start *Outlook Express*. 𝓮𝓮 35

✔ Create a new e-mail message addressed to yourself. 𝓮𝓮 36

✔ Send it. 𝓮𝓮 37

✔ Check if your e-mail is in the *Outbox*. 𝓮𝓮 38

✔ Send and receive your e-mail. 𝓮𝓮 39

✔ Check if you've received e-mail in the *Inbox*. 𝓮𝓮 41

✔ Read your e-mail message. 𝓮𝓮 42

✔ Close *Outlook Express*. 𝓮𝓮 43

Exercise: Do You Have Mail?

In this exercise, you're just going to check if you have any new e-mail messages.

✔ Start *Outlook Express*. 𝓮𝓮 35

✔ Send and receive your e-mail. 𝓮𝓮 39

✔ Check if you've received e-mail in the *Inbox*. 𝓮𝓮 41

✔ Close *Outlook Express*. 𝓮𝓮 43

Exercise: Deleting an E-mail

✓ Start *Outlook Express*. 🦶35

✓ Send and receive your e-mail. 🦶39

✓ Look in the *Inbox*. 🦶41

✓ Delete your test e-mail. 🦶44

✓ Close *Outlook Express*. 🦶43

Exercise: E-mail in the Drafts Folder

✓ Start *Outlook Express*. 🦶35

✓ Create a new e-mail message addressed to yourself. 🦶36

✓ Save it. 🦶45

✓ Close the window containing the new e-mail. 🦶32

✓ Check if your e-mail is in the *Drafts* folder. 🦶46

✓ Delete your new e-mail. 🦶44

✓ Close *Outlook Express*. 🦶43

Background Information

How Does E-mail Work?

All e-mail messages are delivered to a *mail server*. This is a computer at your Internet Service Provider that is dedicated to processing electronic mail.

If you've written to someone and the e-mail has been sent, then it's transported by your ISP's mail server until – after passing through a number of intermediate stations – it reaches the mail server at the addressee's ISP and is stored there.

It works the same way in reverse. E-mail for you is saved on your ISP's mail server until you pick it up with *Outlook Express*.

The Parts of *Outlook Express*

You can display or hide the following parts of the window.

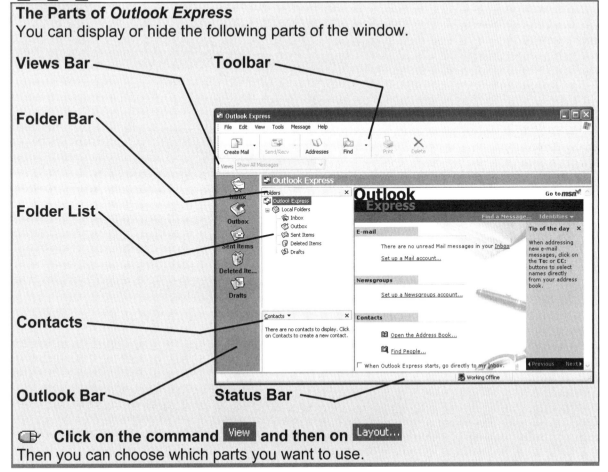

☞ **Click on the command** View **and then on** Layout...

Then you can choose which parts you want to use.

Netiquette

The word *netiquette* is an abbreviation of the phrase "*Internet etiquette*". It denotes a collection of rules that people who use e-mail are advised to follow. It is particularly advisable for *newbies* (beginners on the digital highway) to take note of netiquette. Anyone who writes an e-mail message should realize that many of the aids we use during a conversation, such as facial expression, vocal inflections and gestures, are now unavailable. This can lead to situations in which comments that were meant to be funny or ironic are completely misinterpreted.

The use of e-mail has also led many people to assume a kind of telegram style. A writing style that is too succint can make a curt or grumpy impression.

You should also take the lack of opportunity for an immediate reaction into account. During a conversation, you can immediately correct an unfortunate comment; that's not possible with e-mail.

In general, it's a good idea to write your e-mail just as you would a letter sent by regular mail. You should also realize that not every subject is appropriate for e-mail. For example, the addressee might share his or her computer with other people who also have access to the e-mail program.

Make use of the normal rules for capitalization while writing. A sentence that's all in capitals can be interpreted as shouting.

If you're writing a "difficult" e-mail, take the time to read it through again a few hours later. Once you've sent a message, there's usually no going back.

Make sure to write your name and address, if applicable, at the bottom of your e-mails. Then the addressee will know who sent the e-mail.

Tips

 Tip

Do you want to avoid seeing this window again?
You see this window every time you send a new e-mail message:

 Click on the box next to Don't show me this again.

 Then click on
⬜ OK

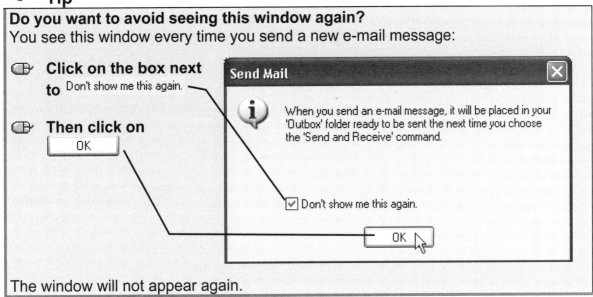

The window will not appear again.

 Tip

A Good View
You can best read an e-mail if you temporarily maximize its window:

 Click on 🔲

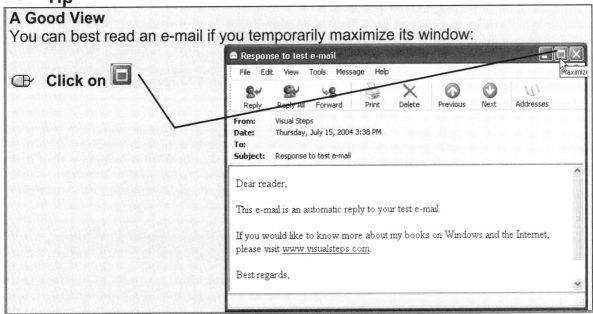

Tip

Printing an E-mail
You can easily print an e-mail message on paper.

☞ **First check if the printer is on**

👆 **Click on** Print

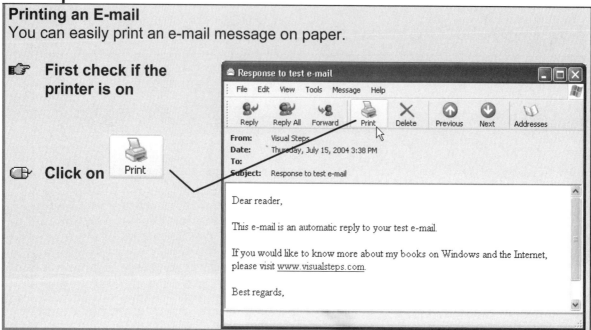

 Tip

Do you want to send only, or receive only?
By default, all e-mails are sent and recieved at the same time when you connect to the Internet. You can, however, tell *Outlook Express* to only send messages, or only receive messages. Here's how you do it:

👆 **Click on** ▾ **next to**
Send/Recv

You can then choose to Receive All of Send All .

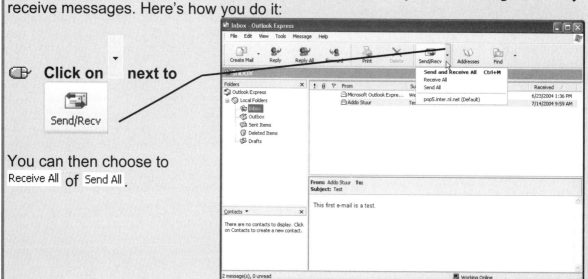

6. Addresses, E-mails and Attachments

In the 1970s, people thought the computer would come to occupy such a central position that a paperless society would arise. All information would be read on (portable) monitors. Paper would become superfluous. In reality, things have turned out differently. In fact, more paper than ever is being used. After all, it's very easy to print out an e-mail message, and people do it quite often.

Nonetheless, the rise of the Internet has contributed to a change in communication. E-mail is slowly replacing the function of the telephone, the letter and the fax. This is in part a result of the fact that, not only short messages but all kinds of other information can be sent by e-mail, such as photographs or drawings.

The speed of communication has also increased dramatically: An e-mail can arrive within seconds. A photo can be sent in minutes. Extensive exchange of e-mails also occurs in work environments.

The increase in e-mail usage has led to an increased importance for its management. The computer is being used more and more as an archive for our correspondence.

In this chapter, you'll learn how you can organize your e-mail messages neatly. You'll also learn how to save your e-mail addresses in an address book, and how to keep them organized so you can quickly retrieve them.

You'll learn how to send an attachment with an e-mail message. In this way you can exchange photos with family and friends, wherever in the world they may be.

In this chapter, you'll learn:

- how to use the Address Book
- how to add a new e-mail address
- what happens with a bad e-mail address
- how to use a signature in your e-mails
- how to sort your e-mails
- how to search within your e-mails
- how to send an attachment
- how to view an attachment
- how to open an attachment
- how to save an attachment

Starting Outlook Express

First, start the program *Outlook Express*:

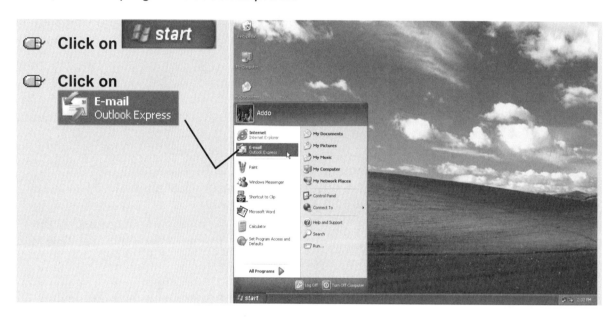

In this chapter, *Outlook Express* doesn't need to connect to the Internet. Of course, you can check your e-mail if you'd like.

You see the welcome screen for *Outlook Express*:

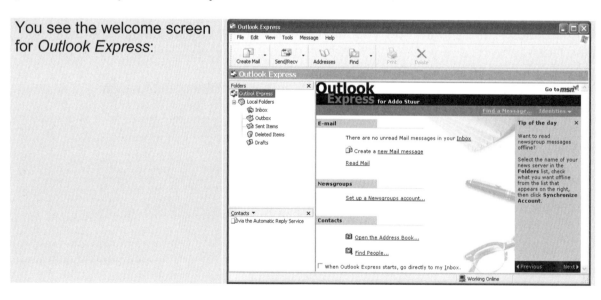

The Address Book

Windows has linked an address book with the *Outlook Express* program.
In this address book, *Outlook Express* automatically saves all the e-mail addresses from e-mails you've answered. Here's how you view the Address Book:

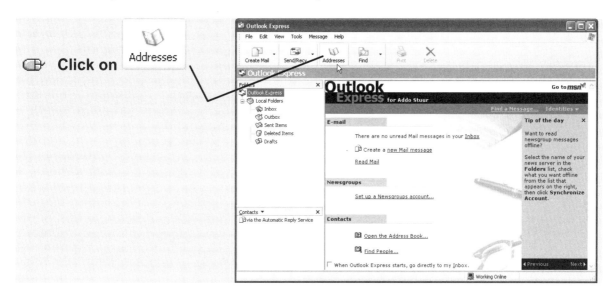

Click on Addresses

In the previous chapter, you replied to the test mail from test@visualsteps.com. This e-mail address should therefore be stored in your Address Book.

The Address Book has its own window.

If everything's gone well, there should be at least one address here, the address of test@visualsteps.com:

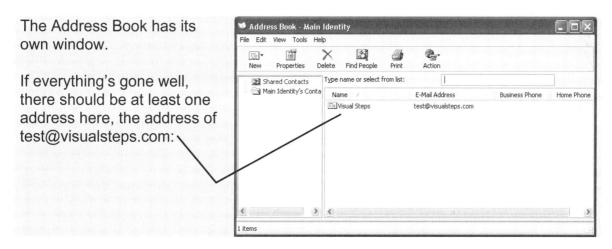

 HELP! There isn't any address.

You don't see the address in the window above? Then you didn't answer the e-mail in the previous chapter, or your *Outlook Express* is set up differently.
☞ **Just keep reading up to the section *Adding a New E-mail Address***

Filling in an Address

An automatically-saved address contains at least the e-mail address. The rest of the name and address information usually needs to be added or corrected.
You can edit the e-mail address information as follows:

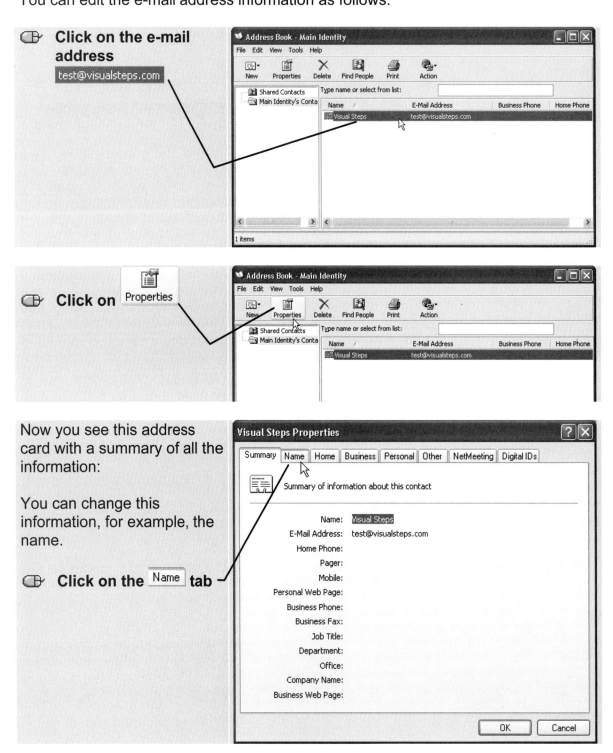

Click on the e-mail address

test@visualsteps.com

Click on Properties

Now you see this address card with a summary of all the information:

You can change this information, for example, the name.

Click on the Name **tab**

The first and last names have already been filled in by the program, but they won't be right in this case. You can fix that yourself.

Now you see these entries for the name.

First erase the first name; it's already selected:

Press

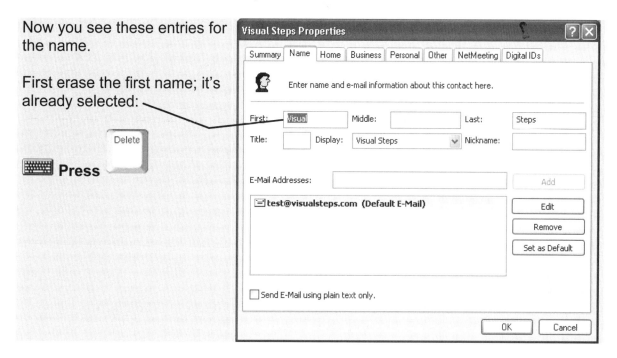

Now you can change the last name. You can move to that field using a key.

Press twice on

Tab

Now the last name is selected:

Press

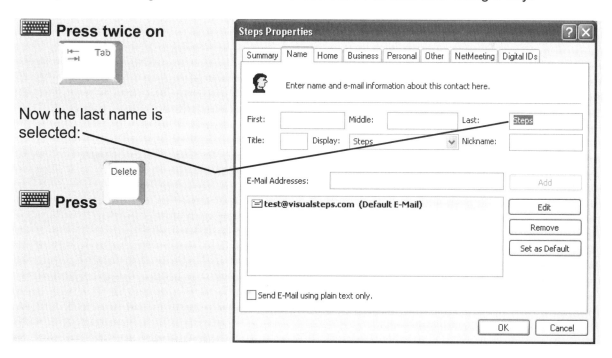

The last name has been deleted, and you can type in a different name:

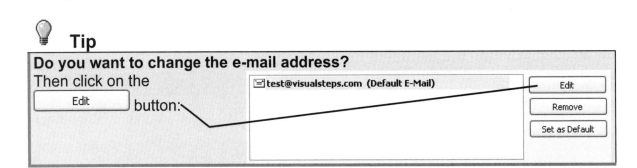

⌨ **Type:**
Test e-mail

You can see that the e-mail address has been filled in correctly:

Test e-mail Properties

Summary | Name | Home | Business | Personal | Other | NetMeeting | Digital IDs

Enter name and e-mail information about this contact here.

First: _____ Middle: _____ Last: Test e-mail

Title: ___ Display: Test e-mail ▾ Nickname: _____

E-Mail Addresses: _____ Add

test@visualsteps.com (Default E-Mail)   Edit
                                         Remove
                                         Set as Default

☐ Send E-Mail using plain text only.

OK   Cancel

💡 **Tip**

Do you want to change the e-mail address?
Then click on the
[Edit] button:

test@visualsteps.com (Default E-Mail)   Edit
                                         Remove
                                         Set as Default

The e-mail address is usually stored correctly when it's automatically saved. In contrast, the other information usually needs correcting. In this example, you've given the e-mail address a made-up last name (*Test e-mail*), but in general this will be the name of an existing person or organization.

If you are satisfied with the information, you can close this window:

☞ **Click on** ⌷ OK ⌷

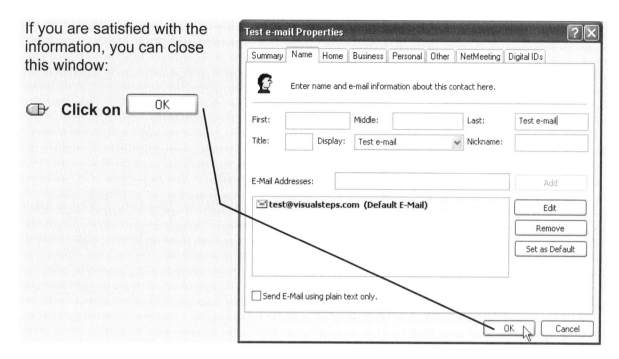

You can also close the Address Book window:

☞ **Click on** ☒

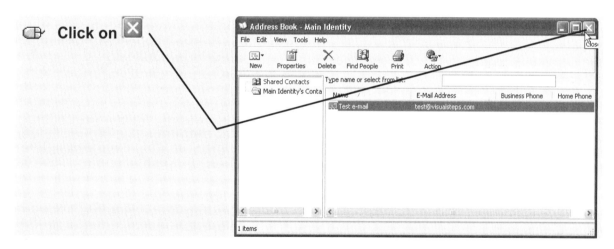

Once a name is in the Address Book, you can use it every time you send this person an e-mail.

Using an Address

Now that the e-mail address has been saved in the Address Book, you can easily use it to create a new e-mail message:

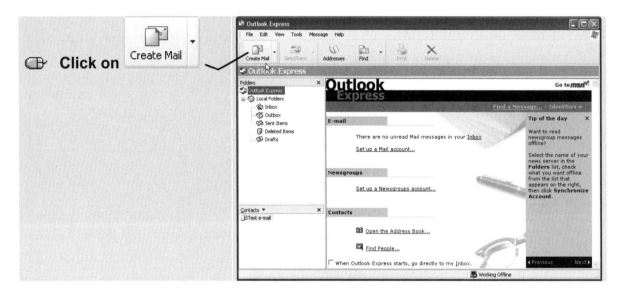

Here's how you choose an address from the Address Book:

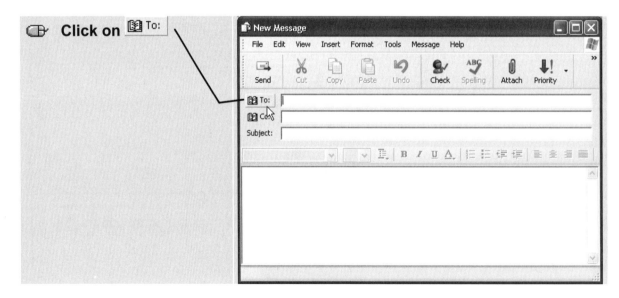

Now you see this window.
First choose a name from the
list on the left-hand side:

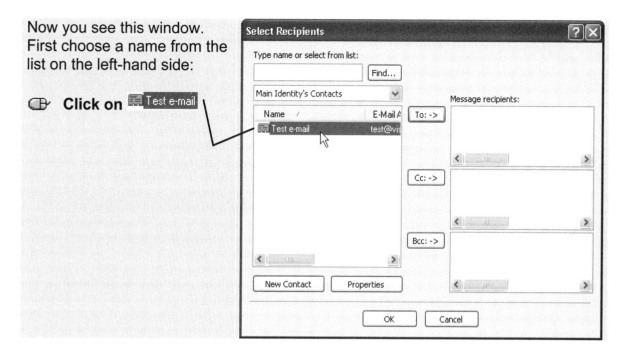

Then you can add the address to the *Message recipients* box:

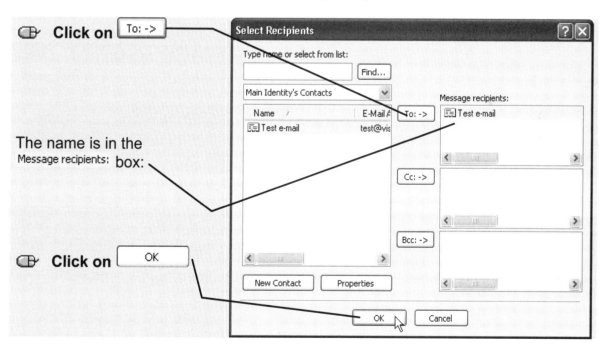

The name is in the
Message recipients: box:

Click on [OK]

 Tip

Multiple Addressees?
You can also use this window to send the same e-mail to multiple addresses. You do
this by selecting the names in the left-hand list in the above window, and clicking on
the [To: ->] button.

You see that the name has been filled in next to 📖 To: :

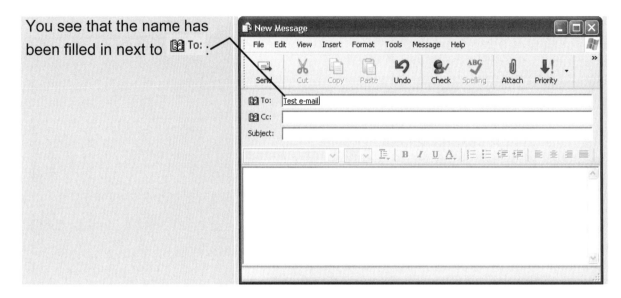

You don't actually have to send this e-mail. You can close the window without saving the e-mail message:

👆 **Click on** ☒

👆 **Click on** [No]

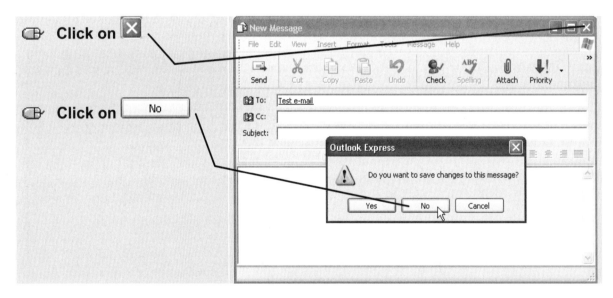

Now you've seen how you can use an e-mail address from the Address Book.

In *Outlook Express*, the e-mail address of every person to whom you've replied is automatically stored. Of course, you don't have to wait until you get an e-mail from someone. You can add an e-mail address to the Address Book right away.

Adding a New E-mail Address

You can directly add the e-mail addresses of your family, friends and acquaintances to the Address Book. This is how:

Click on Addresses

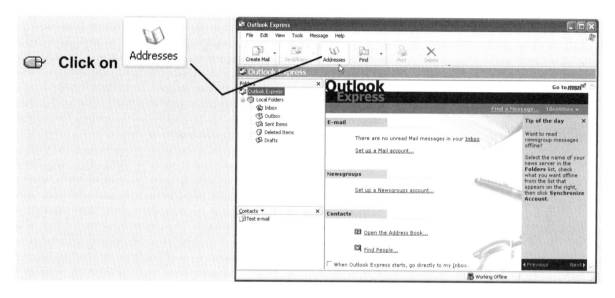

Once the Address Book is open, you can add a new name. In *Outlook Express*, that's called a *contact*:

Click on New

Click on New Contact...

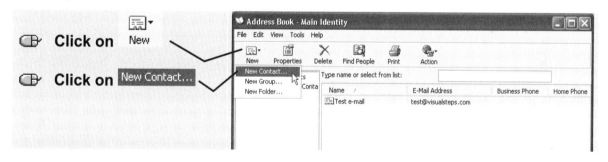

You see this window again for filling in the name and e-mail address:

A Wrong E-mail Address

Most likely it will happen at least once that you use a wrong e-mail address. People frequently change their Internet Service Provider, and ISPs themselves go out of business or change their names. In addition, you can always make an error typing. A single letter or period in the wrong place means the e-mail will never arrive.
It's a good exercise to send an e-mail to a wrong address and see what happens:

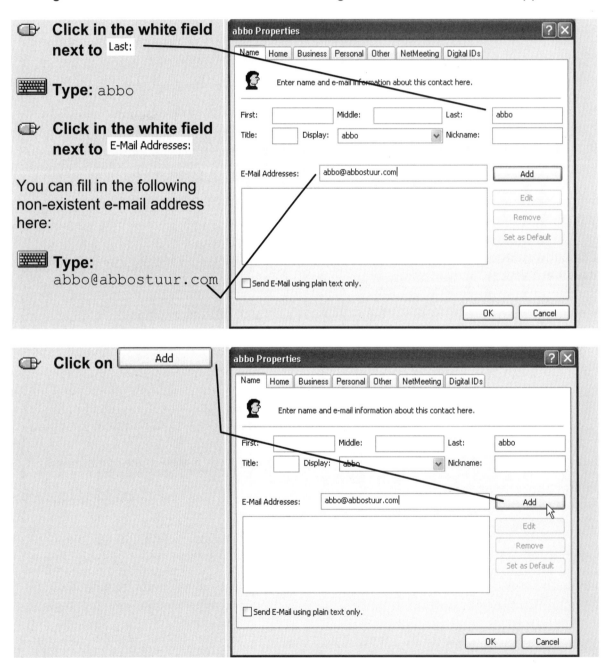

Click in the white field next to Last:

Type: abbo

Click in the white field next to E-Mail Addresses:

You can fill in the following non-existent e-mail address here:

Type:
abbo@abbostuur.com

Click on Add

Tip

> **Multiple addresses?**
> The Address Book has been designed so that a person can have multiple e-mail addresses, for example, a private address and one for work. You can add multiple e-mail addresses for one person.

You see that the e-mail address is filled in here:

☞ **Click on** OK

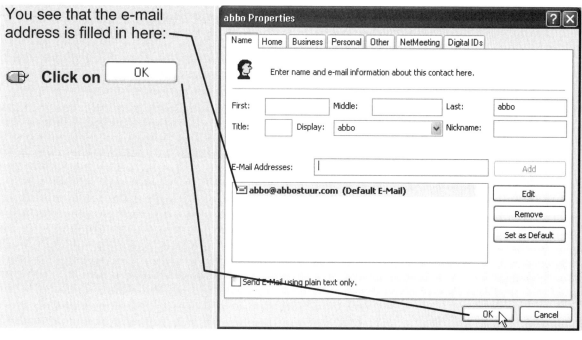

The name has been added to your Address Book; now you can close it:

☞ **Click on** ☒

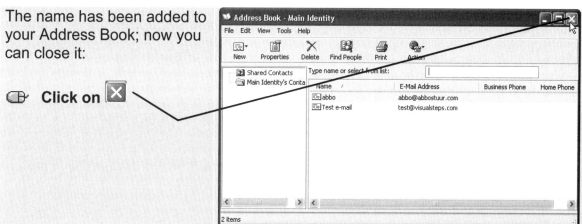

You can create a test mail and send it to the wrong address *abbo@abbostuur.com*. Then you can see what happens:

☞ **Create a new message** 🦶**36**

☞ **Choose from the Address Book:** abbo (abbo@abbostuur.com) 🦶**54**

☞ **Type for the subject:** `Wrong address`

☞ **Type for the body:** `This is an e-mail to a wrong address.`

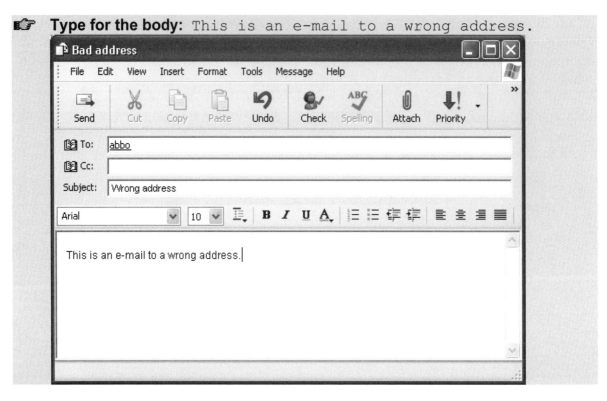

☞ **Send your e-mail to the *Outbox*** 🦶³⁷

☞ **Send and receive your e-mail** 🦶³⁹

After a while, you'll automatically receive a message about this wrongly addressed e-mail. This occurs quickly with some ISPs, and takes longer with others.

☞ **Check your mail later in the *Inbox*** 🦶³⁹

 HELP! I haven't gotten any mail.

There's no message in your *Inbox*?
Maybe it hasn't been received yet. Try again later. If necessary, continue on with the next section and check again tomorrow.

☞ **Check your received e-mail again later** 🦶³⁹

Once you've received mail, you should have an automatic message from a *Mail Server* or a *Mail Delivery Subsystem.*

For example, a message like this:

The technical terms describe what went wrong during delivery. In this case, the name is unknown:

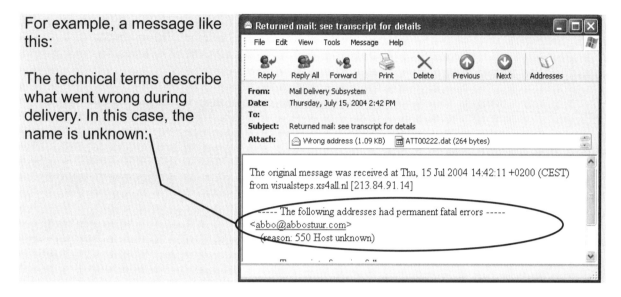

When you get this kind of error message, check in the *Sent Items* folder to see if the e-mail address you used is correct. Check:

  Are there any spaces in the e-mail address?
Are all the periods in the right places?
Is there a typing mistake in the e-mail address?

Tip

Type Again?
You don't have to retype an incorrectly-addressed e-mail. You can select the text and copy it. Then you can paste it into a new message, and send this to the right e-mail address.

Your Signature

In some cases, e-mail will replace your regular correspondence. Just as in every letter, your full name and address information should appear in these messages. You don't have to type these in with every new message. You only have to type them once, into a "signature". Here's how you create one:

Click on Tools

Click on Options...

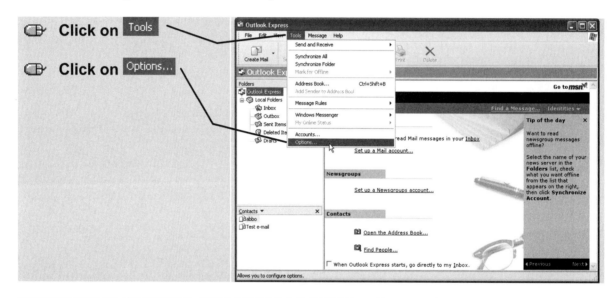

Click on the Signatures **tab**

Now you see the window where you can type in your signature.

Click on New

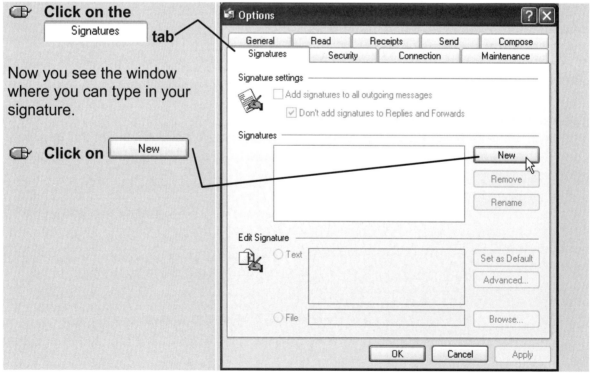

In *Outlook Express*, you can create and save multiple signatures.

You see that Signature #1 has been created:

In the white box next to ⊙ Text you can type in your information:

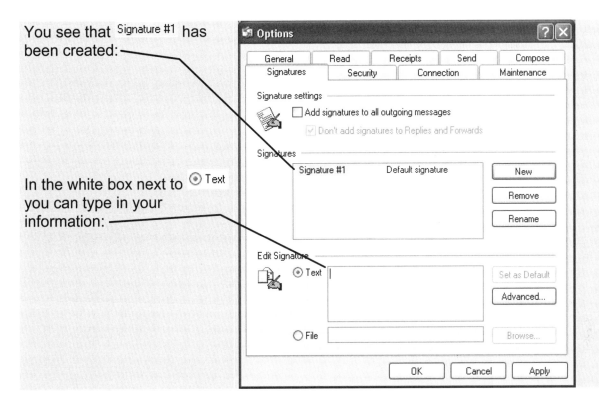

The signature doesn't look like a signature you would write with a pen. This signature consists solely of text and contains your address. Now you can type in your information:

⌨ **Type your full name and address**

🖰 **Click on** Apply

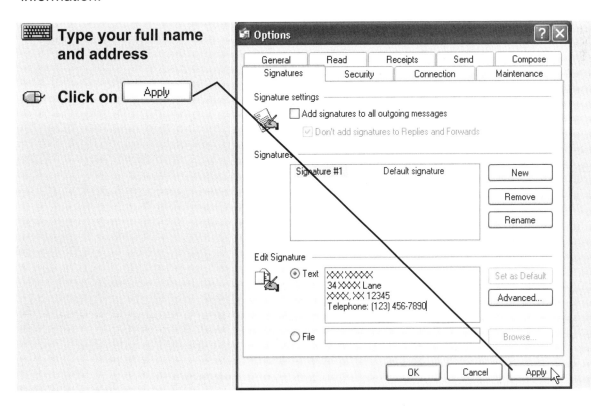

You can also decide whether you want the signature to appear automatically at the bottom of every new e-mail.

You do this by checking this box:

You can also choose to only add your signature manually when you want to. In that case, make sure the box is not checked.

☞ **Click on** OK

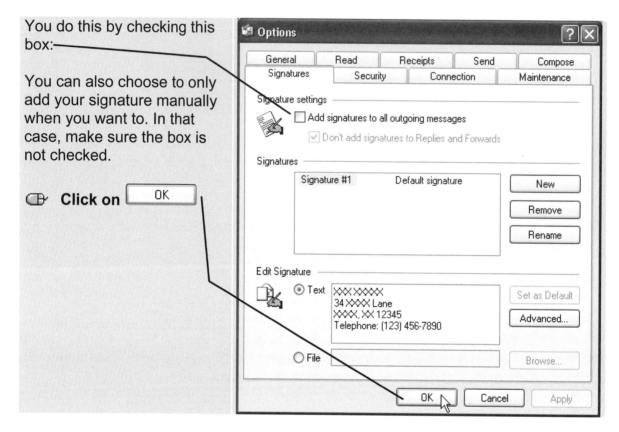

Now you can add your signature to any e-mail message. First, create a new e-mail message.

☞ **Create a new e-mail message** 36

☞ **Click in the text box**

You can add the signature at the location of the cursor.

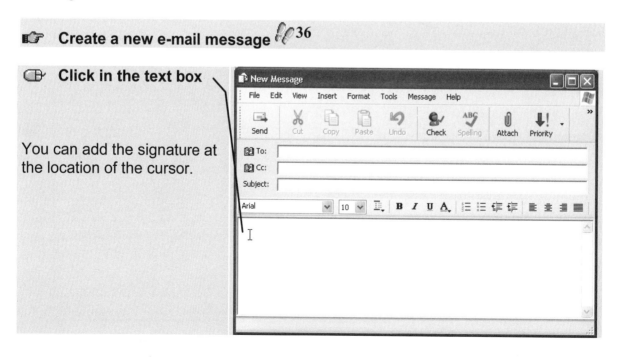

Click on Insert

Click on Signature

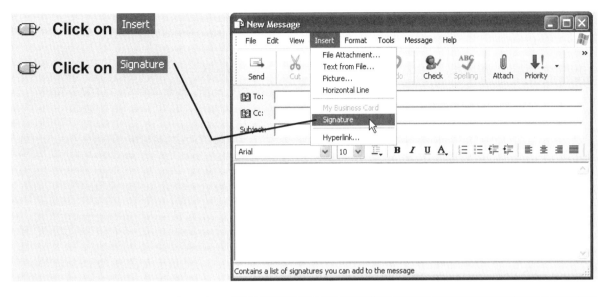

You see that your signature has been inserted:

You don't have to save this message.

Click on ☒

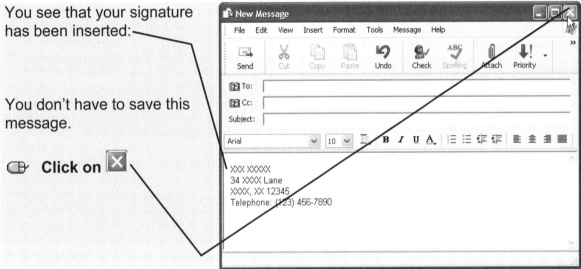

☞ **Don't save the e-mail message** 📖 55

The Inbox, Your Archive

All the messages you receive are saved in the *Inbox*. You'll notice that your *Inbox* soon begins to function as an archive. Especially if you do a lot of e-mailing, the number of e-mails will grow quickly and it will become more and more difficult to find a particular message. There are two ways you can find an e-mail. You can *sort* the list of e-mails, or you can *search* through the messages.

Sorting E-mails

Your e-mail messages are usually sorted by date received.
You can sort them differently, however, such as by the sender's name. Here's how
you do that:

Click on 🖾 Inbox

Click on View

Click on Sort By

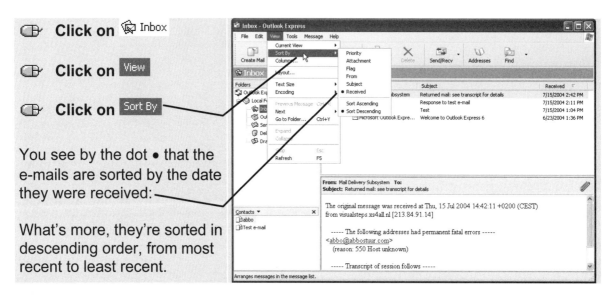

You see by the dot • that the
e-mails are sorted by the date
they were received:

What's more, they're sorted in
descending order, from most
recent to least recent.

Now you can sort them by sender's name. This is in the *From* field:

Click on From

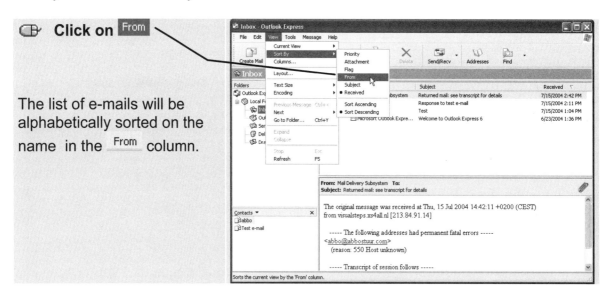

The list of e-mails will be
alphabetically sorted on the
name in the From column.

If your e-mails are alphabetically sorted by sender, it's easier to find an e-mail from a
particular person. E-mails from the same person will be next to each other.

 Please note:

Have you chosen a different sorting method?
Outlook Express stores this setting, and uses it the next time you open the program.

The default setting is to sort on date received, with the most recently received e-mails at the top. That's pretty useful, so you can restore the old setting:

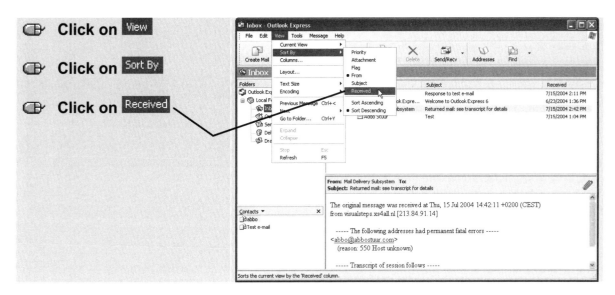

The e-mails will again be sorted by date received.

Searching Your E-mails

Outlook Express has an extensive search function with which you can search through your e-mails. Here's how you start:

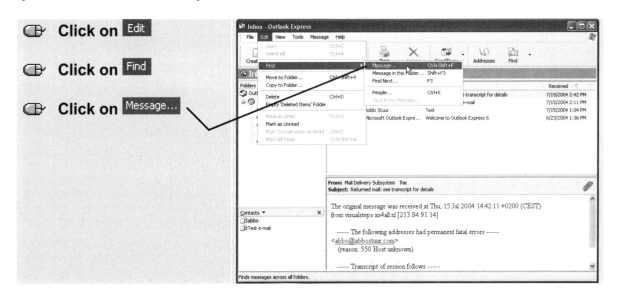

Now you see this window with
various fields:

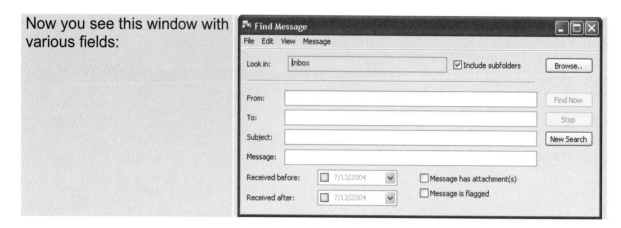

You can search every part of an e-mail message: *From*, *To*, the *Subject* or within the *Message* itself. In addition, you can refine the search, such as specifying the date of receipt.

If you know what the content of the e-mail message is, you can search for it by using a search term. For example, you can use the word "Internet"; that word should be in a test mail you've received.

Click in the white field next to Message:

Type:
Internet

Click on Find Now

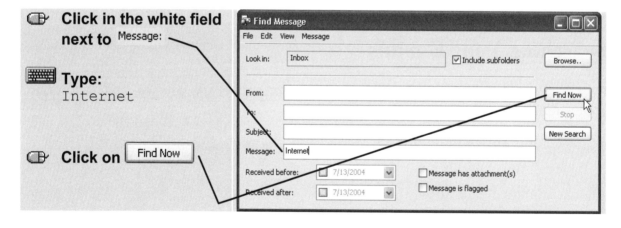

At the bottom of the window, you see the e-mails in which the word "Internet" appears:

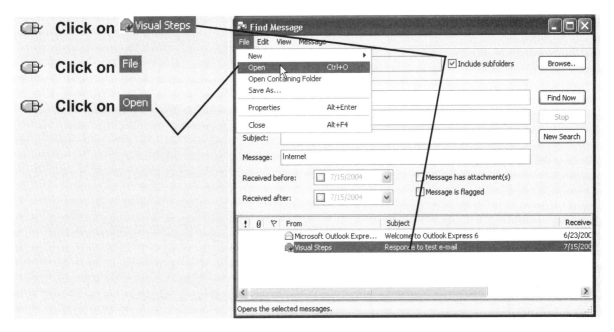

HELP! I don't see any e-mails.

If you don't see any e-mails in the above window, then you may not have received the test mail in the previous chapter.

☞ **Just keep reading**

You can view the message as follows:

 Click on Visual Steps

 Click on File

 Click on Open

Tip

If there are multiple e-mail messages in a list and you want to view one of them, you must first select the message you want to see. You do that by clicking on it one time.

The message opens and you can read it. At any rate, the word "Internet" appears somewhere in this message.

When you're finished, you can close the message window.

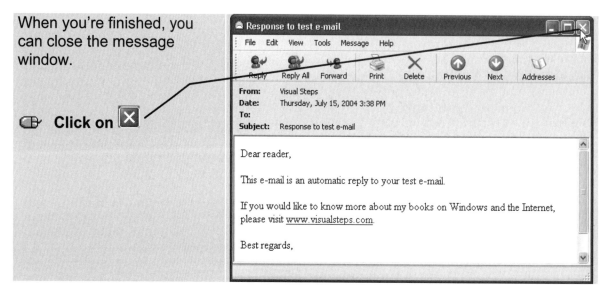

👉 **Click on** ☒

You can also close the *Find Message* window:

👉 **Click on** ☒

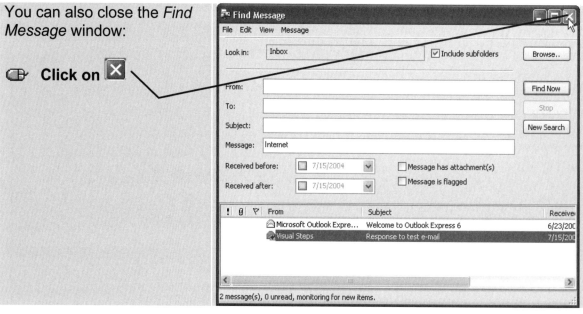

Tip

In *Outlook Express*, there's an icon next to every e-mail. Their meanings are:

✉   an unread message
✉   a message you've already read
✉   a mesage you've already answered
✉   a message you've forwarded

📎   the message contains an attachment
🚩   a message you have marked ("flagged")
❗   a message marked as important by the sender

Sending an Attachment

The nice thing about e-mail is that you can send all kinds of things along with an e-mail message. For example, you can send a photograph, a drawing, or a document. Something you send along with an e-mail message is called an **attachment**.

➡ **Please note:**

As an exercise, you're going to send the photo of Hoorn you saved in Chapter 4 as an attachment.
Did you not save this photo?
☞ **Then just read through this section**

You can practice sending an attachment by sending another e-mail to yourself.

 Click on Create Mail

You see the window you use to create a new e-mail:

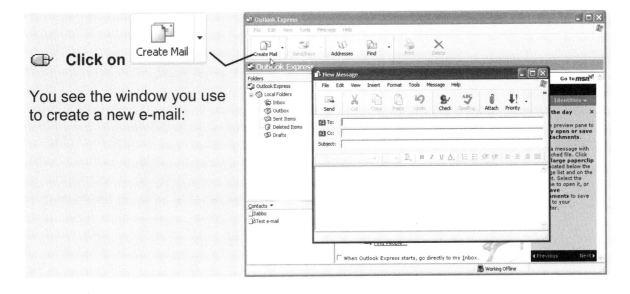

Type your own e-mail address next to ⬚ To:

Every e-mail message has a subject.

👉 **Click next to** Subject:

Type:
Test with
attachment

👉 **Click in the large white area**

Type:
Here's a photo of
the tower in
Hoorn.

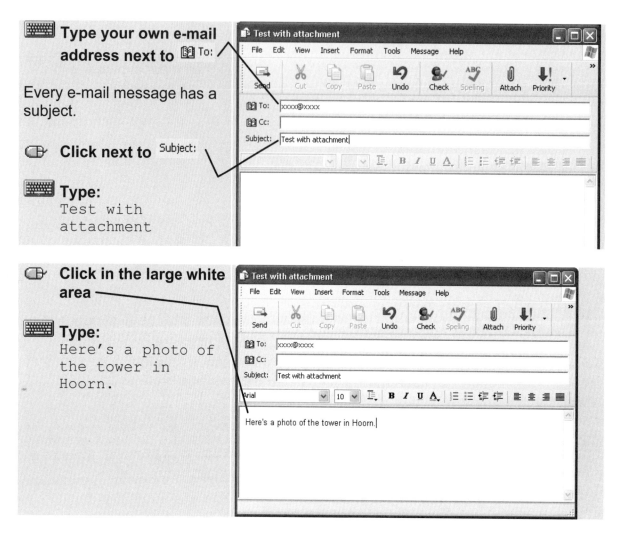

Now you can add the attachment: in this case, the photo of Hoorn.

👉 **Click on** Insert

👉 **Click on** File Attachment...

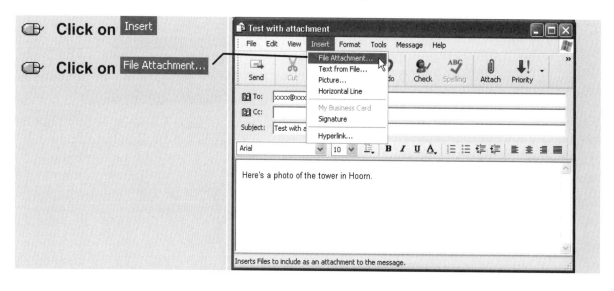

Now you see a window with which you can open a folder or a file:

The photo was saved with the name 📷 photo Hoorn in the folder 📁 My Pictures :

☞ **Next click on**
📷 photo Hoorn

☞ **Click on** [Attach]

You see that the attachment has been added to your message:

☞ **Click on** [Send]

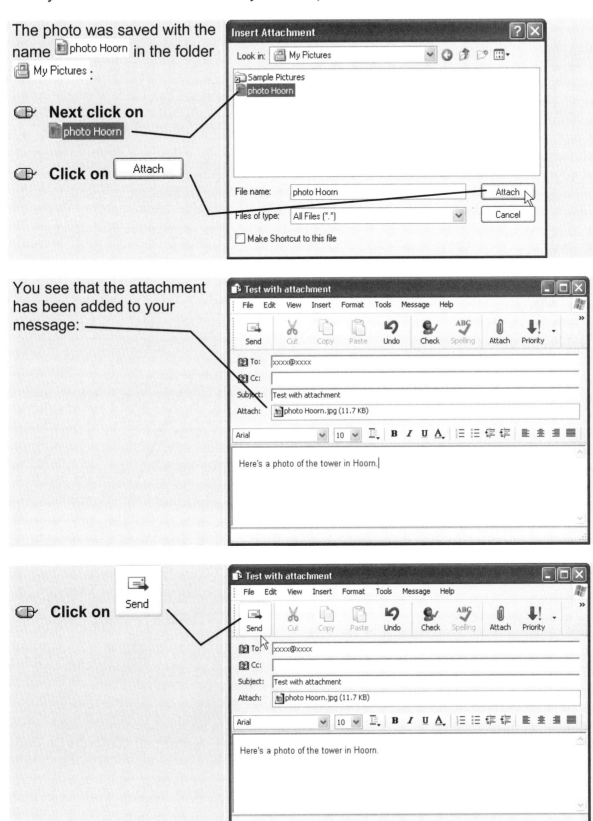

Your message is placed in the *Outbox*. You can send it. If all goes well, you'll also receive it right away.

☞ **Send and receive your e-mail**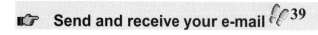

⇨ **Please note:**

Sending an e-mail with a photo attached takes more time than sending an e-mail consisting only of text.
On the taskbar you can see by the blinking little computers that information is being sent intensively:

Viewing an Attachment

The e-mail with an attachment that you sent will probably also be delivered immediately. You'll see it in the *Inbox*:

☞ **Click on** 🐭 **Inbox** (1)

On the right-hand side, you see your own message:

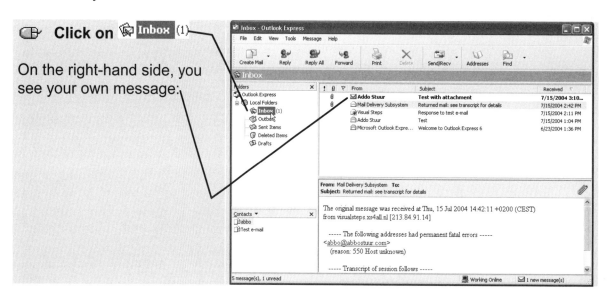

HELP! I don't have any mail.

Is there no new message in your *Inbox*?
Maybe it hasn't been received yet. Try again later:

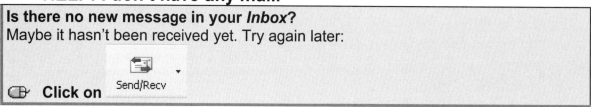

☞ **Click on**   Send/Recv

There's a paperclip in front of the message to show that it has an attachment:

☞ **Double-click on the message**

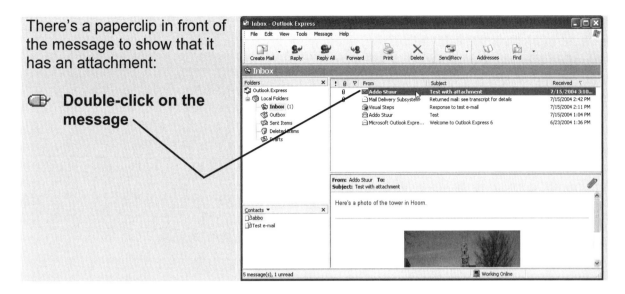

The message opens in a separate window:

You see the attachment in a separate section:

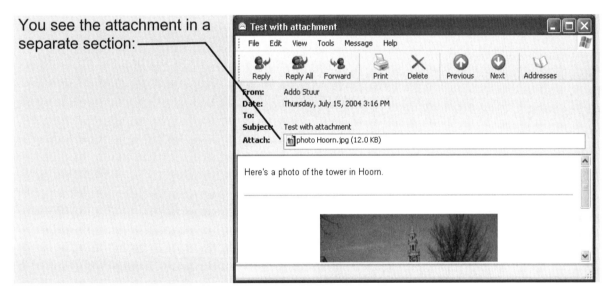

You can do two things with an attachment:

- save it to your hard drive
- just leave it in the e-mail after you've viewed it

You can see your choices as follows:

Double-click on the name of the attachment

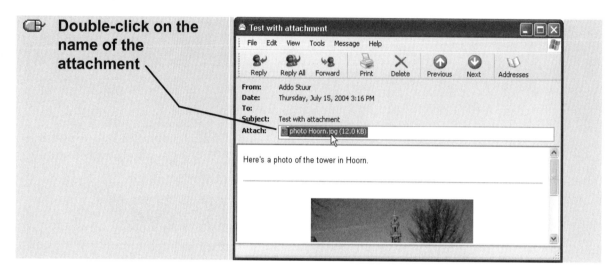

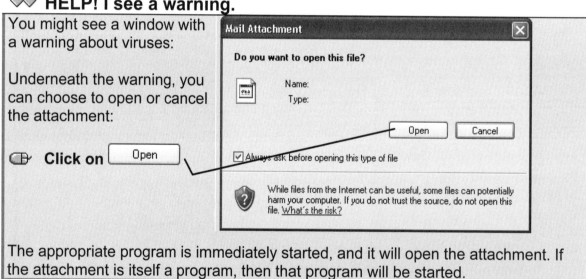

HELP! I see a warning.

You might see a window with a warning about viruses:

Underneath the warning, you can choose to open or cancel the attachment:

Click on Open

The appropriate program is immediately started, and it will open the attachment. If the attachment is itself a program, then that program will be started.

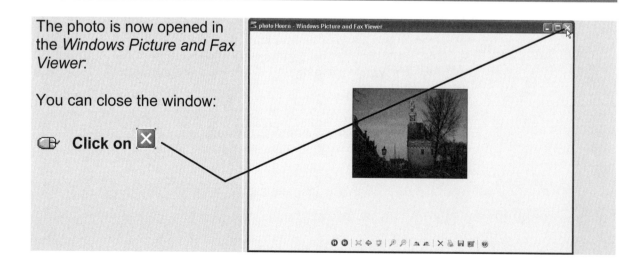

The photo is now opened in the *Windows Picture and Fax Viewer*.

You can close the window:

Click on ☒

Help, a Virus!

A computer virus is a very small program that can copy itself to another computer. Once present on a computer system, it can do a lot of damage. Not all viruses are equally dangerous. Because the virus arrives together with another file, you can't tell without using a special program whether or not you've been infected.

There are several ways to become infected. We'll limit ourselves here to infections coming over the Internet.

You can become infected by downloading a file from the Internet. If it's a program, it must first be installed. At the time of installation, any accompanying viruses become active. For this reason, you should always be careful about the websites from which you download files. The risks are smaller when you visit a respected company than when you visit an obscure address.

You can become infected by an e-mail with an attachment. If the e-mail was sent by someone with whom you frequently correspond, the risks are smaller than if it comes from someone you don't know. Nonetheless, caution is always advisable.

☞ **Never open an attachment if you are suspicious.**
If necessary, send your acquaintance an e-mail requesting clarification.

☞ **If you're suspicious of an unknown sender: Delete the e-mail and its attachment immediately without opening.**
If the attachment didn't contain a virus, that's too bad, but the sender should have been more clear about his subject. In situations like these, the sender can always resend the e-mail.

☞ **If you receive a "strange" e-mail from a known sender: Delete the e-mail without opening it.**
If necessary, ask for clarification from the sender.

☞ **Don't forget to empty the *Deleted Items* folder.**
Only then is the e-mail finally deleted.

Viruses like the infamous "I love you" virus not only do great damage, but also read your entire Address Book and send an e-mail containing a copy of themselves to all the addresses inside. This is also the reason why you can't always trust e-mail from people you know.

In any event, if you regularly use the Internet be sure you use a good **anti-virus software**. This software will give a warning in most cases before the virus can do its work. It's very important that you keep this software up-to-date. Consult the software's documentation for this.

Saving an Attachment

In general, viruses are not present in photos or drawings. In this case, you can safely save the photo.

After you've saved an attachment such as a photo, you can use it again in various ways. For example, you can open it in a program like *Paint* or another photo-editing program. There you can edit and change the photo. Maybe you want to use the photo in a club newsletter you've written in *MS Word*. You can also send the photo by e-mail to someone else.

An e-mail can contain various attachments. The easiest way to save attachments is as follows:

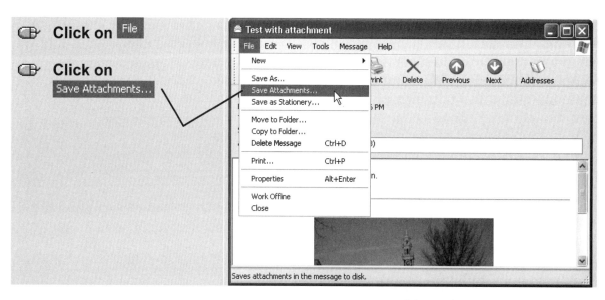

☞ **Click on** File

☞ **Click on**
Save Attachments...

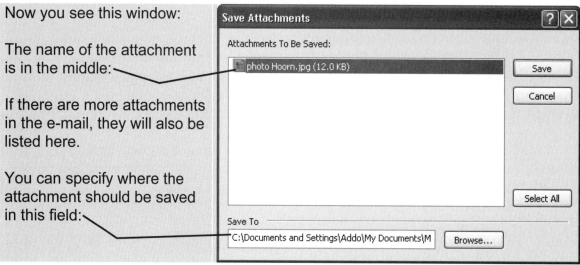

Now you see this window:

The name of the attachment is in the middle:

If there are more attachments in the e-mail, they will also be listed here.

You can specify where the attachment should be saved in this field:

In this case, it isn't necessary to save the photo; after all, it's already on your hard drive.

☞ **So click on** Cancel

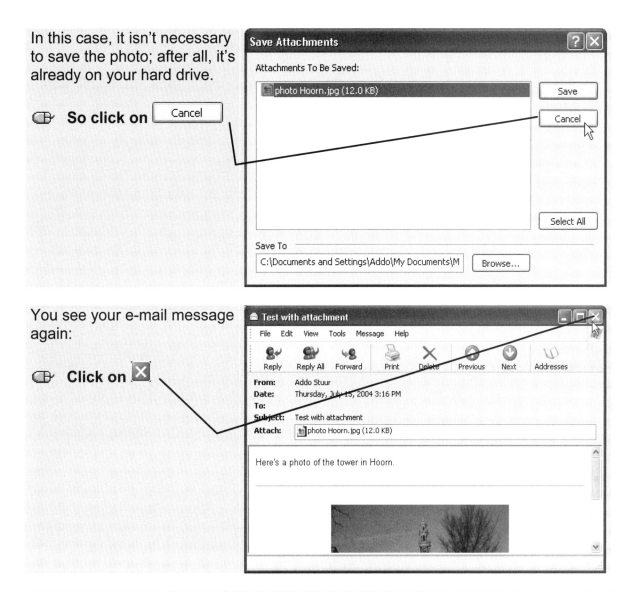

You see your e-mail message again:

☞ **Click on** ⊠

☞ **Also close the *Outlook Express* window** 👣 **32**

Now you've seen how you can send an attachment through e-mail, and how to save an attachment you've received. The following exercises will help you master what you've just learned.

Exercises

Have you forgotten how to do something? Use the number beside the footsteps to look it up in the appendix *How Do I Do That Again?*

Exercise: Sending an Attachment

In this Exercise, you'll practice writing a new e-mail message with an attachment.

✓ Start *Outlook Express*. 𝒻𝒸**35**

✓ Create a new e-mail message addressed to yourself. 𝒻𝒸**36**

✓ Add the photo of Jan Pieterszoon Coen (from Chapter 4) as an attachment. 𝒻𝒸**40**

✓ Send the e-mail message to the *Outbox*. 𝒻𝒸**37**

✓ Send and receive your e-mail. 𝒻𝒸**39**

Exercise: Viewing an Attachment

✓ Start *Outlook Express*. 𝒻𝒸**35**

✓ Check your mail. 𝒻𝒸**39**

✓ See if you have new mail in your *Inbox*. 𝒻𝒸**41**

✓ Open your e-mail message. 𝒻𝒸**42**

✓ View the attachment. 𝒻𝒸**57**

✓ Close the e-mail message window. 𝒻𝒸**32**

Background Information

The Smaller, The Faster

On the Internet, the following rule holds: the smaller a message is, the faster it will be sent. This is also true for an attachment.

If you send an e-mail without an attachment, therefore containing only a text message, it will be sent in a fraction of a second.

If you send a small attachment such as a passport photo, it takes only a few seconds. If you send a large drawing, it takes longer.

You always see the name and size of an attachment such as a drawing or text document:

Attach: photo Hoorn.jpg (12.0 KB)

The size of a photo, document or program is always given in kB or MB. This is a unit of measurement, just like inches and pounds.

A **kilobyte** is a thousand bytes.
So: 20 kilobytes is 20,000 bytes.
The abbreviation for kilobyte is **kB**.

A **megabyte** is a thousand kilobytes.
A megabyte is therefore a million (a thousand times a thousand) bytes.
The abbreviation for megabyte is **MB**.

How long does it take to download or send something?

The speed with which you download or send something depends on several things, such as the speed of your modem, the kind of connection and how busy it is on the Internet.

Just for the sake of argument, let's say you can download **6 kB** per second with a regular modem. That's 360 kB or 0.36 MB per minute.

You can download a 12 kB message in about 2 seconds.
A simple drawing is about 370 kB. It would take 1 minute to download. An extensive text with illustrations might be 1.31 MB and take approximately 4 minutes. You can see that it takes a pretty long time.

In addition to photos and drawings, you can send all kinds of other files with an e-mail. You can even send sounds or videos. But be careful: sound and video files are usually very large. It will take a long time for these kinds of files to be sent or received.

A Faster Modem: Internal or External?

Do you have an older computer? Are you dissatisfied with the speed of your internet connection? You might consider buying a faster modem.

The fastest modem that uses the regular telephone line right now is a modem with a *speed* of *56K.* If you want to go even faster, you'll have to switch over to ISDN, DSL or cable Internet access. In all four cases, you can choose either an internal or an external modem:

Internal modem

External modem

An external modem has certain advantages:

- You can connect the modem easily. The computer doesn't have to be opened in order to install the modem, so you don't need a computer mechanic.
- An external modem has little lights that let you see what's happening on the telephone line. This is useful when the connection isn't functioning properly.
- You can easily connect an external modem to a different computer.

But there are also disadvantages:

- An external modem is more expensive.
- The modem has more cables and often a separate power supply which has to be plugged into an outlet.
- You always have to turn the modem on.

Unwelcome E-mails

It's bound to happen at least once that you receive e-mail from businesses trying to sell you something. This can happen, for example, after you've asked for information about a particular product.

Perhaps the e-mails even "fall out of nowhere" and you have no idea how such a company has gotten your e-mail address. There's a thriving trade in e-mail addresses, and you may have ended up on such a list.

This kind of unwelcome e-mail is called *spam*.

What can you do?

- Usually, the e-mails contain instructions on how to stop their being sent again in the future. Often you have to send an e-mail with a subject or text consisting of a particular sentence or command. This command is processed by a computer without any human intervention.

  There's often no other way to unsubscribe.

- If you can't stop the messages by the above method, you can think about filtering them out. Some ISPs allow you to set up this kind of filter. All messages from a particular sender are then filtered out and destroyed.

- If your ISP doesn't offer this kind of service, you can also set it up in *Outlook Express*. You do this with the command `Message` , `Block Sender...` .

Zipping
Everything sent over the Internet has a specific size. Files containing only text are relatively small. Photos in particular are much larger, and it also takes longer to download them. Because this download time can be frustrating, programs have been developed that can shrink files.
This technique is called *compressing* or *zipping*. A compression program takes all the "extra air", so to speak, out of a file, making it smaller. In order to be able to use the file again later, the reverse function must be applied. The "air" must be put back in the same places.
In this way, a photo (*bitmap*) with a size of 1400 KB (or 1.4 MB) can be reduced to 23 KB, a reduction of 98%!

A very well-known program which is often used for *zipping* and *unzipping* is called *WinZip*.

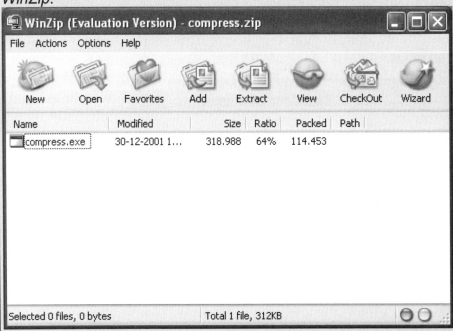

The program WinZip

There is a free trial version of this program that you can download from the Internet. You can read the details on the *Internet for Seniors* website in the Recommended Software section. Particularly if you want to send photos or drawings by e-mail, it's advisable to zip them first before sending them. This saves you and the recipient a lot of time. Make sure the recipient also has *WinZip*.

Tips

  Tip

Opening

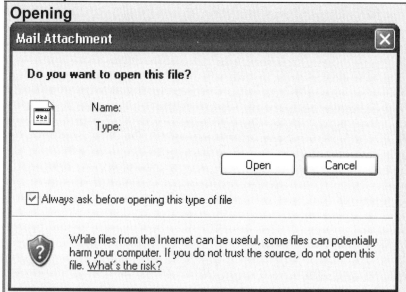

When you choose *Open* in the above window, the program to open the attachment in question is automatically started.

Which program is started depends on your computer's settings. Different programs may be installed on one computer than on another. Your computer may have a different program assigned to open a particular type of file.

If the attachment is a text document, *MS Word* will automatically be started. If you don't have *MS Word* on your computer, then *WordPad* will be started.

If the attachment is a photo, a photo-editing program will be started if there's one on your computer.

If it's a drawing, *Paint* may be started.

If the attachment is a computer program (an *.exe-file for example), then that program itself will be started.

Tip

CC and BCC
You can send an e-mail to multiple addresses in different ways. In the Address Book, you see two more buttons beneath the [To: ->] button.

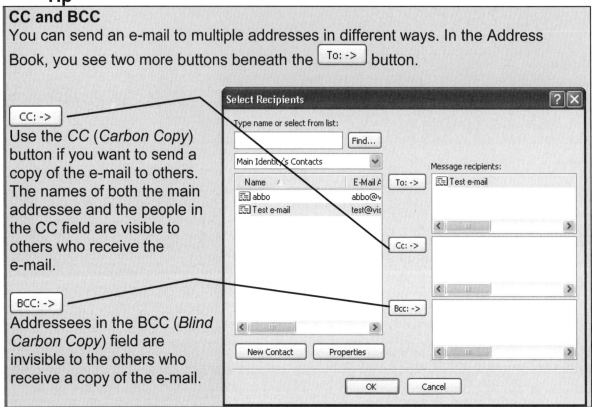

[CC: ->]
Use the *CC* (*Carbon Copy*) button if you want to send a copy of the e-mail to others. The names of both the main addressee and the people in the CC field are visible to others who receive the e-mail.

[BCC: ->]
Addressees in the BCC (*Blind Carbon Copy*) field are invisible to the others who receive a copy of the e-mail.

 Tip

How do I find an e-mail address?
The Internet is such a dynamic medium that there is no telephone book containing everyone who has an e-mail address. People also frequently change Internet Service Providers. When you switch to a new ISP, you usually get a new e-mail address.
In addition, not everyone wants his or her private e-mail address to be published, to avoid unrequested e-mails, for example.
There are telephone-book-like websites where you can submit your own e-mail address.

Tip

Searching for E-mail Addresses

There are some companies on the World Wide Web that try to gather as many e-mail addresses as possible.

One such company is *Bigfoot Directories*:

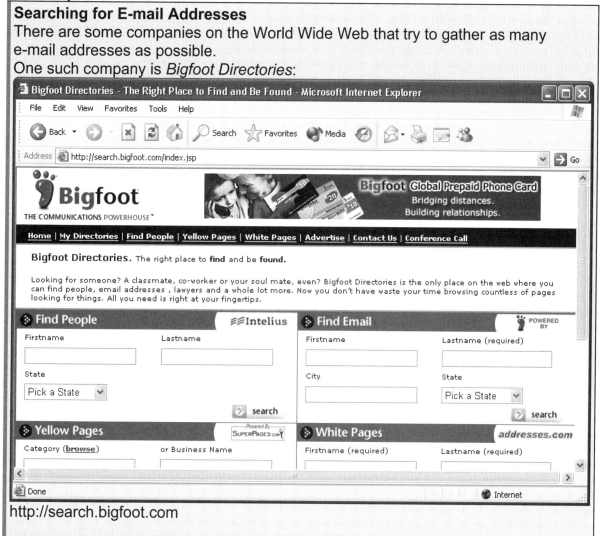

http://search.bigfoot.com

By typing in a name, you can see if it has an associated e-mail address. You can also use the *fuzzy search*. Then it will also search for names that are similar to the name you typed in. This is useful if you don't know exactly how a name is spelled.

Tip

Searching with Search Engines

Some well-known search engines also offer the option to search for e-mail addresses. For example, you can use *Yahoo*'s *People Search*:

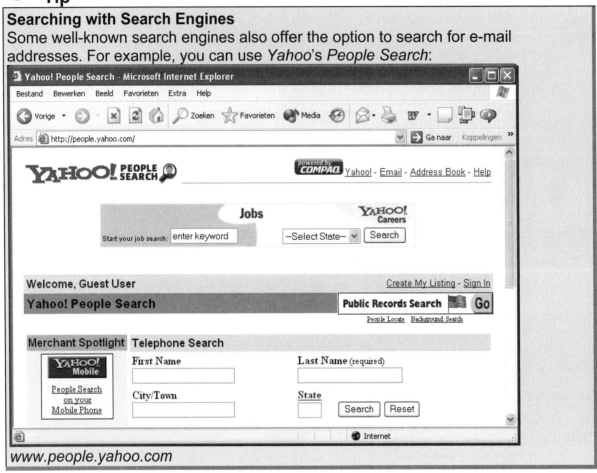

www.people.yahoo.com

Tip

Keyboard Control

If you prefer, you can use the keyboard to operate *Outlook Express* rather than the mouse. The most important keys and their functions are listed below.

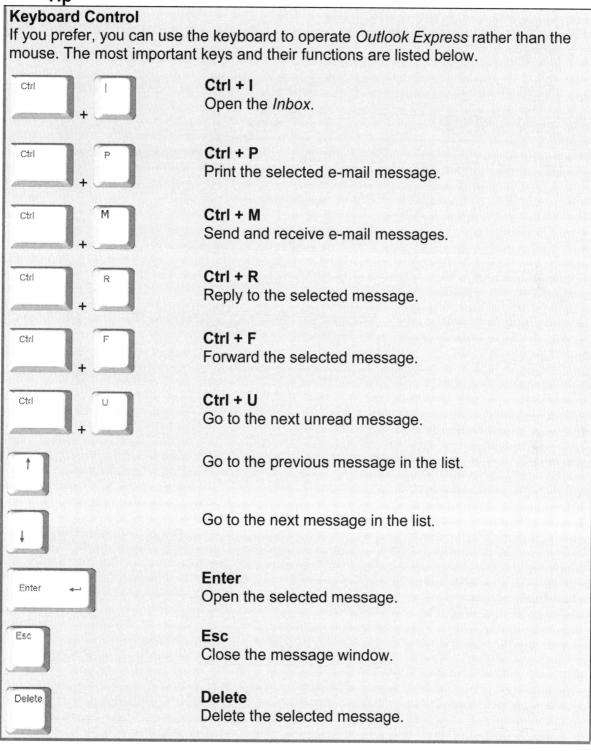

Ctrl + I
Open the *Inbox*.

Ctrl + P
Print the selected e-mail message.

Ctrl + M
Send and receive e-mail messages.

Ctrl + R
Reply to the selected message.

Ctrl + F
Forward the selected message.

Ctrl + U
Go to the next unread message.

Go to the previous message in the list.

Go to the next message in the list.

Enter
Open the selected message.

Esc
Close the message window.

Delete
Delete the selected message.

Tip

Security Settings in Outlook Express
When you install *Windows XP Service Pack 2*, a few security settings are automatically activated in *Outlook Express*. You can take a look at these settings:

👆 **Click on** Tools

👆 **Click on** Options...

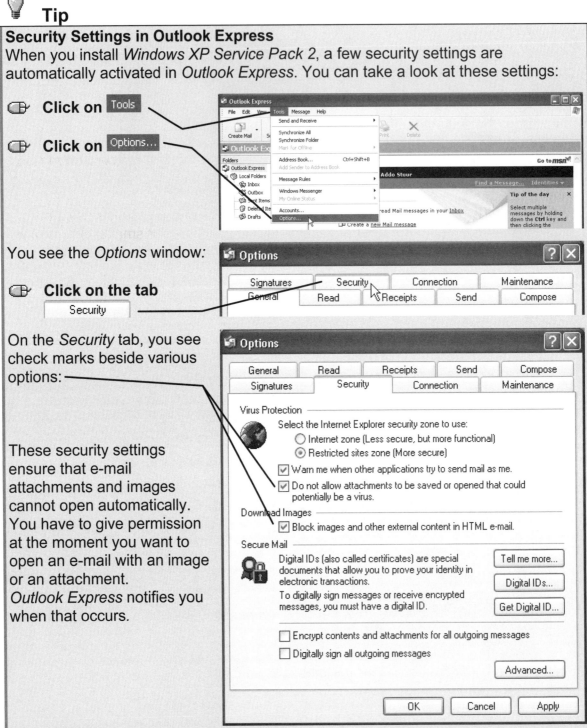

You see the *Options* window:

👆 **Click on the tab**
Security

On the *Security* tab, you see check marks beside various options:

These security settings ensure that e-mail attachments and images cannot open automatically. You have to give permission at the moment you want to open an e-mail with an image or an attachment. *Outlook Express* notifies you when that occurs.

It's advisable to leave the security settings on this page just as they are. That keeps you in control of any undesirable e-mails.
Check whether you trust the content or attachment on a per e-mail basis. If you have any doubts, ask the sender for clarification about the e-mail, or delete it without opening. Don't forget to empty the *Deleted Items* folder afterward.

7. Personalizing Your E-mail

Up to this point, you've created e-mails that consist only of text without any formatting. It's customary in the business world to send e-mails containing short texts without frills. For personal use however, it can be a lot of fun to send more interesting mail to your friends, children or grandchildren.

In fact, almost all the formatting you can use in a text-editing program can also be applied to an e-mail. You can choose different fonts and larger or smaller letters. An interesting background color or pattern is also possible. This is called *Rich Text*. *Outlook Express* also provides various kinds of stationery. A formatted e-mail message is actually a kind of web page that is then sent as an e-mail. You can also use photos and images in your e-mail messages.

E-mail is becoming increasingly important for communication between people. It's also possible to quickly create an e-mail message using *Internet Explorer* to let someone know about an interesting website.

People are also increasingly using e-mail services such as *webmail*. When you're on vacation, you might still like to be able to read and send e-mail. This is easy to do with an e-mail service you can use over the *World Wide Web*, called *webmail*. With webmail, you can read and send e-mail wherever you are in the world.

In this chapter, you'll learn how to:

- format an e-mail
- choose a different font and size
- change the background color
- use stationery
- use smileys
- send e-mail using *Internet Explorer*

Formatting E-mail

There are two kinds of e-mail:

- e-mail with unformatted text and no images, also called *plain text*
- e-mail with formatted text and images, also called *Rich Text* or *HTML*

You can format your e-mails. *Outlook Express* offers all the same options as a text-editing program like *WordPad* or *MS Word*. In fact, it has more options, for example: the use of stationery. First, create a plain new e-mail message:

☞ Start *Outlook Express* 35

In this chapter, *Outlook Express* doesn't need to connect to the Internet. Of course, you can check your e-mail if you'd like.

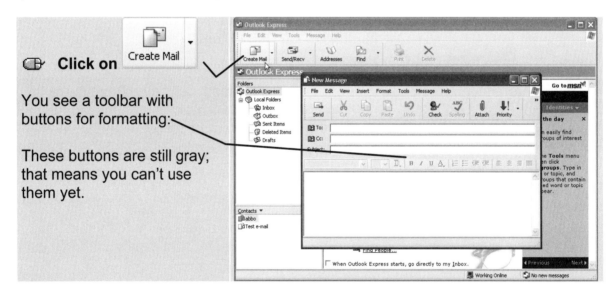

☐ Click on Create Mail

You see a toolbar with buttons for formatting:

These buttons are still gray; that means you can't use them yet.

HELP! I don't see any toolbar buttons.

Is the toolbar not visible?
Then your *Outlook Express* has been set up differently:

☐ Click on View

☐ Click on Toolbars

☐ Click on Formatting Bar

These buttons won't become active until you place the cursor in the white box where you type the text of your e-mail:

 Click in the box where you type your message

You see that all the buttons are now active:

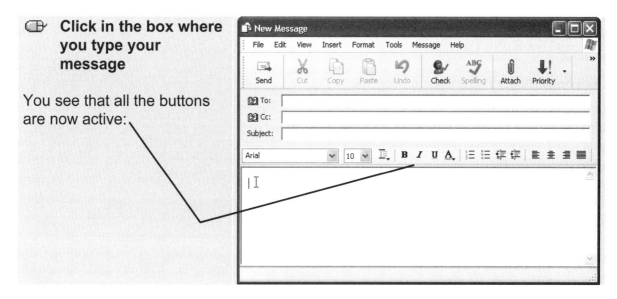

 **HELP! The buttons are still gray.**

Does the toolbar stay gray?
Then your *Outlook Express* has been set up differently. You need to choose another format for your e-mail message:

 Click on Format
 Click on Rich Text (HTML)

Most of the formatting you can do in *WordPad*, for example, is also available in *Outlook Express*.
You can see your options on the toolbar:

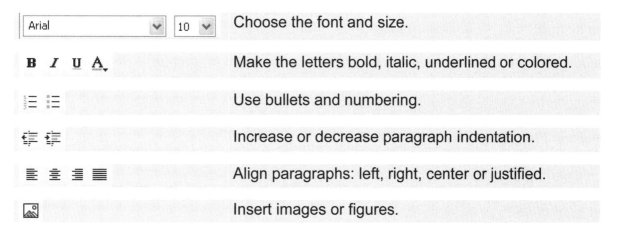

Arial 10	Choose the font and size.
B *I* U A	Make the letters bold, italic, underlined or colored.
≣ ≣	Use bullets and numbering.
⇷ ⇸	Increase or decrease paragraph indentation.
≣ ≣ ≣ ≣	Align paragraphs: left, right, center or justified.
🖼	Insert images or figures.

Tip

> **Would you like to know more about text formatting and fonts?**
> Read the *Visual Steps* book *Windows XP for Seniors*.
> See **www.visualsteps.com/winxp** for more information.

The Font Size

You can write your e-mails using a larger font size to increase readability. The default setting is a smaller font. You can choose a larger font size like this:

You see a number on the toolbar.
That's the size of the current font. You see that this is only 10 (*points*) large:

☞ **Click on** ⌄ **next to the number**

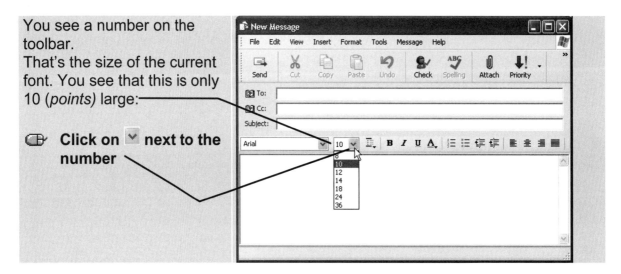

Now you see a list of numbers. A low number means smaller letters; a large number larger letters:

☞ **Click on e.g.** 14

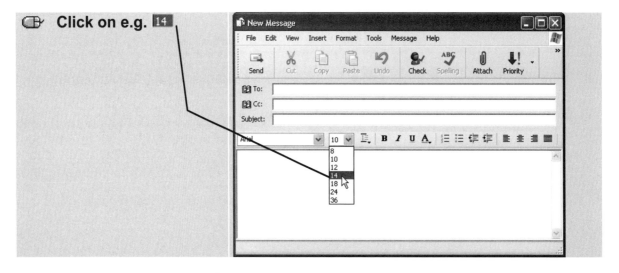

From now on, the text you type will be in a larger font.

Type:
This is a larger
font size, 14
points.

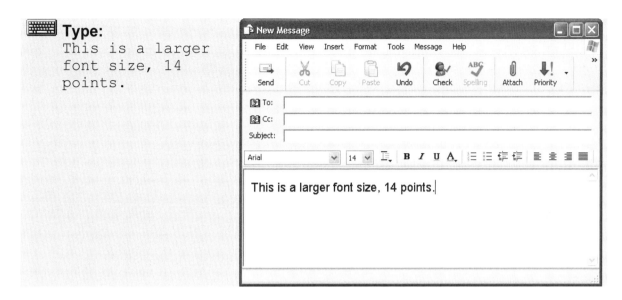

You see that the letters are larger.

The Background Color

You can also change the background color if you'd like. For example, you can make it gray:

Click on Format

Click on Background

Click on Color

You see a list of colors from which you can choose:

Click on Gray

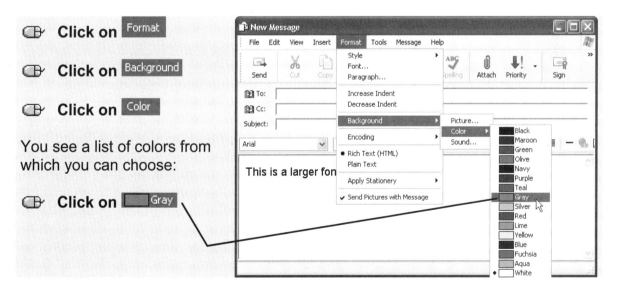

The background is now gray:

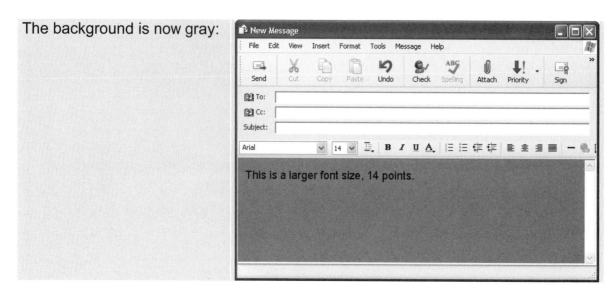

You can do all kinds of formatting this way. You can also draw a line or place an image into the e-mail text. Go ahead and experiment all you like.

Stationery

Outlook Express also has ready-made stationery that you can use as a background. You can use it to give your e-mail message a whole different look. Here's how you choose stationery:

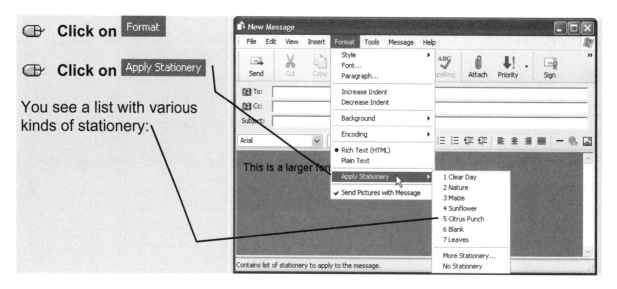

Click on `Clear Day`

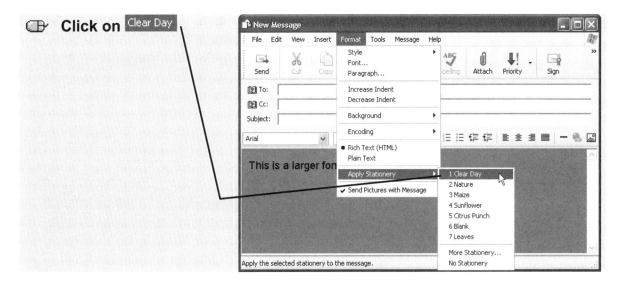

HELP! I don't have *Clear Day*.

It's possible that *Clear Day* isn't on the list in your computer.

☞ **Choose a different stationery from the list**

You see e.g. a light, summery background for your e-mail message:

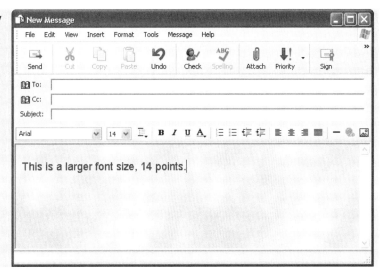

You can also remove the stationery:

🖱 **Click on** Format

🖱 **Click on** Apply Stationery

🖱 **Click on** No Stationery

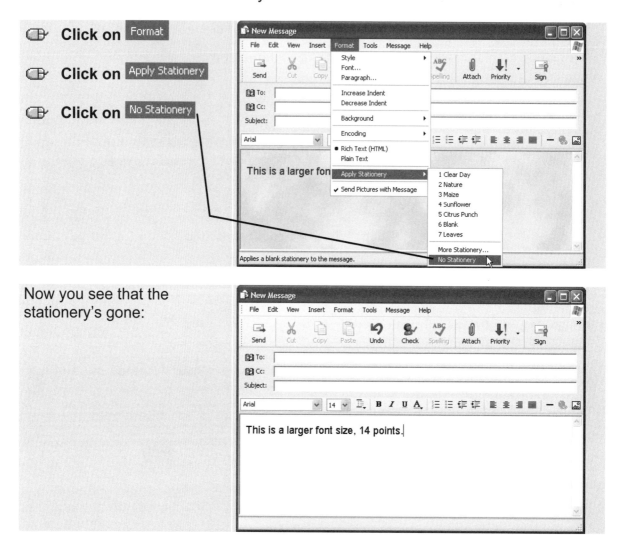

Now you see that the stationery's gone:

You can close this e-mail message now without saving it:

🖱 **Click on** File

🖱 **Click on** Close

You're then asked if you want to save the changes:

🖱 **Click on** No

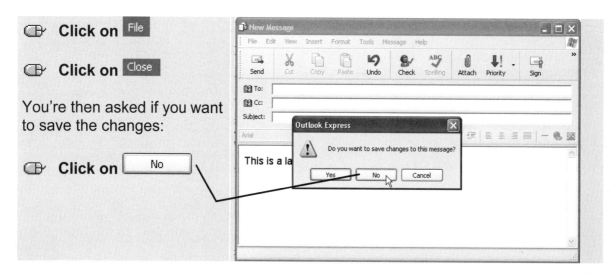

Ready-made Stationery

You can also use ready-made stationery right when you create a new message. You'll see that the font has been altered to go with the stationery.

Click on next to

Create Mail

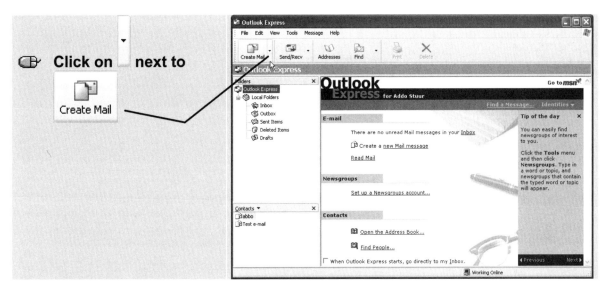

You see a list containing various kinds of stationery:

Click on Sunflower

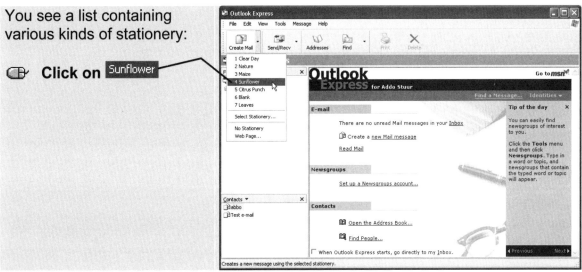

You see this attractive
stationery:

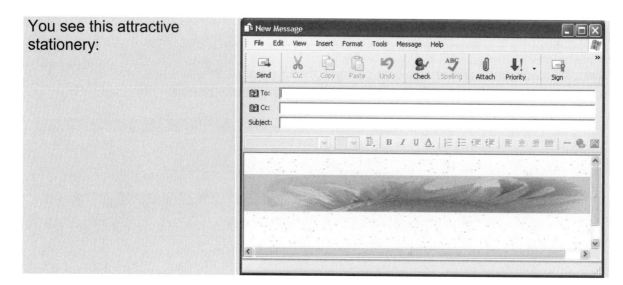

Now you can add your own text, both above and below the colored banner:

**Click below the
colored banner**

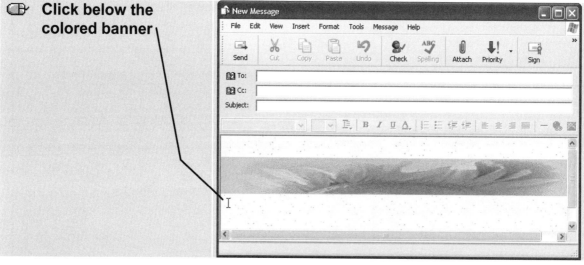

Type:
A sunny
background.

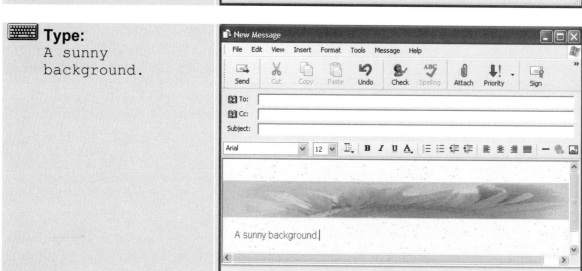

Smileys

E-mail is primarily used to send short letters and messages. You usually type shorter sentences than you would in a regular letter. In order to make your intentions clear, you can use *smileys*. These little icons show what you think of something, without using words. These *smileys* are often used on the Internet:

:-)	happy	;-)	wink
:-(	sad, unhappy	{:-<	surprised
:-D	very happy	:-c	very unhappy
>:-<	angry	:-x	kiss
%-)	crazy	{:-@	angry
:/)	not funny	:,-(	crying

If you lean your head to the left, you can see that these icons could be little faces. You can type these smileys using the letters and symbols on the keyboard.

Type:
; -)

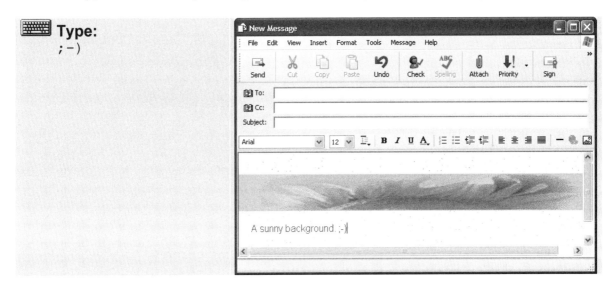

You can use these techniques to send an eye-catching e-mail to someone for special occasions like birthdays and holidays.

You can close this practice message now without saving it:

☞ **Click on** `File`

☞ **Click on** `Close`

You'll be asked again if the changes should be saved:

☞ **Click on** `No`

💡 **Tip**

Will they be able to see it?
You can easily send a formatted e-mail to anyone that has *Windows* and uses *Outlook Express* for their e-mail program.
If you aren't sure whether the recipient uses this program, it's possible he or she won't be able to view your handsome e-mail.
You can send them a test e-mail first. They will let you know if they were able to read the message.

☞ **Close *Outlook Express*** 🦶43

E-mail Using Internet Explorer

The program *Internet Explorer* contains several functions that make it easy to send an e-mail when you're out on the *World Wide Web*. This can be useful if you've found an interesting website and want to send the web address to a friend. You can make use of this function as follows:

☞ **Start *Internet Explorer*** 🦶1

☞ **Open the *Internet for Seniors* website for this book** 🦶52

Now you see this page:

☞ **Click on** File

☞ **Click on** Send

You see two options for e-mail:

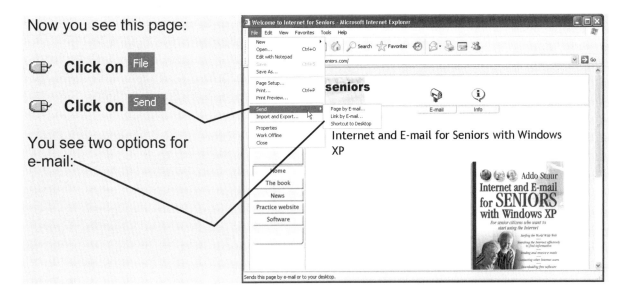

These two options are:

○ send the page by e-mail
○ send the web address (the link) by e-mail

You can send an *entire webpage* to someone by e-mail. It's handier, however, to send only the web address (the *link*). By clicking on the web address, the recipient of your e-mail can connect to the Internet and view the page in question. The great advantage of sending the link by e-mail is that the chance for error from typing the address is minimized.

Take a look:

☞ **Click on** Link by E-mail...

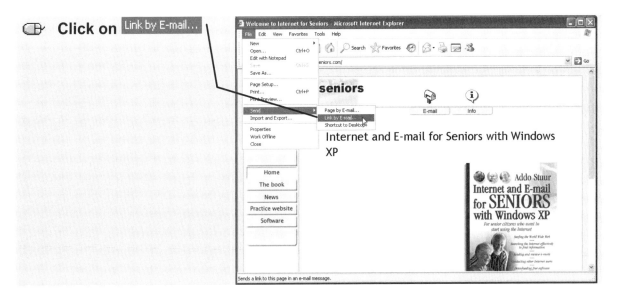

Outlook Express starts in the background and a new e-mail message is immediately readied for you. You'll see that a variety of information has already been filled into this new e-mail message:

Fill in the e-mail address of the recipient next to :

The web address (the link) is already listed as an attachment:

The recipient of this message just has to open the attachment to view the webpage.

You don't have to send this message.

⊕ **Click on**

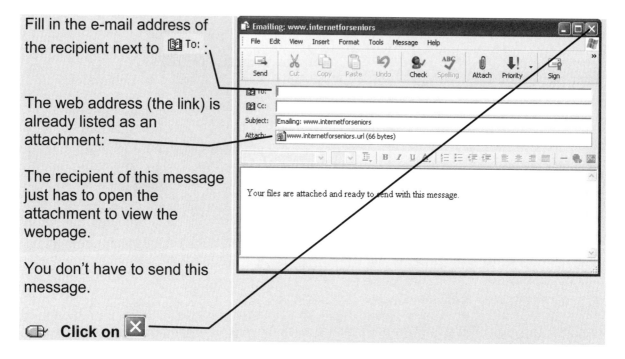

An E-mail Address on a Website

Many websites list e-mail addresses you can use to contact a person, company or institution. Sometimes this is set up so that *Outlook Express* is started on your own computer with a new message. Give it a try:

⊕ **Click on**

Practice website

There's a special link for creating an e-mail message:

⊕ **Click on** • Test e-mail

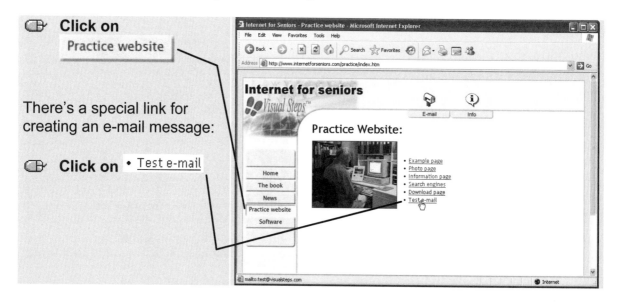

A window for a new e-mail message opens.

The correct e-mail address has already been filled in:

You don't need to send this message, so:

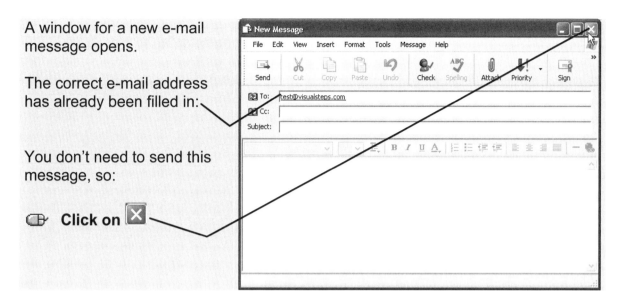

☞ **Click on** ✕

Now you can continue with the Exercises, which will help you master what you've just learned.

Exercises

Have you forgotten how to do something? Use the number beside the footsteps to look it up in the appendix *How Do I Do That Again?*

Exercise: Creating an E-mail

In this exercise, you'll practice creating a formatted e-mail.

- ✔ Start *Outlook Express.* 🦶³⁵

- ✔ Create a new e-mail message addressed to yourself. 🦶³⁶

- ✔ Choose a larger font size of 14 points. 🦶⁴⁷

- ✔ Type in the following message:
  `Larger letters are easier to read.`

- ✔ Choose a gray background. 🦶⁵⁰

- ✔ Send this e-mail to the *Outbox.* 🦶³⁷

Exercise: An E-mail on Nice Stationery

In this exercise, you'll practice creating e-mail messages using ready-made stationery.

- ✔ Create a new e-mail message and choose a ready-made stationery. 🦶⁴⁹

- ✔ Address the e-mail message to yourself.

- ✔ Send this e-mail to the *Outbox.* 🦶³⁷

Background Information

E-mail Abroad

Almost everywhere in the world, you can find public places with access to the Internet. There are Internet cafés where you can access the *World Wide Web* for a fee. Many libraries have Internet-enabled computers, and more and more hotels are offering similar services.

For sending and receiving e-mails while you're away from home, it's useful to have an e-mail address you can access via the *World Wide Web*. This is called *webmail*. The most well-known webmail service is *Hotmail*.

If you have a webmail address, you can read your e-mail anywhere in the world.

Internet Abroad

If you'll be traveling abroad for a long time and want to have Internet access while you're away, you'll need to arrange for local access. It would be very costly to have your computer connect through your dial-up number in the United States. There are several options.

- Ask your ISP if it has dial-up numbers in the countries where you'll be traveling. This is called *roaming*. Many American ISPs have foreign dial-up numbers. If your Internet Service Provider doesn't have options for dialing up locally where you'll be traveling, you can explore other options.
- You can consider using an ISP with a worldwide presence. For example, *Compuserve* is a worldwide organization with local dial-up numbers around the world. If you have a subscription in the US, you'll also have access abroad.
- Another possibility is a temporary subscription with a free ISP abroad, such as *FreeSurf* in France, *Wanadoo* in the Netherlands, or *LiveDoor* in Japan. You can keep your regular Internet subscription and have your mail forwarded to your new free e-mail address in the other country. One disadvantage is that the instructions and installation software will probably be in a foreign language.

E-mail Services from ISPs

Many ISPs offer various kinds of services for processing your e-mail.

- **Webmail**

  Many Internet Service Providers offer the option of using *webmail*. With it, you can view and send e-mail from a special website belonging to your ISP. You do this using *Internet Explorer*. The big advantage of this is that you can do it on any computer that has access to the Internet.

- **Forwarding your e-mails**

  Every incoming e-mail is sent through (forwarded) to an e-mail address you specify. For example, you can have your e-mails forwarded to your *Hotmail* address if you have one.

- **Automatic reply**

  Every incoming e-mail is automatically answered with a message you've written beforehand. This is useful if you're on vacation, to let people know that you're away and won't be able to reply immediately to an e-mail. This service is also called *Vacation Service*.

- **A second e-mail address**

  Many ISPs give you the opportunity to request multiple e-mail addresses for your family members, for example.

  It can also be useful to have multiple e-mail addresses if you want to keep your e-mails separated; for example, your private correspondence and the e-mail you receive as secretary for a club. You can read how to set up multiple e-mail addresses (accounts) in *Outlook Express* at the *Internet for Seniors* website.

- **Changing your e-mail address**

  You can usually change your e-mail address later if it works better for you. You might need to do that if you use multiple e-mail addresses, for example.

- **Changing your password**

  Your ISP probably gave you your own password for your e-mail account. In most cases you didn't choose this password yourself. It can be useful, however, to choose a password you can easily remember.

- **Links to other communication media**

  Some ISPs provide a service for sending e-mail to cellular phones, for example. This can be done through *SMS*: short text messages that can be read on the cell phone screen.

- **E-mail filtering**

  Some ISPs can filter out unwelcome e-mails for you.

You can read which services are available on your ISP's subscriber service web pages.

Newsgroups

There's a special kind of e-mail called *newsgroups*, or *discussion groups*. These are comparable to bulletin boards where people place messages and others can react to them. There are thousands of newsgroups covering nearly every subject imaginable. If you've subscribed to one of these newsgroups, you can read its messages and reactions to them in *Outlook Express*, and participate in the discussion by posting a message of your own if you so desire.

In order to set up *Outlook Express* to read newsgroups, you must first have the name of a *news server*. You can get this from your Internet Service Provider. Then you can download all available newsgroups from that server. That's an enormous list containing thousands of groups:

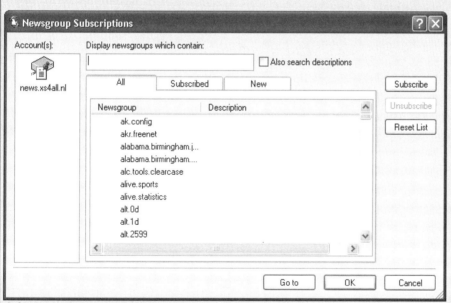

A few newsgroup names

You can then subscribe to one or more of these newsgroups. "Subscribe" is actually a confusing word, because your name and so forth aren't recorded. The only thing that happens is that all the messages in the newsgroup you've chosen are downloaded.

When you open the newsgroups in *Outlook Express,* you can *synchronize* the messages. That means that your list is updated with the current list of messages on the news server.

The content and quality of the newsgroups differs tremendously from one subject to the next, and a word of warning is in order. In some newsgroups, the "dark side" of the Internet emerges: the most extreme subjects are "discussed" by strangers, and it often becomes clear that someone is hiding behind anonymity. On the Internet, you can never be certain of someone's identity.

Tips

 Tip

A Photo as Background
You can use any image at all as a background for your e-mail:

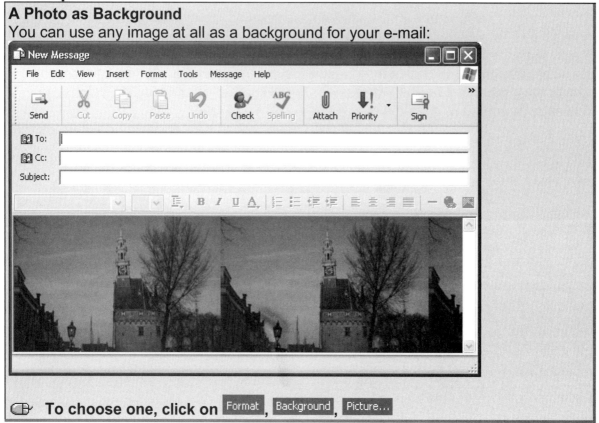

 To choose one, click on Format , Background , Picture...

 Tip

Unusual Fonts
Use only well-known fonts such as *Times New Roman* and *Arial* in your e-mails. Not everyone has the same fonts installed on his or her computer. Some drawing programs, for example, will install the most beautiful fonts, but that doesn't mean the recipient of your e-mail has the same font on his computer. In that case, your handsome e-mail will be shown in a default font.

8. Downloading Files

There's a treasure trove of information on the Internet that you can copy onto your own computer. This copying is called *downloading*. The opposite of *downloading* is *uploading* (sending files from your computer to the Internet).

You can download just about anything: computer programs, music, video films and more. After you've downloaded something, you usually save it to your computer's hard drive so that you can use it again later.

For computer programs, the second step after downloading is usually installing the program onto your computer. Installation makes the program ready for use so that you can work with it. For example, the program gets added to the Start menu so you can start it easily.

There's a separate web page for this chapter on the *Internet for Seniors* website. Here you'll find different kinds of files and also a small computer program, the *Alarmclock*, with which you can practice downloading and installing programs. Once you know how to do this, a wealth of (free) computer programs lies waiting for you on the Internet. Not only programs that are enjoyable or useful for you, but also for your grandchildren, for example.

The Internet is also becoming an increasingly important medium for computer and software manufacturers. You can often download the latest versions of software from the Internet, and it's frequently the best way to replace faulty software with the most recent improved version. In short, downloading is becoming more and more important for maintaining your computer.

In this chapter, you'll learn how to:

- download the *Alarmclock*
- install the program
- remove a file from the Desktop

The Practice Website

There's a practice page for this chapter on the *Internet for Seniors* website. To work through this chapter, you'll first connect to the Internet and then open this web page.

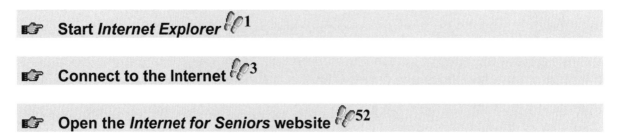

☞ **Start** *Internet Explorer* 🦶¹

☞ **Connect to the Internet** 🦶³

☞ **Open the** *Internet for Seniors* **website** 🦶⁵²

There's a page for practicing downloading on the website. Take a look at this page:

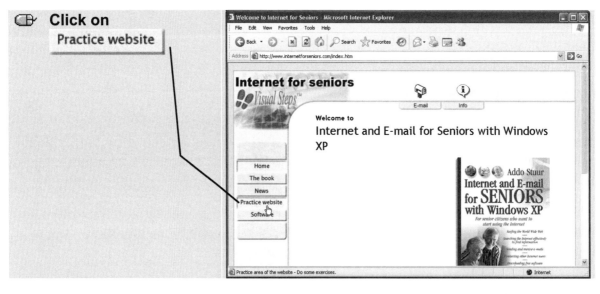

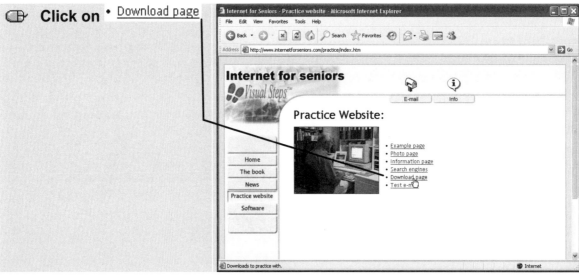

Downloading the Alarm clock

In order to practice downloading software, there's a small program on the website called the *Alarm clock*. You'll see how to download this program and then install it.

You see a page with different kinds of files:

Among them is the *Alarm clock* program. You can start downloading it by clicking on the name:

☞ **Click on** <u>Alarm clock</u>

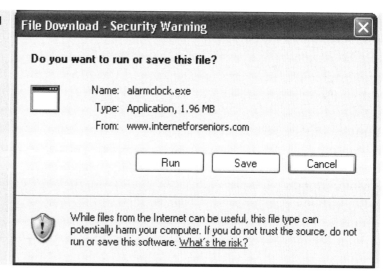

A window appears where you can choose between two options:

You can choose to:

- *run* the file.
  In this case, the installation program is immediately started (runned);
- *save* the file.
  Then the file will be saved to your computer first. Afterwards, you have to start the installation program yourself.

In this case, it's a good idea to save the file first:

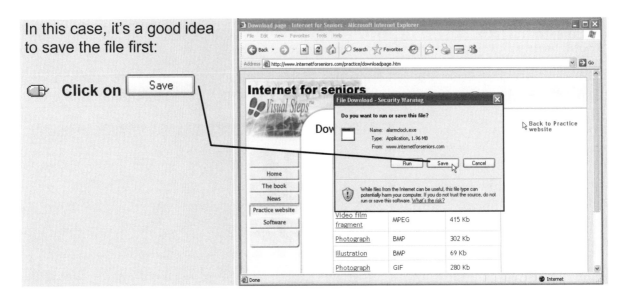

⊞► **Click on** | Save |

A window appears in which you can specify where you want to save the file:

We'll put the installation program on the *Desktop*.

⊞► **Click on** | Desktop |

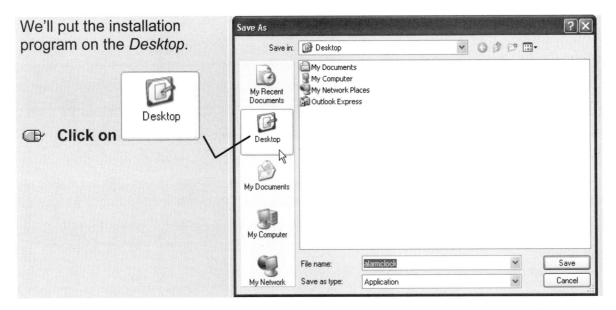

Always pay attention to the folder where you're going to save a file; otherwise you might not be able to find it again later.

The installation program already has a name: `alarmclock`

☞ **Click on** `Save`

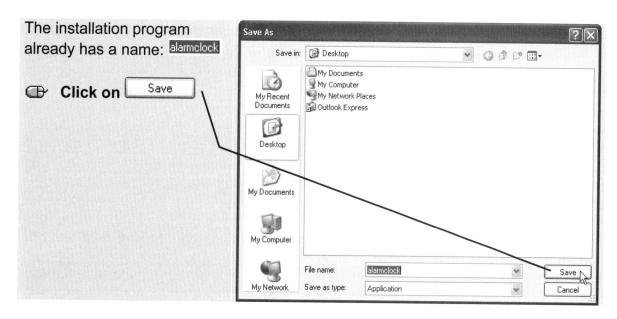

The file download begins automatically.

You can follow the progress of the download by watching the green bar:——

In the window, you can see roughly how long the download will take and how large the file is (1.96 MB).

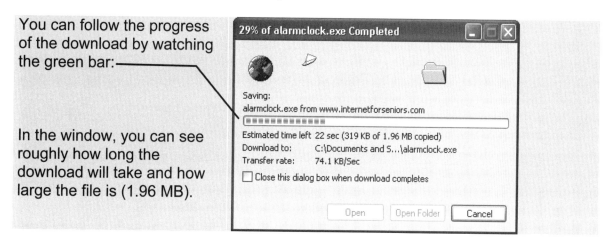

Has the whole file been downloaded?

☞ **Click on** `Close`

Now you can close *Internet Explorer* and disconnect from the Internet.

☞ **Close *Internet Explorer*** [2]

☞ **Disconnect from the Internet if necessary** [16]

The *Alarm clock* program has been downloaded and is stored on your computer's hard drive. Now you can install the program on your computer.

Installing the Program

Most computer programs contain several parts. In order for the program to work properly, all these parts have to be correctly "installed" on your computer. The different parts are then copied to the right place on your hard drive and the program name is added to the *Start* menu in *Windows*. All this work is done by the installation program. This is also how the *Alarm clock* installation works.

You saved the installation program to the *Desktop*. That's the mainscreen in *Windows*. You can start the installation program like this:

Somewhere on the desktop you should see the icon for the *Alarm clock*:

☞ **Double-click on the icon** alarmclock

Windows appear one after another as the installation is being set up:

Then you see this window:

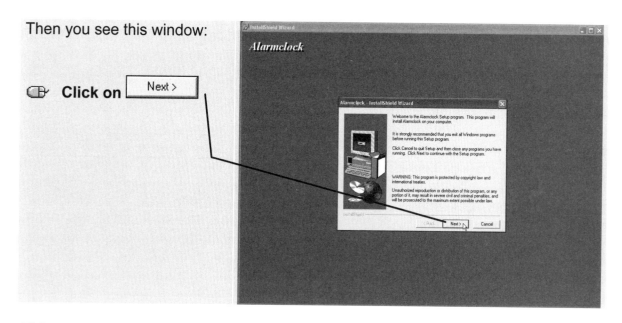

CB▸ **Click on** Next >

This program uses the word *setup*. This means the same thing as *installation*. You'll see four more windows in a row, all of which can be left unchanged. This means you can keep going to the next window:

CB▸ **Click in the next four windows on** Next >

Then you see a window with the *Alarm clock* icon:

You can close this window:

CB▸ **Click on** X

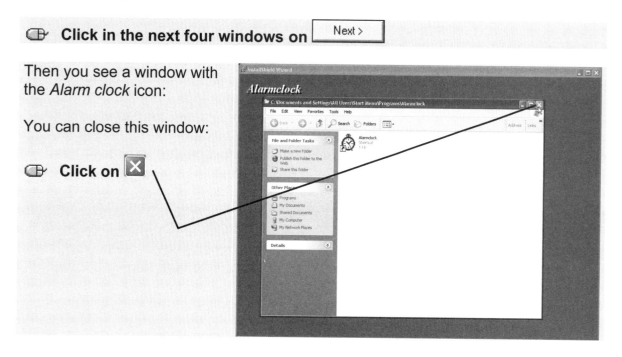

Finally, you see this last window:

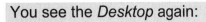

Click on [Finish]

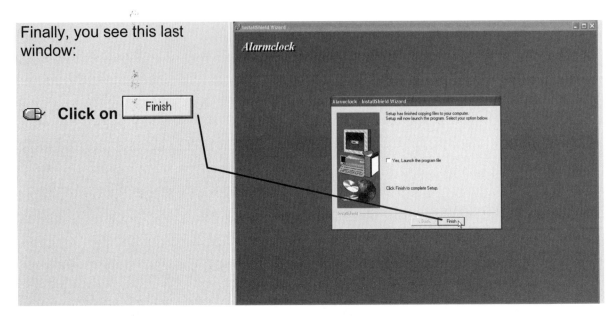

You see the *Desktop* again:

Most installation programs work more or less the same way as the *Alarm clock*. You've seen how this kind of installation works. Now you can start the *Alarm clock* program.

⇨ **Please note:**

The icon on the *Desktop* is the installation program, not the *Alarm clock* program itself.
In fact, you don't need the installation program anymore. A little further in the book, you'll read how you can remove the installation program.

Starting the Alarm clock

You use the *Start* button to start a new program:

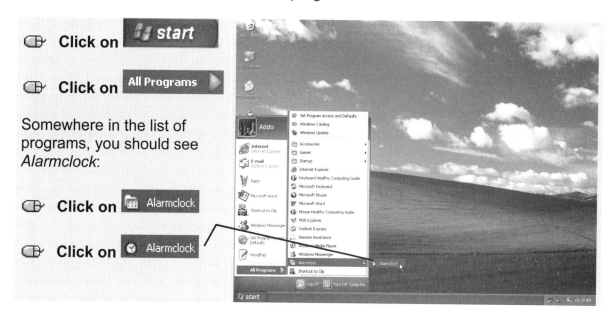

☞ **Click on** `start`

☞ **Click on** `All Programs`

Somewhere in the list of programs, you should see *Alarmclock*:

☞ **Click on** `Alarmclock`

☞ **Click on** `Alarmclock`

The program starts.

You see this little window:

💡 **Tip**

How does the *Alarm clock* work?

You can type in the alarm time:

🖱 **Click on**

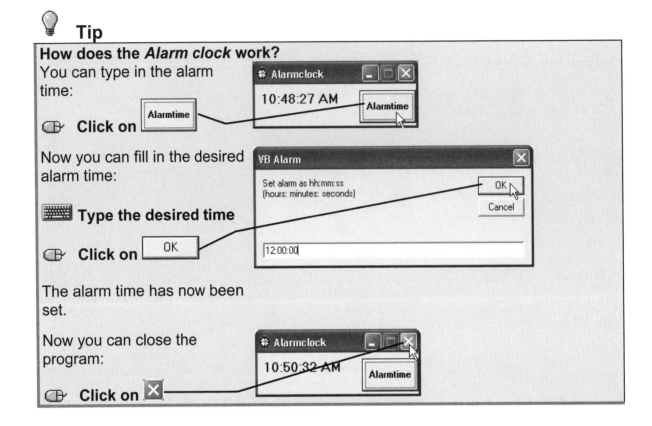

Now you can fill in the desired alarm time:

⌨ **Type the desired time**

🖱 **Click on** OK

The alarm time has now been set.

Now you can close the program:

🖱 **Click on** ✕

Deleting the Installation Program

Now that the *Alarm clock* works, you can now remove the installation program. You no longer need it. Because it's on your *Desktop* in plain view, it may only lead to confusion. You can delete it as follows:

🖱 **Click with the right mouse button on the**

icon alarmclock

Now you see a list of commands:

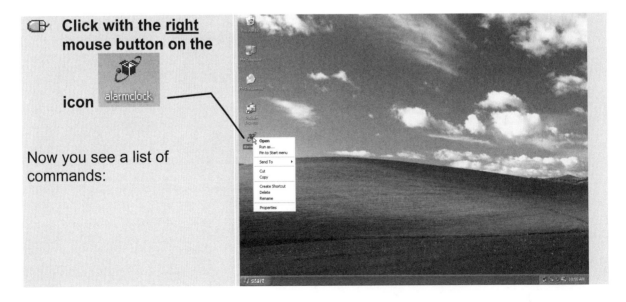

Click with the left mouse button on Delete

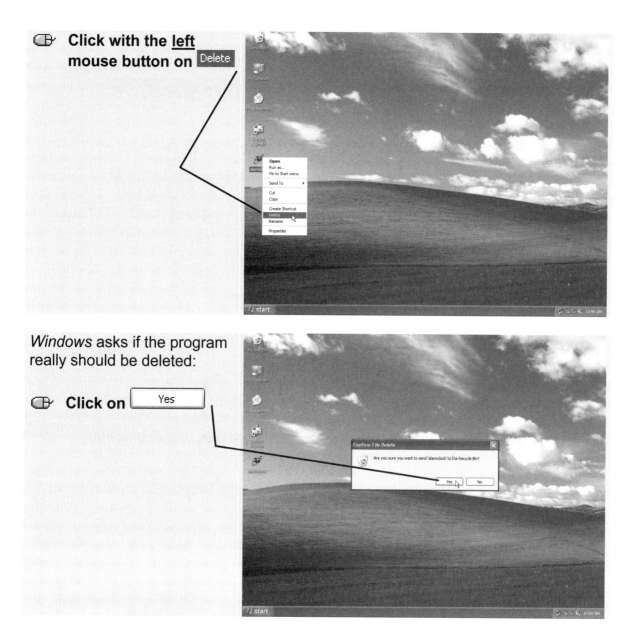

Windows asks if the program really should be deleted:

Click on Yes

The icon for the installation program is removed.

Open or Save?

When you download a file, you'll usually be asked if you want to *run* it or *save* it on the hard drive. Then you see this window:

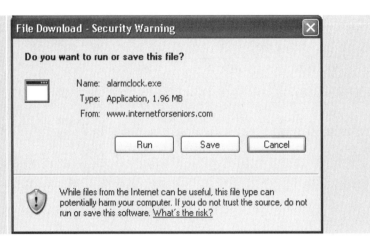

You've seen how you can save an installation program and then start it. If you download a different type of file, however, what happens depends upon the kind of file and your computer's settings.

- If your computer recognizes the file type, the file will sometimes be opened right away, and you won't be able to choose between *run* and *save*.
- Depending on the programs available on your computer, the appropriate program may be started and the file opened.

A large number of different types of files are on the *Internet for Seniors* practice page:

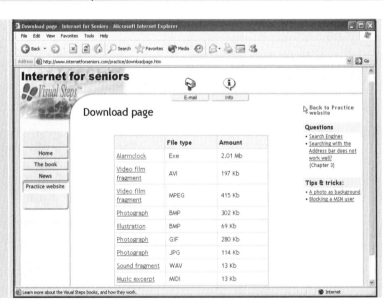

There are photos and music in different file types, so you can see which program is started when you download the file.

In the following exercises, you can download these files and see what happens with them on your computer.

Exercises

Have you forgotten how to do something? Use the number beside the footsteps to look it up in the appendix *How Do I Do That Again?*

Exercise: Downloading

In this exercise, you'll practice downloading files.

✓ Start *Internet Explorer.* 👣1

✓ Connect to the Internet. 👣3

✓ Open the favorite: *Internet for Seniors.* 👣17

✓ Click on `Practice website`.

✓ Click on • `Download page`.

✓ Open a video clip (AVI) 👣51 and
   see which program is started.

✓ Open a photo (JPG) 👣51 and
   see which program is started.

✓ Open a photo (GIF) 👣51 and
   see which program is started.

✓ Open a music file (MIDI) 👣51 and
   see which program is started.

✓ Close *Internet Explorer.* 👣2

✓ Disconnect from the Internet if necessary. 👣5

Background Information

Types of Software
Various types of software are available on the Internet:

Freeware
This software may be freely used and copied. It's sometimes also called *Public Domain* software.

Shareware
The program may be used free of charge for a period of time so you can try it out. If you'd like to keep using it after the trial period, you must pay.

Cardware
You may freely use the software, but the maker wants you to recognize that this is his or her intellectual property. The user is expected to send a postcard indicating that he or she is using the program.

Demos
Demos are free software in which some functions have been disabled. The functions that still work give a good idea of the software's capabilities.
Sometimes the demo works fully, but only for a limited time.

Updates
These are additions or improvements to existing software. They are provided free of charge to people who have a license for the original program.

Cookies
Cookies are bits of information that are stored on your computer. This information can be requested by websites in order to determine various things, such as your settings or username for that website.
By using cookies, you only have to enter that information once.
Cookies can be misused, however. They can be used to store personal information such as name, address and buying behavior.

Plug-ins

A *plug-in* is an accessory program which can be installed as an extra in *Internet Explorer*. *Plug-ins* are often required for viewing video clips and animations or listening to music. You usually download them free of charge from the Internet. The following programs are required in order to open specific file types:

- *Macromedia Flash*: for viewing and interactive use of animations on websites.

- *RealPlayer:* for playing sound and music; among other things, this program makes it possible to follow radio broadcasts over the Internet.

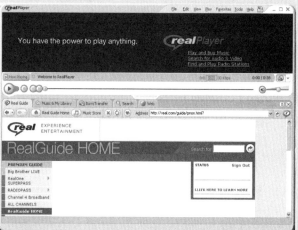

- *MP3-Player*: plays highly-compressed music files at near-CD quality.

- *Adobe Reader*: reads PDF documents; many manuals and brochures on the Internet are distributed in this file format.

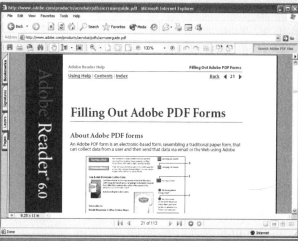

Windows Media Player

You can play music and video without *plug-ins*, too: the *Media Player* is installed when you install *Windows*.

This program can play a number of file types:

- WAV   music and sound
- MIDI   recordings of musical instruments
- MPEG   audio and video in compressed form
- AVI   sound and moving video images

MSN Messenger

You can use the *Messenger* program to let friends, colleagues and family know that you're online.

The principle is simple. When you connect to the Internet, the *Messenger Service* notes that you're online. This information is passed on to your contacts. In this way, you can see who is also online at the same time.

You can start up an online conversation with one of them; this is called *chatting*. You can also send them a short message. You can download the *Messenger* program free of charge at www.msn.com.

The Cable Modem
Internet access through cable is a fairly recent development. It makes use of the cable TV setup with which you also receive your television images.

The cable TV outlet   *An external cable modem*

The way in which your computer connects differs greatly from one cable provider to the next. Sometimes a mechanic will install an **internal cable modem** into your computer. Alternatively, an **external modem** might be placed between your computer and the cable outlet. The modem is then connected to your computer with another cable.

The ISDN Modem
ISDN has a number of advantages over the regular telephone line. First, its speed is greater than that of the regular telephone network. This is particularly evident when you're surfing the Internet. Another advantage is that you have two telephone lines. This means that you can use the telephone and the Internet at the same time.
If you choose ISDN, you'll need to buy an ISDN modem in order to benefit from the increased speed. There are external and internal ISDN modems. They look just like regular modems, with a slightly different telephone jack. An internal modem is sometimes called an *ISDN card*.

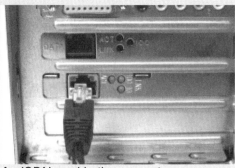

An ISDN card in the computer   *An external ISDN modem*

DSL
The most recent development is DSL. With DSL, the telephone line coming into your home is split. Your telephone connects to one jack, and your computer connects to the other through a modem. The big advantage of DSL is that, just as with a cable connection, you're connected to the Internet twenty-four hours a day. The DSL connection is very fast and you can call on the telephone and use the Internet at the same time.

Tips

 Tip

Updating *Windows XP*
Updating means replacing your system files with the very latest versions. The *Windows Update* program scans your computer, creates a list of files that can be updated, and then installs the files. These files are automatically downloaded from the *Microsoft* website.
Here's how you start *Windows Update*:

Click on **start**,
All Programs, **Windows Update**

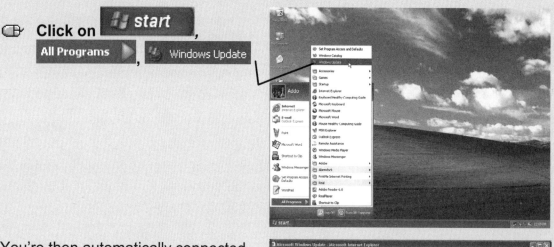

You're then automatically connected to a special *Microsoft* website on the Internet:

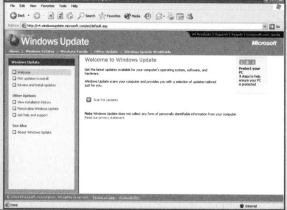

Tip

Where can I find programs?
There are websites with huge software libraries.
On the *Internet for Seniors* website, you'll find a special software page with up-to-date information on locations where you can find interesting programs.

 Tip

Downloading? Always save to the same folder.
It's a good idea to always save files you've downloaded in the same folder, for example in 📁 My Documents . That way you can always find your files. Many people make a separate folder inside this one just for downloads, for example 📁 My Downloads .

9. Optimizing Your Internet Settings

In previous chapters, you've acquired a lot of experience with the Internet. This chapter describes several settings that can make it easier to work on the Internet. We aren't going to discuss how to set up a "bare bones" computer in this chapter; the differences among computers, modems and ISPs is too great for that. You can contact your ISP for help in this case.

In this chapter, you'll find an answer to the following problems and questions:

- Dial-up connection settings:
  - Should I connect automatically to the Internet?
  - Should I save my password?

- *Internet Explorer* settings:
  - How do I change the text size?
  - How do I clear my history?
  - How do I remove temporary files?
  - How do I disconnect automatically from the Internet?

- *Outlook Express* settings:
  - How do I send and receive mail immediately?
  - How can I disable the Outbox?
  - How do I include the original message in my reply?
  - How can I check my account information?

Adjusting the Dial-up Connection

You can adjust a number of things related to connecting to the Internet, such as:

- whether or not you connect to the Internet automatically
- whether or not your password is saved

You can do this by starting *Internet Explorer*:

Do you have an external modem?
☞ **Turn on the modem**

☞ **Start *Internet Explorer*** 📖¹

After it starts, you see this window for the dial-up connection:

You can adjust the settings mentioned above in this window.

Dial-up Connection ☒

Select the service you want to connect to, and then enter your user name and password.

Connect to: NL net Hoorn ▾
User name: xxxxxx
Password: ●●●●●●●●●●●●●●●●
☐ Save password
☐ Connect automatically

[Connect] [Settings...] [Work Offline]

Connecting Automatically

Whether or not to connect automatically is a matter of personal preference.

Connect Automatically
Naturally, it's convenient if the connection occurs on its own; that way you don't always have to click on the *Connect* button every time. If you have a permanent connection to the Internet, for example over the cable or another network, this is certainly the preferred setting.

Don't Connect Automatically
In some cases, it's useful to have a "stop option". Then you have the choice whether or not to make the connection.
Some programs will try to make a connection to the Internet without asking. This setting prevents that from happening, which avoids undesirable and unexpected telephone costs (to e.g. 900 numbers) and keeps your telephone line free for calls.

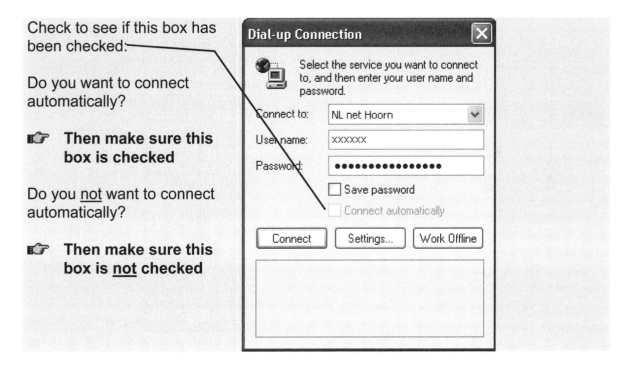

Check to see if this box has been checked:

Do you want to connect automatically?

☞ **Then make sure this box is checked**

Do you <u>not</u> want to connect automatically?

☞ **Then make sure this box is <u>not</u> checked**

Saving Your Password

Whether you should save your password or not depends a great deal on how accessible your computer is to others. If you're the only user and no one else has access to your computer, the situation is very different than when the same computer can be used by others.

Don't Save
If you choose not to save your password, you'll have to type it in yourself every time. This is recommended when you want to be certain that no one else can use your Internet connection.

Do Save
If you're the only person who uses your computer and you're reasonably certain no one else can use it, you can choose convenience and let your password be saved.

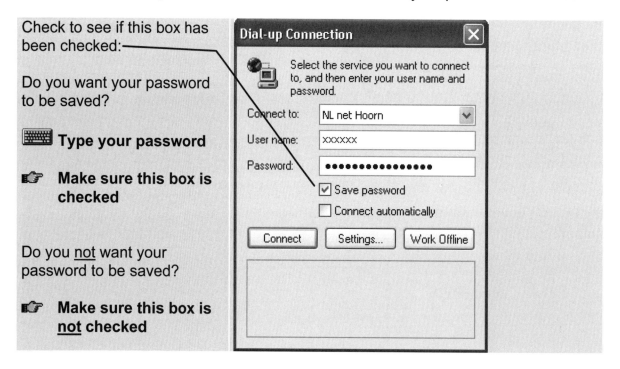

Check to see if this box has been checked:

Do you want your password to be saved?

⌨ **Type your password**

☞ **Make sure this box is checked**

Do you **not** want your password to be saved?

☞ **Make sure this box is not checked**

To store these settings for your connection, you have to connect to the Internet:

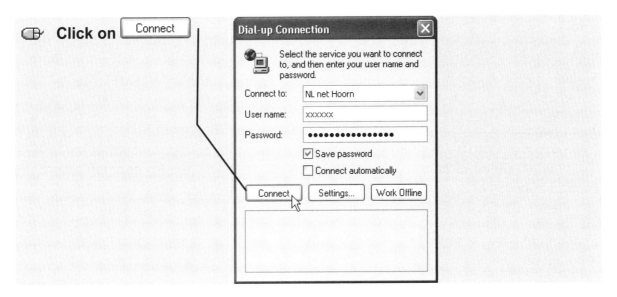

Click on Connect

Wait until the connection has been completed. Then you can disconnect again:

☞ **Disconnect from the Internet** 🦶 16

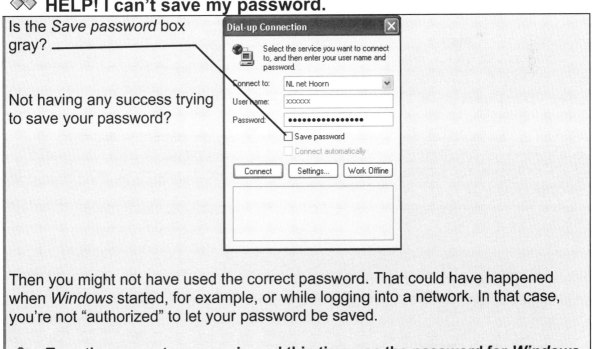

HELP! I can't save my password.

Is the *Save password* box gray?

Not having any success trying to save your password?

Then you might not have used the correct password. That could have happened when *Windows* started, for example, or while logging into a network. In that case, you're not "authorized" to let your password be saved.

☞ **Turn the computer on again and this time use the password for *Windows* or the network**

If this doesn't help, contact your computer supplier or your ISP.

Tip

Changing Your Password
The password you type into the dial-up connection window is the password your ISP gave you.
You can't just change it, or you won't be able to connect to the Internet anymore. What you can do is change your password on the service page of your ISP's website.
Once you've received confirmation of the new password from your ISP, you can type it into the dial-up window and save it.

Choosing a Password
A password is an agreed-upon identification word. By providing the password, you let your ISP's computer know that you really are who you say you are. At any rate, you'll need a password if you want to send or receive electronic mail, or enter the *World Wide Web*.
A password is only intended for use by people who have the right to access. That's why you should keep your password a secret. If you want to write it down somewhere just to be safe, do it somewhere that makes sense to you, so you can find it again.
Choosing a password is a painstaking task. Make sure in any case that your password:
- meets your ISP's requirements
- is not an existing word
- does not consist of letters that are next to each other on the keyboard

Because many people have trouble coming up with a good password and then remembering it, it's often suggested that you create your password from the first letters of an existing sentence. How about: Mccnbc ("My computer can not be cracked")?

Last but not least, it's a good idea to change your password regularly.

Internet Explorer Settings

You can do various things in *Internet Explorer* such as:

- adjust the text size
- clear your history
- delete temporary files
- automatically disconnect from the Internet

Adjusting the Text Size

You can change the size of the text while you're working in *Internet Explorer. Internet Explorer* saves this setting. If you chose larger letters last time, then the text will be displayed in larger letters the next time you open the program. If the text is too small for you to read it easily, you can adjust it like this:

Click on View

Click on Text Size

Click on Largest

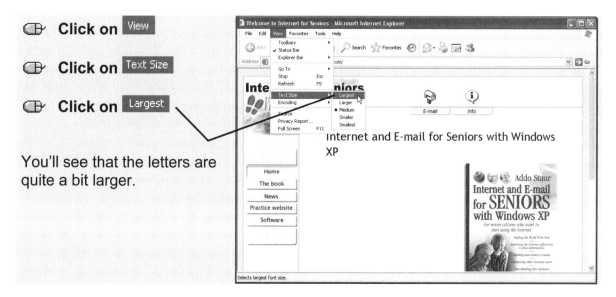

You'll see that the letters are quite a bit larger.

If you don't change this setting again, *Internet Explorer* will start up next time with large letters.

 Tip

Not everything's gotten larger?
The text size setting only works on pure text. Text on images and buttons will not be affected. You may be amazed to see how many things on some web pages are actually images. Unfortunately, you can't enlarge or shrink these elements.

Clearing Your History

It can be useful sometimes to clear out the list of websites you've visited: for example, if someone else will be using the computer after you and you don't want them to see which websites you've visited.
In that case, you can clear your history:

🖘 **Click on** Tools

🖘 **Click on** Internet Options...

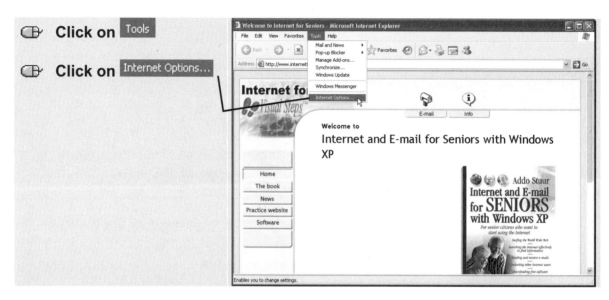

Now you see this window:

🖘 **Click on** Clear History

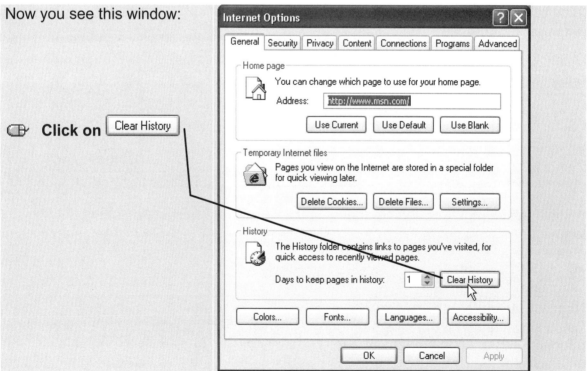

Just to be sure, you're asked if you really want to clear:

Do you want to clear the history?
☞ **Then click on**
| Yes |

Do you want to keep the history?
☞ **Click on** | No |

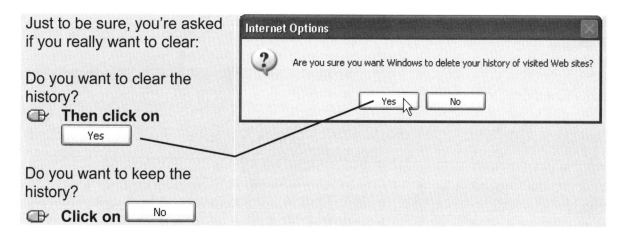

At the bottom of the window, you can change the number of days that the web pages should be saved if you'd like. We won't do that now:

☞ **Click on** | OK |

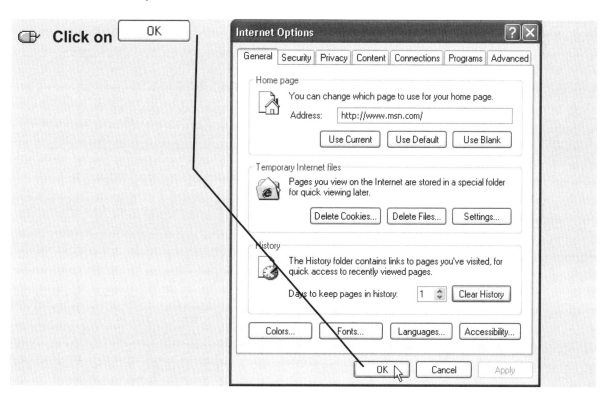

Once you've cleared your history, the folder will be empty. You can check this yourself:

☞ **Click on**

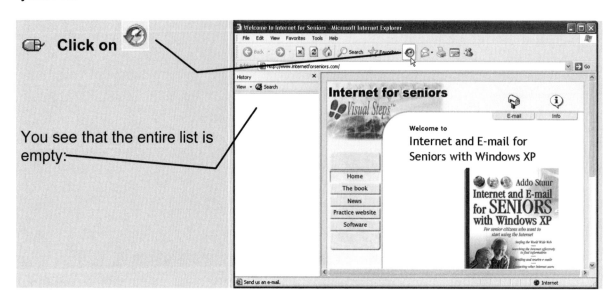

You see that the entire list is empty:

All the websites you've recently visited have been erased from memory.

💡 **Tip**

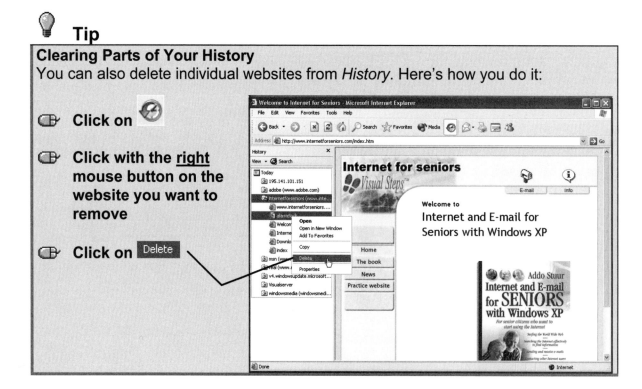

Clearing Parts of Your History
You can also delete individual websites from *History*. Here's how you do it:

☞ **Click on**

☞ **Click with the right mouse button on the website you want to remove**

☞ **Click on** Delete

Deleting Temporary Files

Every time you visit a website, web pages (including text and images) are temporarily stored on your computer's hard drive.
You'll notice this while you're surfing if you use the *Back* or *Forward* buttons to browse through web pages. The second time you visit the same page, it appears on the screen more quickly. That's because the page has been saved on your computer and nothing is being transferred over the telephone line.

These saved pages are called *temporary files*. There are different reasons why you might want to delete your temporary files, for example:

- *Internet Explorer* keeps getting slower.
- You want to erase all traces of your previous activity on the *World Wide Web*.

You can erase all temporary files from your computer like this:

☞ **Click on** Tools

☞ **Click on** Internet Options...

You see this window again:

☞ **Click on** Delete Files...

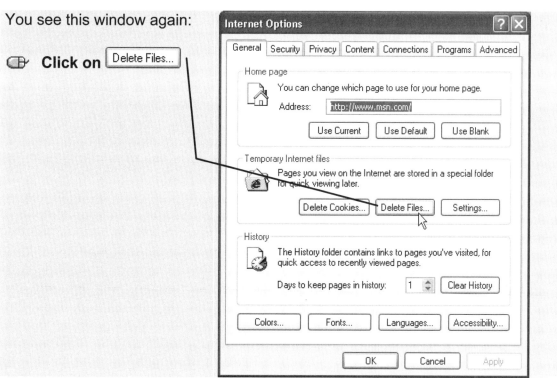

Then you see a warning window:

Do you really want to clear them out?

☞ **Then click on**
  OK

Have you changed your mind?

☞ **Then click on**
  Cancel

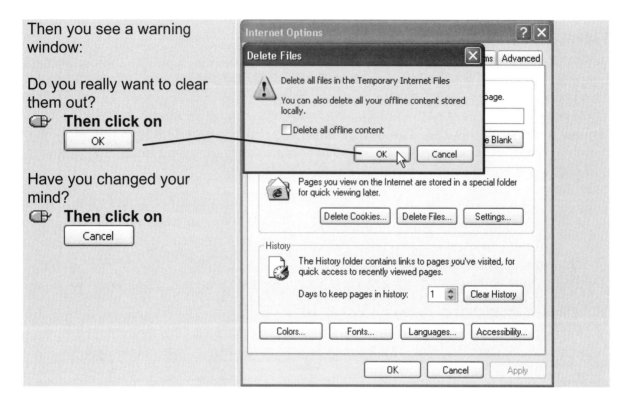

You'll have to wait a bit, and you'll see a little hourglass. Once it disappears, *Internet Explorer* has finished deleting the files.

Disconnecting Automatically

It's useful if *Internet Explorer* disconnects automatically when you close it, or when you haven't used it for a while.
Especially if you connect over the telephone line, this can prevent unnecessarily tying up your line and blocking incoming phone calls.

Click on the tab
Connections

Now you see this window you can use to adjust the connection:

Click on Settings...

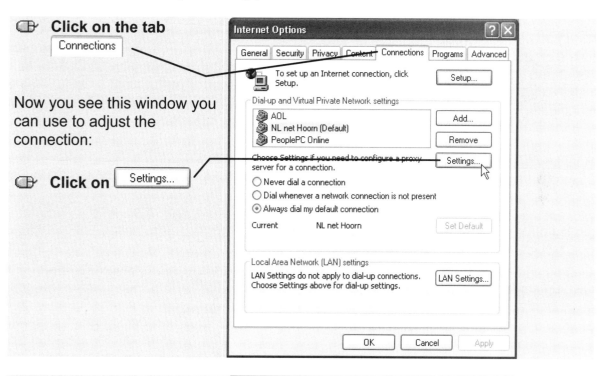

Now you see this window:

Click on Advanced

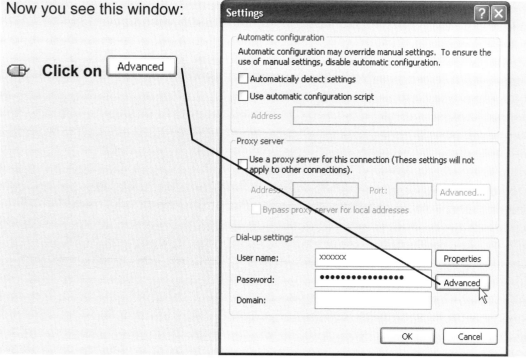

A little window opens:

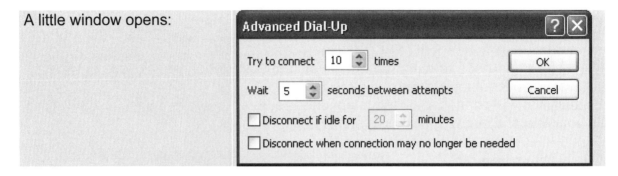

In this window, you can adjust two things:

- Disconnect automatically if you haven't used the connection for a while.
- Disconnect automatically when you close *Internet Explorer*.

If you connect over the telephone line, it's a good idea to turn both settings on. First, set up to disconnect automatically when you're not using the Internet:

You can choose the time period after which the connection will be broken:

- ☞ **Click on the box beside** Disconnect if idle for

- ☞ **Choose the time period, e.g. *10* minutes**

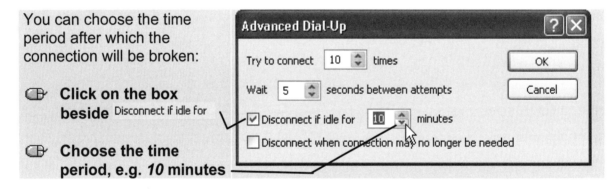

Now you can set *Internet Explorer* to disconnect automatically when you stop:

- ☞ **Click on the box beside** Disconnect when connection may no l

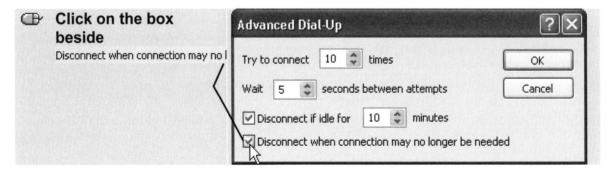

Tip

Is *Internet Explorer* confused?
It might happen that *Internet Explorer* suddenly stops working the way you expect.
For example, the program might stop displaying images on websites.
Then you can return to the default settings. Here's how you do it:

☞ **Click on** Tools

☞ **Click on** Internet Options...

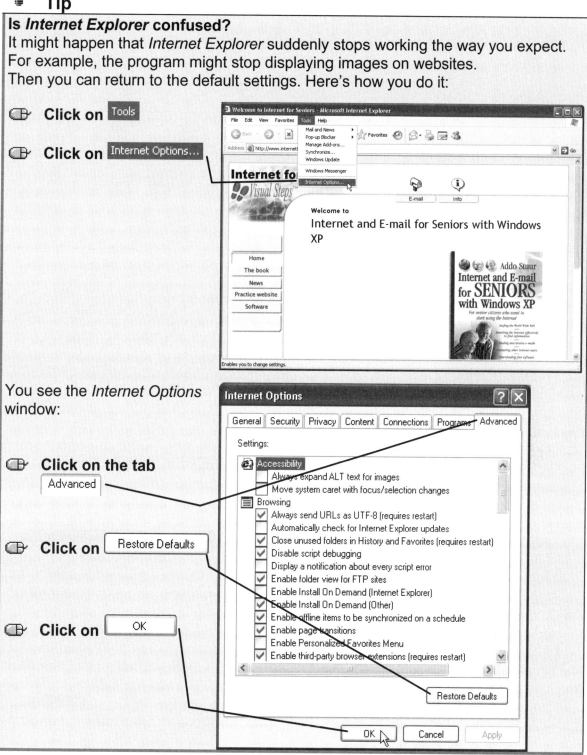

You see the *Internet Options*
window:

☞ **Click on the tab**
Advanced

☞ **Click on** Restore Defaults

☞ **Click on** OK

Outlook Express Settings

You can adjust various things in *Outlook Express* such as:

- your mail delivery
- the way in which your e-mail messages are sent
- your e-mail data

☞ **Start *Outlook Express* ⁇ ³⁵**

Mail Delivery

Outlook Express can be set up in one of two ways:

- It connects automatically to the Internet and sends and receives mail when it opens.
- It does <u>not</u> connect automatically to the Internet. You must manually give the command to send and receive.

It's a matter of personal preference which setting you'd like to use.

You can adjust this as follows:

Click on Tools

Click on Options...

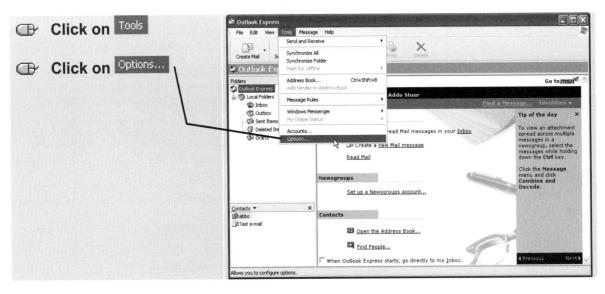

Now you see this window with a large number of settings:

See if the box beside Send and receive messages at startup has been checked:

Do you want to send and receive mail immediately at startup?
☞ **Make sure this box is checked**

Do you **not** want to automatically connect to the Internet when it opens?
☞ **Make sure this box is not checked**

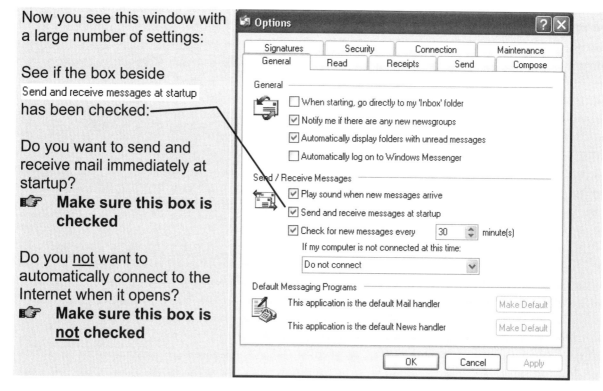

 Tip

Automatically Check Your E-mail
You can set up *Outlook Express* to connect automatically to the Internet and check your e-mail after a certain number of minutes.

You can turn this on by checking this box:

Then you can set the number of minutes, and what should happen if you aren't already connected.

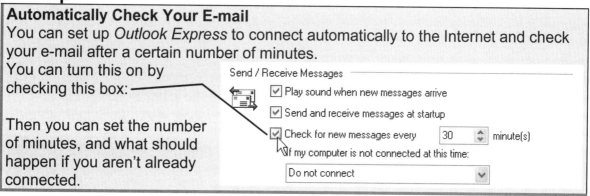

 Tip

Starting Up
You can set up *Outlook Express* to open the *Inbox* automatically when it starts.

You can turn this on by checking this box:

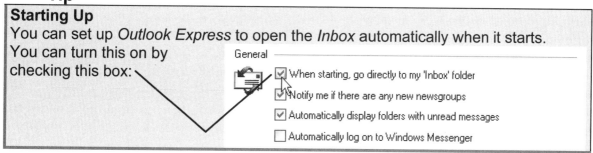

Send Options

Outlook Express has several settings for answering your e-mail. You can view these as follows:

Click on the tab

Send

You see several check boxes:

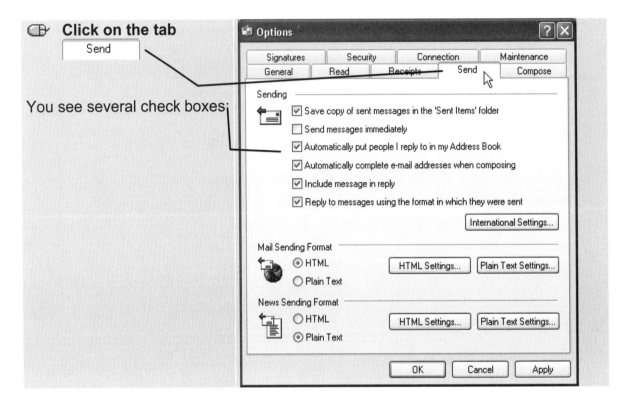

Not all these settings are equally important; they're often a matter of personal preference. For that reason, we're only going to discuss the most important ones here:

- sending your mail immediately, instead of putting it in the *Outbox* first
- not including the original message in your replies

You can try out all the other options if you'd like. These kinds of changes are easy to undo.

No Outbox

You can choose not to use the *Outbox*. When you've written an e-mail message and you click on the *Send* button, you'll connect automatically to the Internet. This does have the disadvantage that you can't write all your e-mail messages first and then send them all at the same time.

Do you want to send your e-mail immediately?

☞ **Then check the box beside**

Send messages immediately

Do you **not** want to do that?
☞ **Make sure the box is not checked**

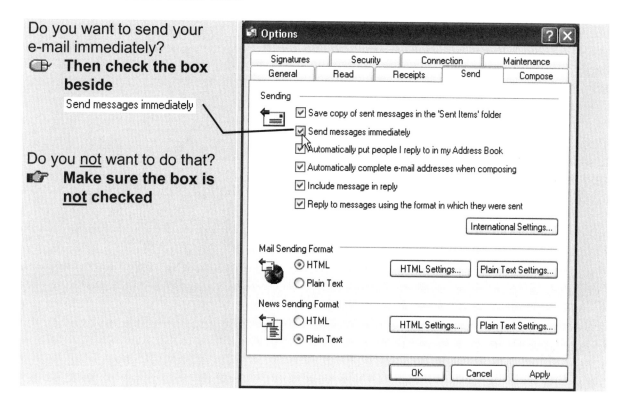

Your Reply

You can choose to include the original message in your reply to an e-mail.

You do this using the
checkbox Include message in reply :

Do you want to include the
original message in your
reply?
☞ **Make sure this box is
   checked**

Do you **not** want to include
the original message in your
reply?
☞ **Make sure this box is
   not checked**

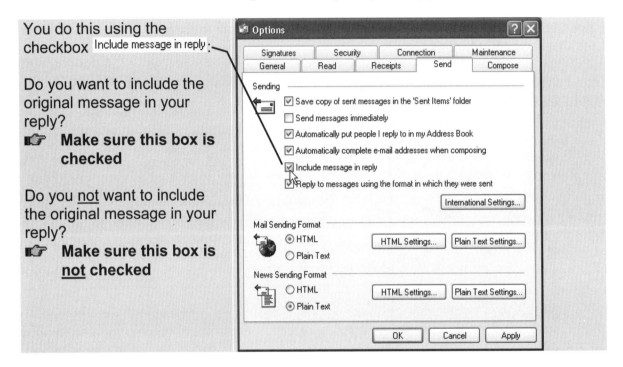

If you don't check this box, you'll begin with an empty message and the original
message will not be shown.

You can save the settings
and then close the window.

🖰 **Click on** OK

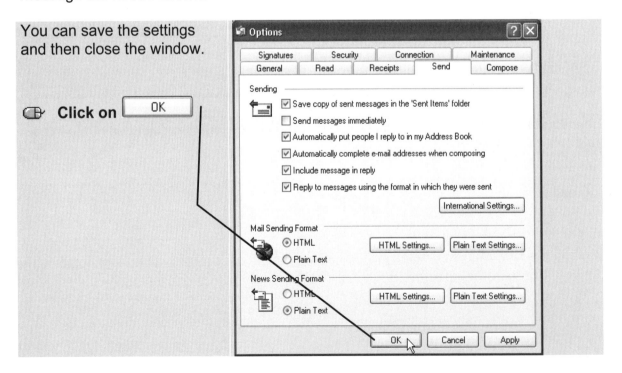

Checking Your Account

By *account*, we mean your mailbox at your ISP. It's a good idea to check your e-mail account information from time to time.
Here's how you do it:

👉 **Click on** `Tools`

👉 **Click on** `Accounts...`

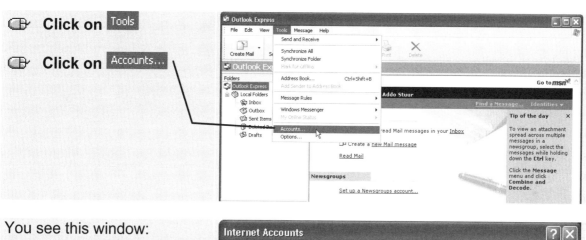

You see this window:

👉 **Click on the tab** `Mail`

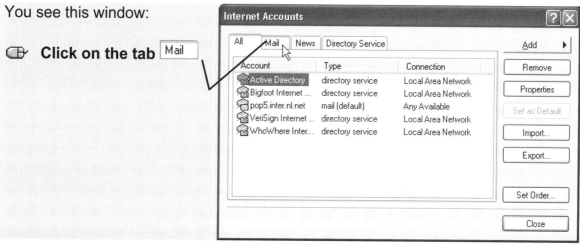

Now you see the name(s) of your e-mail account(s):

👉 **Click on** `Properties`

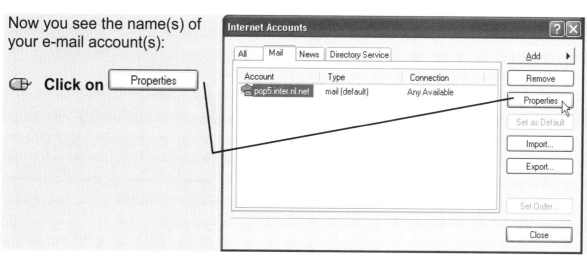

Checking Your Name

When you installed your ISP's software, you probably entered a name that's used as sender's name for your e-mail. You might want to change or edit this name. You can do that in the window below:

☞ **Check your name**

If you're not satisfied, you can change the name.

If you have multiple e-mail addresses, you can also use one of these other addresses as your reply e-mail address. You do that in this box:

☞ **Click on** OK

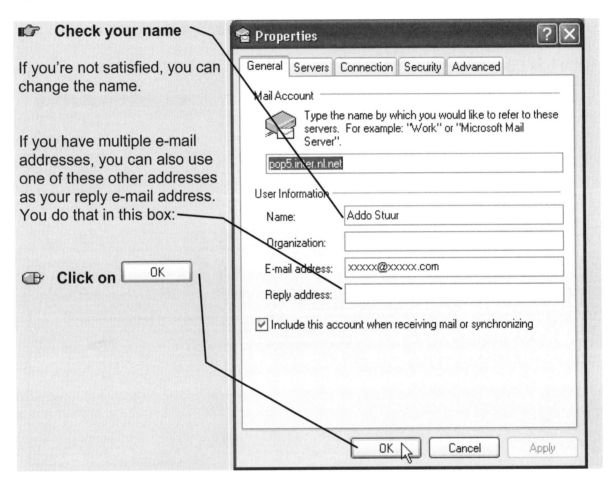

10. Relaxing on the Internet

One of the enjoyable new features of *Windows XP* is the ability to play games on the Internet. *Windows XP* has made that exceptionally easy for the player. Playing all kinds of games together on the Internet is becoming increasingly popular.
One nice aspect of this is that you come into contact with opponents from all over the world. A pleasant side effect is that there are other people on the Internet with whom you can play at any time of the day (or night).
It's definitely worth your while to try out playing games on the Internet.

Games on the Internet

Windows XP offers direct access to a number of games. Here's how you do it:

☞ **Click on** **🏁 start**

☞ **Click on** **All Programs** ▶

☞ **Click on** 🎮 Games

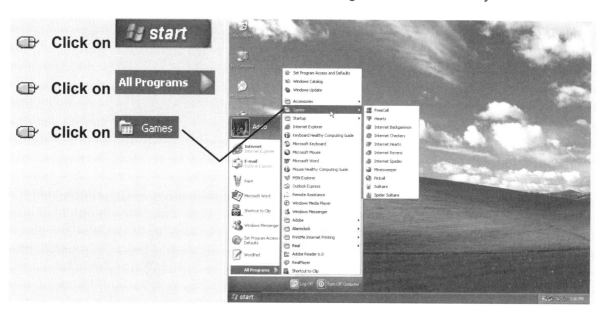

You see that there are various games you can play over the Internet:

- *Backgammon*, the famous board game
- *Hearts*, a card game with three opponents
- *Reversi*, a board game with one opponent
- *Spades*, a card game that's a little bit like bridge

In this chapter, you'll read how to play the popular game *Reversi*. You start it like this:

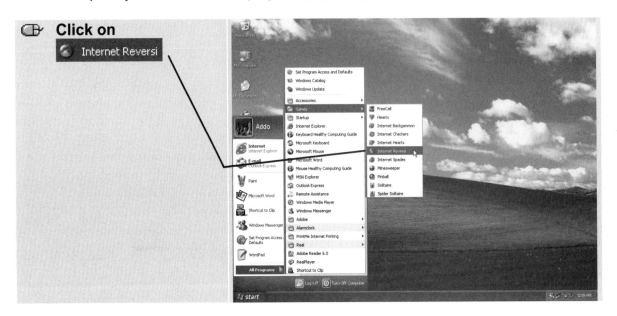

In the next window, you can sign on to play:

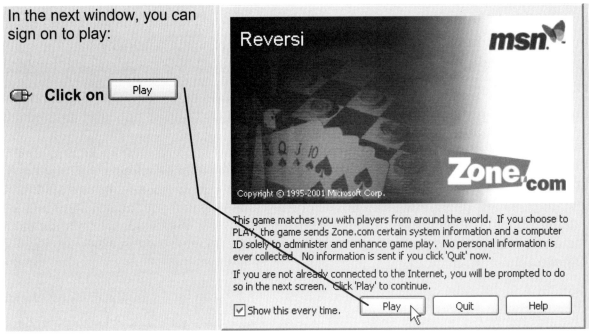

Your computer connects to the Internet in the usual way. Then you're taken to *Zone.com*, part of *MSN*. After you've signed on, you have to wait until other players have been found.

Then you see this game board:

At the bottom, you can see the *chatbox*. You can use it to send short messages to your opponent, thereby communicating with him or her.

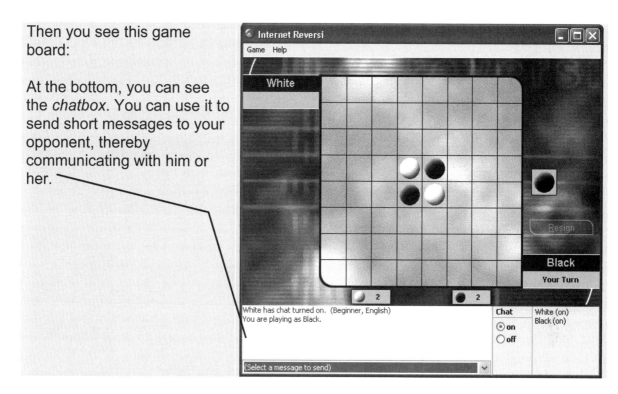

The nice thing about this chat function is that these messages are translated automatically. If you're playing against a Chinese opponent, the messages show up in his chatbox in Chinese.

The Rules of Reversi

It's outside the scope of this book to fully explain the rules of *Reversi*, but here's the short version. You try to turn as many stones as possible into your color (black or white). You do this by enclosing your opponent's stones on both sides. The color of the enclosed stones then changes to your color. You might know this game as *Othello*.

 Tip

Do you want to progress quickly from beginner to expert?
Then always try to win the positions on the edges of the game board. Placing your stones in the corners of the board is even better. Then you'll have a very good chance of ending up the winner.

Stopping

If you want to stop at the end of a game, do the following:

 Click on Game

 Click on Exit

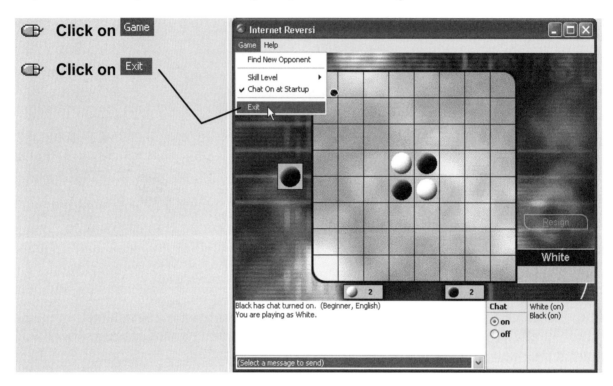

Now you can disconnect from the Internet, or play another game.

⇨ **Please note:**

You have to manually disconnect from the Internet using the taskbar; it doesn't happen automatically.

Other Games

At present, you can choose from the following other games:

Spades

A game that's similar to *Bridge* with one partner and two opponents.
If there aren't enough players, their hands will be played by the computer.

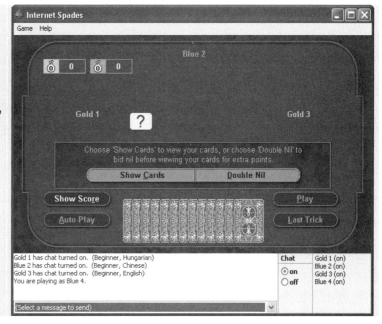

Backgammon

The famous board game. You can choose the level at which you want to play. Then you'll be connected to an opponent on the same level.
You can choose your level in the other games described here, too.

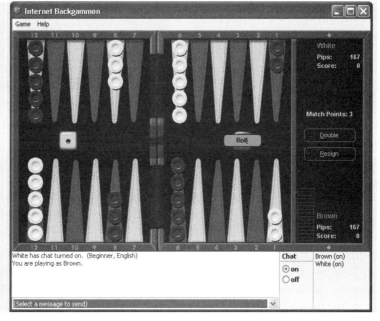

Hearts

A well-known card game with three opponents.

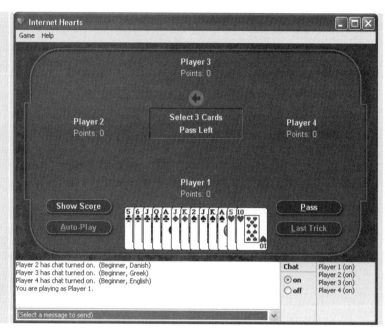

There might very well be other new games available soon at *MSN Zone.com*.

You can choose other online games in *Internet Explorer* by going to **www.zone.com**:

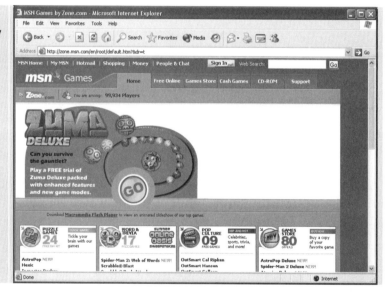

Appendices

Appendix A
Installing Desktop Accessories

If the group *Accessories* isn't on your computer, you can still install it. This is a collection of *Windows XP* programs that's usually installed immediately. You can't work through this book without these programs. The *Accessories* are usually in the installation files on your hard drive. You can install them like this:

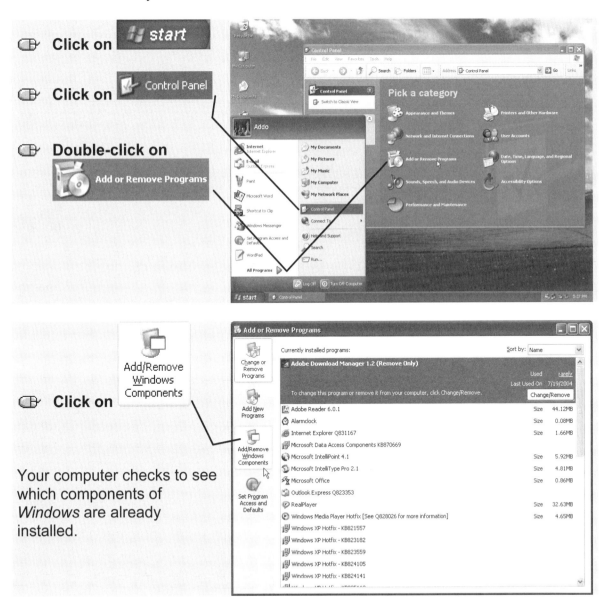

Click on **start**

Click on **Control Panel**

Double-click on **Add or Remove Programs**

Click on **Add/Remove Windows Components**

Your computer checks to see which components of *Windows* are already installed.

If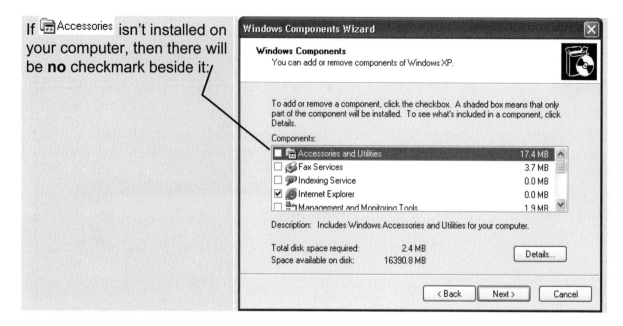

You can select *Accessories:*

👉 **Click in the box beside**

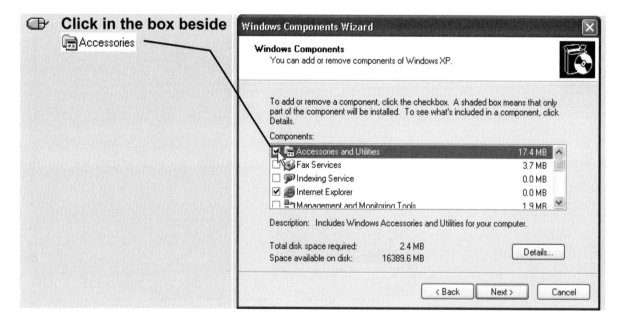

Now you can install the programs:

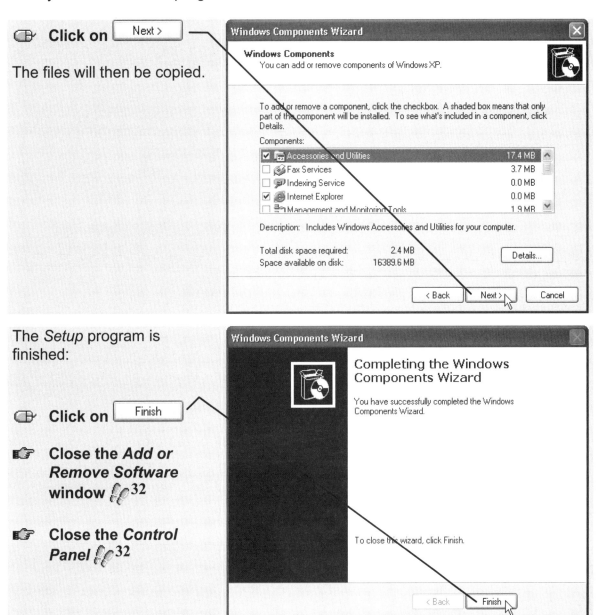

☞ **Click on** [Next >]

The files will then be copied.

The *Setup* program is finished:

☞ **Click on** [Finish]

☞ **Close the *Add or Remove Software* window** ⫫³²

☞ **Close the *Control Panel*** ⫫³²

Appendix B
Address Bar Search Settings

Does your computer respond differently than described in Chapter 3? For example, the *Search* frame doesn't appear on the left-hand side? Then your computer has been set up differently. This is easy to change. Here's what you do:

☞ **Start** *Internet Explorer* ⬚¹

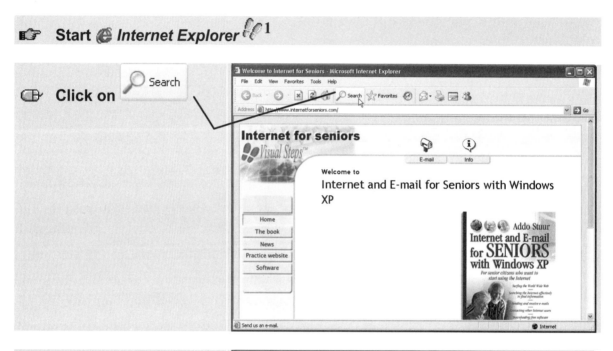

Click on 🔍 Search

Click on Customize

Now you see the *Search* frame on the left-hand side:

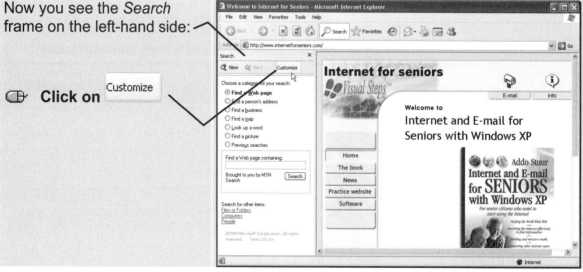

Then you see the *Customize Search Settings* window:

👆 **Click on**
    Autosearch settings

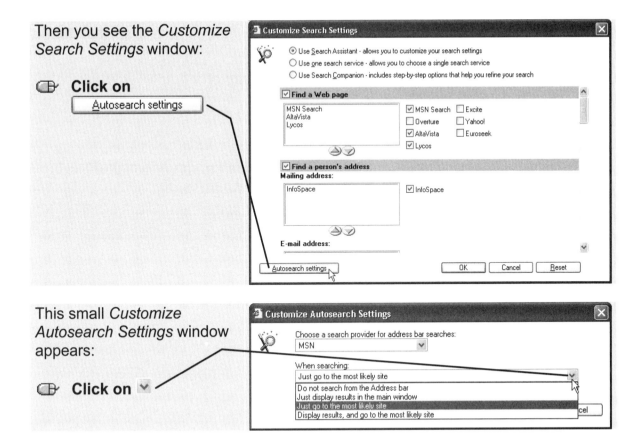

This small *Customize Autosearch Settings* window appears:

👆 **Click on** ✓

Now you can choose the right setting:

👆 **Click on**
    Display results, and go to the most likely site

👆 **Click on** [OK]

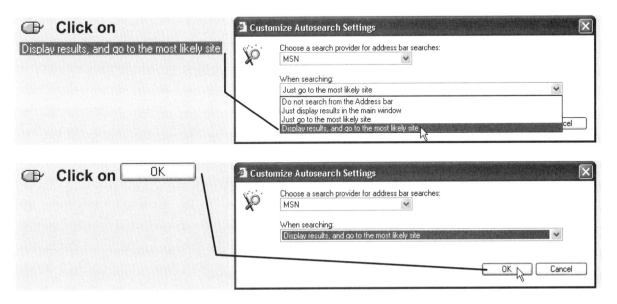

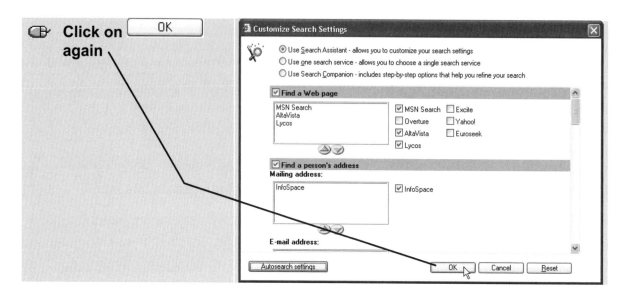

Now you can type **? bike** into the address bar again. This time, the program will respond as described in Chapter 3.

Appendix C
Using Large Buttons in Internet Explorer

Internet Explorer might use small buttons on your computer, like on this bar:

You can easily change these to large buttons like the ones used in this book:

Here's how you change this:

Click on View

Click on Toolbars

Click on Customize...

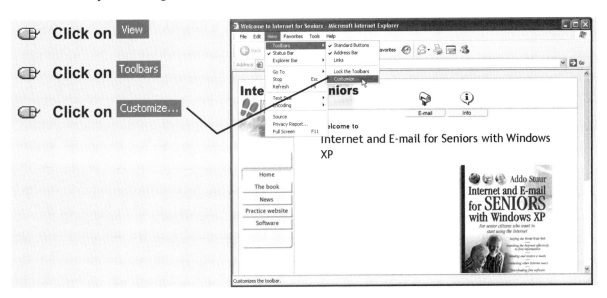

Now you see this window, which you can use to adjust the button bar:

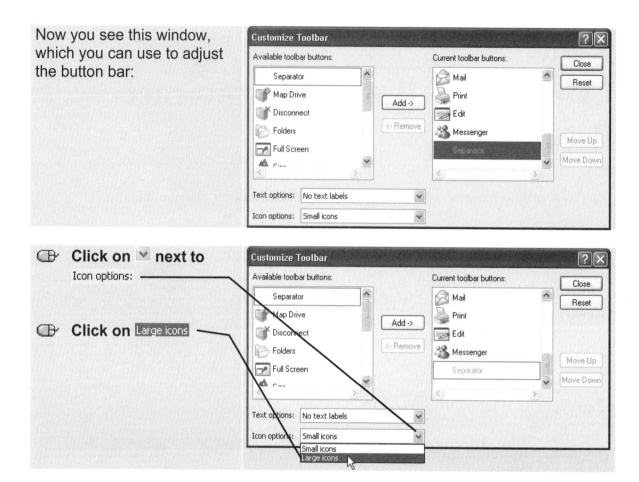

Click on ▼ next to
Icon options: ————

Click on Large icons

You can also give the buttons a label, so that the buttons on your computer look just like the ones in this book:

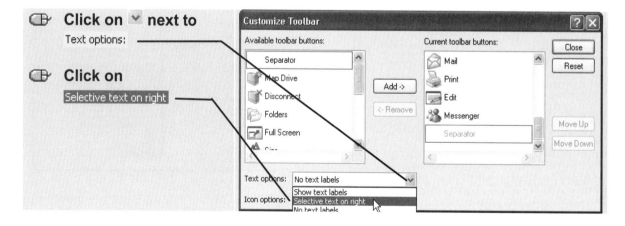

Click on ▼ next to
Text options: ————

Click on
Selective text on right ————

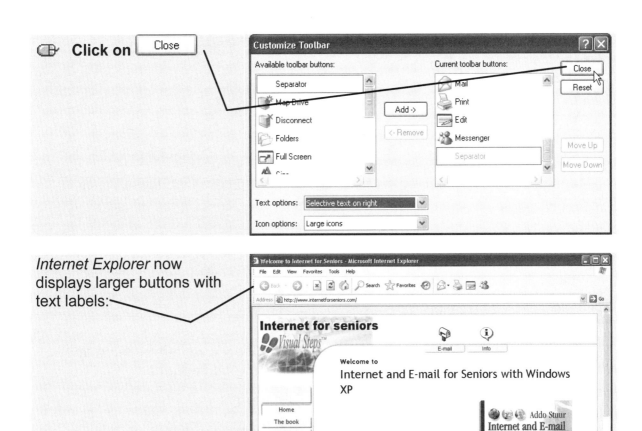

👆 **Click on** ⌷ Close ⌷

Internet Explorer now displays larger buttons with text labels:

Appendix D
How Do I Do That Again?

In this book, many tasks and exercises are followed by footsteps: 👣 x
You can use the number beside the footsteps to look up how to do these things in
this appendix.

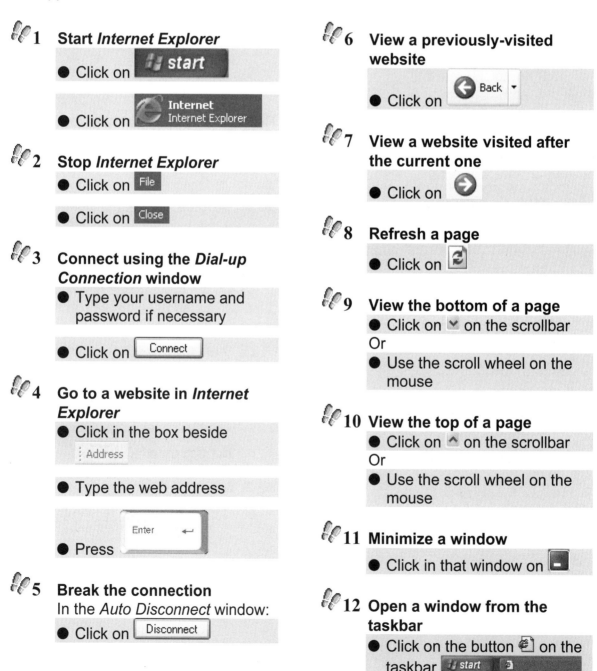

👣1 **Start *Internet Explorer***
- Click on **🏁 start**
- Click on **🌐 Internet Internet Explorer**

👣2 **Stop *Internet Explorer***
- Click on **File**
- Click on **Close**

👣3 **Connect using the *Dial-up Connection* window**
- Type your username and password if necessary
- Click on **Connect**

👣4 **Go to a website in *Internet Explorer***
- Click in the box beside **Address**
- Type the web address
- Press **Enter ⏎**

👣5 **Break the connection**
In the *Auto Disconnect* window:
- Click on **Disconnect**

👣6 **View a previously-visited website**
- Click on **🔙 Back ▾**

👣7 **View a website visited after the current one**
- Click on **➡**

👣8 **Refresh a page**
- Click on **🔄**

👣9 **View the bottom of a page**
- Click on **⌄** on the scrollbar
Or
- Use the scroll wheel on the mouse

👣10 **View the top of a page**
- Click on **⌃** on the scrollbar
Or
- Use the scroll wheel on the mouse

👣11 **Minimize a window**
- Click in that window on **▬**

👣12 **Open a window from the taskbar**
- Click on the button **🗎** on the taskbar **🏁 start**

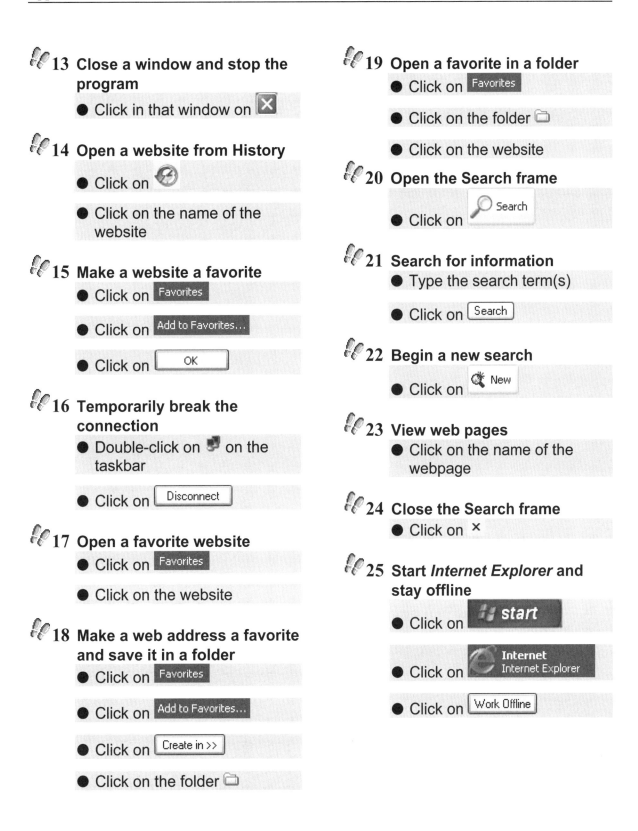

13 Close a window and stop the program
- Click in that window on ☒

14 Open a website from History
- Click on 🕘
- Click on the name of the website

15 Make a website a favorite
- Click on Favorites
- Click on Add to Favorites...
- Click on [OK]

16 Temporarily break the connection
- Double-click on 💻 on the taskbar
- Click on [Disconnect]

17 Open a favorite website
- Click on Favorites
- Click on the website

18 Make a web address a favorite and save it in a folder
- Click on Favorites
- Click on Add to Favorites...
- Click on [Create in >>]
- Click on the folder 📁

19 Open a favorite in a folder
- Click on Favorites
- Click on the folder 📁
- Click on the website

20 Open the Search frame
- Click on 🔍 Search

21 Search for information
- Type the search term(s)
- Click on [Search]

22 Begin a new search
- Click on ⚛ New

23 View web pages
- Click on the name of the webpage

24 Close the Search frame
- Click on ×

25 Start *Internet Explorer* and stay offline
- Click on 🏁 start
- Click on 🅔 **Internet** Internet Explorer
- Click on [Work Offline]

26 Open a web page
- Click on File
- Click on Open...
- Click on Browse...
- Click on the file name
- Click on Open

27 Select text
- Place the mouse pointer in front of the text
- Press the left mouse button and hold it down
- Drag the mouse down the page
- Release the mouse button when everything is selected

28 Copy a selection
- Click on Edit
- Click on Copy

29 Start the program *WordPad*
- Click on start
- Click on All Programs
- Click on Accessories
- Click on WordPad

30 Paste text
- Click on Edit
- Click on Paste

31 Stop *WordPad*
- Click on File
- Click on Exit

Question: Save changes?
- Click on No

32 Close a window
- Click in that window on ⊠

33 Save a photo
- Click with the <u>right</u> mouse button on the photo
- Click on Save Picture As...

34 Give a photo a name
- Next to File name: type the name for your file:

  File name: [   ]
- Click on Save

35 Start *Outlook Express*
- Click on start
- Click on E-mail Outlook Express

36 Create a new e-mail message
In the *Outlook Express* window:
- Click on Create Mail

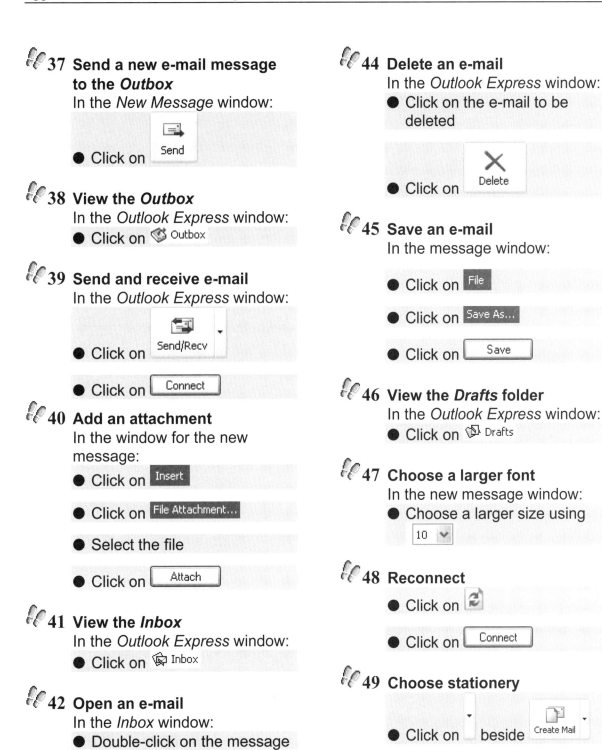

37 Send a new e-mail message to the *Outbox*
In the *New Message* window:
● Click on Send

38 View the *Outbox*
In the *Outlook Express* window:
● Click on Outbox

39 Send and receive e-mail
In the *Outlook Express* window:
● Click on Send/Recv
● Click on Connect

40 Add an attachment
In the window for the new message:
● Click on Insert
● Click on File Attachment...
● Select the file
● Click on Attach

41 View the *Inbox*
In the *Outlook Express* window:
● Click on Inbox

42 Open an e-mail
In the *Inbox* window:
● Double-click on the message

43 Stop *Outlook Express*
In the *Outlook Express* window:
● Click on File
● Click on Exit

44 Delete an e-mail
In the *Outlook Express* window:
● Click on the e-mail to be deleted
● Click on Delete

45 Save an e-mail
In the message window:
● Click on File
● Click on Save As...
● Click on Save

46 View the *Drafts* folder
In the *Outlook Express* window:
● Click on Drafts

47 Choose a larger font
In the new message window:
● Choose a larger size using 10

48 Reconnect
● Click on
● Click on Connect

49 Choose stationery
● Click on   beside Create Mail
● Choose the stationery

50 Choose a background color
In the message window:
- Click on `Format`
- Click on `Background`
- Click on `Color`
- Click on the desired color

51 Download and open a file
- Click on the file name
- Click on `Open`

52 Open the *Internet for Seniors* website
- Type beside `Address` : www.internetforseniors.com

Or:
- Click on `Favorites`
- Click on `Welcome to Internet for Seniors`

53 Save a web page
- Click on `File`
- Click on `Save As...`
- Type beside `File name:` the name for the web page
- Click on `Save`

54 Choose a name from the Address Book
- Click on `To:`
- Click on the name
- Click on `To: ->`
- Click on `OK`

55 Save changes to this message?
- Click on `No`

56 Maximize a window
- Click in that window on ▣

57 View an attachment
- Double-click on the attachment
- Click on `Open`

58 Display the whole page
- Click on ▯

59 Display the page at actual size
- Click on ▯

60 Display *Pages* in the *Options* frame
- Click on `Pages`

61 Open *My Computer* or *My Documents*
- Click on `start`
- Click on `My Computer`

or
- Click on `My Documents`

Appendix E
Index

Notes

Notes

Notes

Notes